MW01616968

PARTING
COMPANY

Praise for the previous edition of *Parting Company*

" A timely manual for surviving the trauma of sudden termination . . .
of incalculable value for the perilous art of negotiating for adequate
severance pay and favorable job references."

—*The New York Times*

" A thoroughly wise and practical book, it couldn't have arrived at a
more appropriate time."

—Consumer Bookshelf, *Los Angeles Times*

" This book is well worth putting on your bookshelf—in anticipation
of the day when the bell tolls for you."   —*USA Today*

PARTING
COMPANY

*How to Survive the Loss of a Job
and Find Another Successfully*

REVISED EDITION

William J. Morin
and **James C. Cabrera**

A DIVISION OF DRAKE BEAM MORIN, INC.
A HARCOURT PROFESSIONAL AND
CORPORATE DEVELOPMENT COMPANY

275 BROAD HOLLOW ROAD
SUITE 300
MELVILLE, N.Y. 11747
800-345-5627

Copyright © 2000, 1991, 1982 by Drake Beam Morin, Inc.

All rights reserved. No part of this publication may be reproduced or transmitted in any form or by any means, electronic or mechanical, including photocopy, recording, or any information storage and retrieval system, without permission in writing from the publisher.

Requests for permission to make copies of any part of the work should be mailed to: DBM Publishing, 275 Broad Hollow Road, Suite 300, Melville, N.Y. 11747

All exercises, instruments, tables, and diagrams used here are the property of Drake Beam Morin, Inc.

Library of Congress Cataloging-in-Publication Data
Morin, William J.
      Parting Company : how to survive the loss of a job and find another successfully / William J. Morin and James C. Cabrera
      p.   cm.
ISBN 0-78-100141-2
      1. Employees—Dismissal of.   2. Executives—Dismissal of.
3. Job hunting.   I. Cabrera, James C.   II. Title.
HF5549.5.D55M673 1991
650.14—dc20   90-25903

Printed in the United States of America

Third Edition 2000

The authors would like to acknowledge the entire Drake Beam Morin staff of professionals who have identified and developed many of the ideas expressed in this book. They are too numerous to list, but without their contributions we would not have been able to complete this work.

We would like to give our special thanks to Tim Lynch and also to Drake Beam Morin's Development Group for their invaluable assistance and collaboration.

Contents

CHAPTER 1

The Seven Danger Signs • Reasons for Termination •
Some General Steps to Take • Should You Quit First? •
Negotiating Your Way Out of a Job • Strengthening
Your Hold

CHAPTER 2

Five Reactions to Termination • Five Common Emotions •
The Art of Getting Fired

CHAPTER 3

Do Nothing • Dealing with Emotions • Practical
Considerations • How Much Severance Should You

Receive? • How Much Severance Will You Receive? •
How Should Your Severance Be Disbursed? • Other
Practical Concerns • Meeting Your Former Employer •
Moving Ahead

CHAPTER 4

*Deciding Your Own Fate—Early Retirement and Voluntary
Separation Programs*   53

Early Retirement Programs • An Offer You May—or May
Not—Be Able to Refuse • Voluntary Separation Programs •
Look, Don't Leap! • How the Company Sees It • How
You See It • How the Company Proceeds • How You
Should Proceed • What If You Leave? • What If You
Stay?

CHAPTER 5

*Career Decision Making—Overview and Phase I:
Managing Personal Reactions*   73

Worrying about Change • A Model for Decision Making •
Phase I: Managing Personal Reactions

CHAPTER 6

*Career Decision Making—Phase II: Gathering
Information*   81

Six Categories of Internal Information • The Role of
Values • Financial Factors • The Importance of Interests •
Psychological Needs • What You've Done: Your
Accomplishments • What You Can Do: Your Skills •

CHAPTER **16**

CHAPTER **17**

CHAPTER **18**

CHAPTER **19**

APPENDIX **A**

Preface to the Third Edition

Much has changed in the parallel worlds of work, employment and careers since we published the first edition of *Parting Company* in the early 1980s. Phrases like downsizing, rightsizing and outsourcing were not yet common in the language of business then. And, even as we tried to convince people that the idea of cradle-to-grave employment with a single company was quickly and inevitably turning out to be a very risky assumption, millions of American workers employed by the nation's leading corporations continued to believe that they were parties to an implicit promise: the notion that, if they did their jobs, their companies would look out for them.

Later, as people in one industry after another started to become intimately and painfully acquainted with all those new "-ing" words, waves of collective anger and sadness were unleashed in the wake of what many of us perceived to be a rash of broken promises. Even as companies insisted, "It's nothing personal; it's all about economics," a collective sense of, "I worked hard for them, and look what they did to me," spread across the corporate landscape.

Today we seem to have gotten the message that the only thing we can really depend on throughout our careers will be constant and continuous change. If Asian economies falter, a U.S. aircraft manufacturer finds itself with little choice but to lay off workers as orders it had booked are canceled. It's difficult to lay the blame for the global financial excesses that inspired the trouble at the airplane company's door.

We also find that the kind of change that has significant implications for careers doesn't just occur when markets turn down. Successful companies in many fields are convinced that they will keep being successful only if they can transform themselves into dominant competitors, organizations whose size and reach produce economies and efficiencies of scale that smaller competitors simply cannot duplicate. The result has been an ongoing wave of mergers and acquisitions, followed by the elimination of duplicate functions at the merged companies. New kinds of companies are emerging as a result, like the financial "supermarkets" that now want to be our bankers, insurance agents, stock brokers, credit card issuers and who knows what else. Finally, when a product doesn't live up to predictions, or a business fails to attain financial goals established for it, companies are far quicker today to kill the product or exit the business than ever before.

As a result, as we look back over the years, perhaps what has changed most dramatically has been the velocity of change, itself.

From our perspective, however, at least one central fact of workplace life is no different today than it was two decades ago. That is our conviction that, while rapidly changing economic and competitive conditions may make it impossible for you to control any one job, you can control your career by demonstrating your conviction and willingness to be responsible for it. This is what we meant years ago when we suggested to people that they not think of employers as concerned parents whose ultimate interests were intricately aligned with those of their employees. It was true then, although certainly not as evident as it is today: no one but yourself will—or in fact should be responsible for your career.

Translated to the specific realm of job loss and job search, this has broad implications for most American workers. Given the continuing volatility of the business environment (and the likelihood that work life is unlikely to get much calmer in a new century), waiting for a job to be taken from you before preparing to replace it is no longer a sensible career approach. This doesn't mean that you should neglect the job or shortchange the employer you have today, but it does call for constantly honing your skills, continuing to build and rebuild a network of professional colleagues and contacts, and always looking out and ahead to new opportunities and possibilities on the career horizon.

Reality calls for a far more active approach to careers and career decisions today. If you wait for someone else to make those choices for you, you'll probably be in for a long hard ride. On the other hand, if you take on the job—and it is a job—of being aggressively responsible for your own career, you have the best chance of achieving real and enduring success, no matter how dramatic the change you encounter along the way.

Throughout this book, you'll see that we have tried to get you directly involved in making career decisions and pursuing an effective job search. The black bar indicates that it's time for you to pick up a pen or pencil and get to work on your own future. Here's your first assignment.

WHAT AM I DOING HERE?

In the space provided here, first describe why you are reading this book, in a few phrases or sentences. Have you just lost your job? Are you worried about keeping your present position? Are you looking for a way out of an employment situation you don't find rewarding? Then, make a note or two about how you want to use the book. Do you want to find a new job? Do you want to test whether your present career is taking you where you really want to go? Date your entries. If your mind, or your situation, changes in the future, refer back to this page and make another entry.

_____

_____

_____

_____

_____

_____

_____

_____

_____

_____

_____

_____

_____

_____

_____

_____

_____

    By putting your thoughts on paper, you've begun to use your copy of *Parting Company* as a guide to creating a personal career journal that can help you take control of your professional future.

One thing has not changed in the business world: the sense of losing control and trust that virtually everyone feels when his or her job is taken away. Fear of being fired has intensified, in fact, as more and more employees discover that doing the job and trusting the company no longer guarantee twenty-five years of employment followed by a sentimental retirement party. This can be a bitter realization. Time and again our clients tell us, "I trusted them, and look what they did to me."

We are convinced that a new trust relationship between employer and employee is both possible and preferable. We believe that the employer/employee union should be based on the skills and accomplishments of individuals, not the presumed good intentions of the company. Employees should take responsibility for their careers by perfecting their skills, becoming visible in their industry, and continually improving their understanding of their business.

Employees' fundamental goal should be to serve themselves. By doing so, they will also serve their companies more effectively than in the past.

We hope this new edition of *Parting Company* will help you serve yourself.

Introduction

The world's leading corporations—companies like Mobil, AT&T, and General Motors—hire us to work with people who no longer work for them. Our business is career continuation (often called outplacement counseling), and we teach ex-employees the skills they need to continue their careers quickly and efficiently, with the least possible amount of emotional wear and tear and with the best chances for professional success and personal satisfaction.

Since 1970 we have worked individually with more than 50,000 people in one-on-one outplacement counseling programs. As leaders of group outplacement sessions and in our roles as chairman and president of Drake Beam Morin, Inc., the number of people we have consulted with surpasses 500,000.

We have good news and bad news about your career. First, breathe a sigh of relief. You will probably never actually get fired. To be fired today, you must do something so devastating that your boss forgets everything he or she has learned about the principles of management, forgets the company's personnel and legal departments, forgets the corporate chain of command, forgets everything but the words "You're fired!"

Most managers are too prudent to act so rashly, and most employees have neither the corporate muscle to commit such remarkable sins single-handedly nor the visibility to call attention to themselves if they do.

But take another deep breath because the chances that you will *lose* your job at least once during your professional career continue to rise. You might be "terminated." You could be "dehired." A neurotic economy or psychotic stock market could land you in the middle of an "across-the-board staff retrenchment." A new management team might arrive and "sever" you, a process that sounds as though it were accomplished with a very sharp retrenching tool. You may be shown the "window" of a "voluntary separation program."

On one level, these new terms reflect business's preoccupation with fancy words. The thought of firing someone seems harsh and old-fashioned. But the new words also indicate that the business of finding, keeping, and losing jobs has changed dramatically in recent years. The "company man" of the '60s was replaced by the "me-first" employee of the '70s and the "yuppie" of the '80s (who has already joined the endangered species list and may be headed for extinction). By the '90s, a sense of uncertainty, confusion, and even resentment had begun to color the employment outlook of many members of the work force.

In the '60s, people lived good corporate lives and married good corporate wives. (Corporate husbands would come later.) When companies said "Move," people packed. By the late '70s, if a corporation offered a man a promotion linked to a relocation, no one was particularly surprised if he said, "My wife won't leave her job, my children won't leave their friends, and I won't leave Cleveland."

But as people made new demands and sought greater control of their careers, they also had to assume greater responsibility for the consequences. When executives demanded faster advancement—and headed to new jobs if they didn't get it—companies had to clear deadwood from the corporate tree or lose their most talented individuals.

Convinced that it had to become more productive and competitive to thrive—or even survive—in the world economy, corporate America became increasingly interested in hiring the best talent available and increasingly unwilling to carry unproductive workers. Since one year's shooting star may become the next year's burnout case, everyone's future became relatively less secure.

When economic pressures forced American companies to make wholesale staff reductions, they learned a curious lesson. Productivity and profits didn't necessarily suffer; in many cases they improved. Rounds of reorganizations, staff reductions, and retrenchments followed, as senior managers pushed to find just how tight they could make their ships and still remain afloat.

This changing competitive environment has made the services provided by firms like Drake Beam Morin increasingly valuable to the nation's major employers.

Companies retain us for a number of reasons. They realize that a smooth transition from one job to another cuts the incidence of legal action brought by angry former employees. They believe that staff loyalty and corporate productivity are enhanced when employees feel they won't be abandoned if the worst should occur and they lose their jobs. They find that employees who remain following a staff reduction, and whose motivation may suffer when former colleagues depart, are reassured that their friends are being looked after.

People who go through our programs almost always find jobs more quickly than individuals who fend for themselves. This frequently saves severance dollars for their former employers. And in an era when nobody's job seems as secure as it used to be, the people who set human resources policies may well be considering their own futures when they plan new and more liberal termination programs for their companies.

But what seems surprising to many people is that many corporations, or more precisely the people who run them, really *do* have consciences. Managers are more likely to agree that, in today's corporate climate, failure on the job usually involves more than one individual. Perhaps there is a lack of direction from above. Maybe there is a lack of support from below. The problem may be caused by people thousands of miles away in Tokyo or Taiwan. The decision to abandon an entire business isn't caused by John Jones's failure to perform.

As one industry after another decides that termination, or whatever they may call it, is a necessary fact of corporate life, they feel fewer constraints against letting people go. No longer the ultimate form of capitalistic punishment, termination has become an easier sentence for corporate judges to execute.

Despite the changing corporate climate, one thing has remained the same: the reaction of the person who loses a job. Almost everyone encounters shock, anger, and surprise, plus a psychological inability to deal with these unpleasant emotions and a host of practical problems connected to finding a new job or choosing a new direction.

Corporation presidents react much the same as middle managers. Both feel that they have lost control of their lives. Elaborate severance packages do not dull the pain.

But if you lose your job today, you can get help. You don't have to go it alone. Your family and friends can help. Professional guidance counselors can help. We can help.

We don't presume to know what you think or feel when you lose your job, but we do know a great deal about the situation that confronts you. You are unique. The situation you face is not. We know that one immediate response is likely to be: This is the end of the world. We know how desperate you can feel. We know that you need and deserve support and encouragement.

We also know that losing a job is *not* the end of the world. There are fates worse than being fired. It's worse for your employer to placate you, to find a corner for you and not give you meaningful, productive work. It's worse for you to abdicate responsibility and turn over control of your life to a corporation.

Most importantly, we know you can turn what feels like a devastating tragedy into a personal and professional triumph. There is no way to escape the pain and anger that accompany the loss of a job, but you can control and dissipate those feelings. You can act rather than be acted upon. You can find a new job, or even a new career, and it can be more satisfying, more challenging, and even more financially rewarding than your previous position.

The process demands hard work and common sense, but no magic is involved. For once, you will be working for yourself, not for someone else. Through severance payments, in fact, your former employer may actually pay you to find a new and better job.

If you plan the search carefully, and if you put the same effort into finding new employment that you spent on your previous job, you will find a good position that is compatible with your skills and interests. You will also gain confidence in yourself and create real security for your future.

PARTING
COMPANY

CHAPTER 1

It Can't Happen to
Me . . . Can It?

Anticipating the loss of a job is like choosing the best way to be hit by a truck. You rarely get to test even the most ingenious ideas, because you usually don't see the truck—or the ax—before it flattens you.

Losing a job is almost always a shock and a surprise. Your boss, your peers, the business media, even your subordinates may anticipate your fate, but they may not pass the word along. And if they do, you may not hear them. People have an extraordinary ability to disregard threatening news. Your boss tells you, "I know how tough things have been, but your work really hasn't been acceptable." You walk away thinking, "Gee, he really *does* understand how tough my job is." Your company may be taking a beating in the marketplace, but you may decide, "That's Marketing's fault. No problems here in Manufacturing."

Frequently, when people leave termination interviews, where they have been told in plain language that they no longer work for the company, they return to their offices and bury themselves in work. What has just occurred seems like a very bad dream, and they hope that, like other nightmares, it will go away if ignored. They are also trying desperately to save the day. "I'll show them," they're saying. "I'll work so hard that someone will notice how valuable I am and save my job."

When corporations hire us to prepare large groups of employees for layoffs caused by reorganization or staff reduction, we suggest the news be made public as quickly as possible. The companies worry: if employees learn that a plant or business will shut down for good in six months, won't everyone jump ship or stop working immediately? We tell them not to be concerned. If operations are to cease on June 1, most employees will begin to think seriously about their futures on June 2.

In fact, when we conduct these sessions, perhaps our most difficult job is convincing people that the plant really *is* going to close. No one likes to admit it, but everyone keeps an eye peeled for individuals riding white horses. Even in today's environment of cost cutting and overhead reduction, which almost always exact heavy tolls on employee levels, one thought lingers: It can't happen here.

And even when people agree that it certainly *can* happen here, they may cling to a final hope: Well, it won't happen to *me.* Many simply refuse to believe that the company where they've worked so hard for so many years will actually take away their jobs.

This unwillingness to accept or acknowledge a terribly unsettling situation is common. Even people who don't like their jobs use them to define themselves and the people around them. We begin conversations by asking, "What do you do?" Our jobs determine when we get up in the morning, how we spend our time, where we live, even how we dress and who our friends are.

The harder we work, and the higher we rise, the stronger this relationship becomes. If we reach the level where being driven around in long black automobiles gets to be part of the job, the suggestion that someone may tamper with things becomes cause for alarm and a good reason to change the subject.

Yet an out-of-work clerk is likely to feel just as threatened as a terminated chief executive officer, so the determination to cling to a job is undoubtedly caused by something much deeper than a need for perks and fringe benefits. One real fear is economic. How will you and your family survive? What if you can't find another job? What will happen to the house, the car, your savings? Another fear is psychological and emotional: the fear of losing the structure provided by employment. Might you simply spin out of control?

Such fears prompt a few people to spend their careers worrying about losing their jobs. If you've ever had to deal with such an individual—trying to get him or her to make a decision, for example, or take a stand on a difficult issue—you may have sworn never to fall into a similar trap. You may even have concluded that any act of watchfulness is negative or counterproductive.

Staying alert is not the same as running scared, however. There are warning signals to watch for, signs that indicate your job is not secure. No one enjoys thinking, "It could happen to me," but business life is so volatile today that it becomes more and more realistic to recognize the relative insecurity of most jobs.

Understanding the warning signs lets you assume a degree of control over your future. You may be able to save your job if you discover it's in jeopardy. A realistic appraisal of the situation may convince you that you don't *want* to save your job and may prompt you to move forward to a more rewarding future. You may conclude that you are in better shape than you imagine. But even if your worst fears are confirmed, and the situation seems hopeless, you can prepare yourself to take an active role in the termination process and not let others make all the decisions for you.

The Seven Danger Signs

1. You Hate Your Job. If you feel really negative about your job and do nothing to remedy the situation, you will probably be terminated within a year. Even if you try to hide these feelings, you will subconsciously telegraph them to the people you work with. Most of us simply don't have very good poker faces. If you do mask unhappiness and dissatisfaction, the only measurable result is likely to be high blood pressure. Something must give, if each morning you climb out of bed and think, "Oh, no, I have to go *there* again."

Job dissatisfaction is the most important danger signal, but since it seems so obvious, and perhaps because it is so widespread, many people never consider it as a reason for losing a job. The very thought makes most of us uncomfortable, because it suggests that what we feel, not what the boss thinks, is the starting point for possible termination. This can be a particularly troublesome issue in periods when massive cutbacks seem to occur with depressing regularity. You hate your job, but you're not at all convinced there's another, better job out there to take its place, so what can you do? If you answer "Nothing," someone else may do something about it for you.

HOW DO I FEEL ABOUT MY JOB?

Write down your current feelings about your job. Be as specific as you can. If you like your job, try to figure out why: is it the people, your industry, the assignments you're being given? If you dislike your current situation, try to pinpoint specific reasons for your feelings. If you feel lukewarm about your job, put those ambiguous feelings into words. If your feelings tend to shift between enjoyment and disenchantment, try to be specific about the situations that evoke both responses.

_____

_____

_____

_____

_____

_____

Did you immediately take the time and invest the effort to complete the exercise above? Or, in your hurry to "get going" on your future, did you skip over it? If you *really* intend to make an efficient, effective career choice but didn't complete the exercise, we strongly urge you to do so now. It's important to complete each activity in this book as you reach it.

Career continuation is a systematic process: you gather information, analyze the data to create a plan, and, finally, implement your plan. Skip any stage in the process, and you jeopardize the results. All the information we're asking you to develop is important. Actually putting your thoughts down on paper improves them: you're forced to organize and analyze the material. In a month or two, you might find yourself sitting in a job interview where you'll be amazed to realize how a note you write down today or tomorrow helps you confidently answer an interviewer's tough question.

2. You Lose Your Voice. If people at work—superiors, co-workers, or subordinates—stop communicating with you, your job is in danger. Perhaps you anticipate bad news and have isolated yourself to avoid hearing it. Maybe your associates sense that your days are numbered and are pulling away from you. Either way, you should heed the advice of everyone's high school coach: "Don't worry when I'm yelling at you. Worry when I'm *not* yelling at you." If you are no longer invited to committee meetings, if you cease to be assigned to tough projects, even if you find yourself excluded from work-related social events, you should hear an alarm.

WHAT AM I HEARING?

Think back over the past six months or so. Have you been at the center of things at work? When people have had a difficult problem, have they come to you for help? Do your peers, subordinates, and superiors ask your opinion regularly? Note specific examples.

_____

_____

_____

_____

_____

_____

3. You Get Negative Feedback. It seems obvious that more
than one negative performance appraisal should be cause for concern. If you aren't doing your job, you certainly run the risk of
losing it.

But you may only listen for positive remarks during performance reviews and forget that the most important comments are
the ones that are the toughest to accept. Or, like many people, you
may convince yourself that you won't be fired no matter what the
boss says about your work: "He'd never fire me; he likes me too
much."

That's a very risky assumption.

HOW AM I DOING?

If your company has a formal performance appraisal process that
includes written reports for employees, review your last few reports.
Note the main points of each report—both positive and negative—and then summarize whether, in the eyes of your boss, your
performance has been improving, staying about the same, or deteriorating.

_____

_____

_____

_____

_____

_____

We should warn you of one unpleasant fact. While poor appraisals certainly represent a real warning sign, superior reports
don't always indicate the opposite. One of the most common re-
frains we hear from clients entering our programs is "This doesn't
make sense. On my last performance review I got high marks in
every category."

The performance appraisal systems at many companies are

notoriously unreliable indicators of the real feelings superiors have for their subordinates' contributions. Often it's simpler for supervisors to give a fair-to-good report than to confront real problems and thorny issues. But when the crunch comes and the superior is told to cut four people from his or her staff, reality intrudes with a vengeance. It may take the form of a single question: "If they're telling me to get the same job done with four fewer people, who do I really want around me?"

4. The Economy Is Working Against You. Today, it should come as no surprise to any American that doing the job doesn't necessarily make the position secure. Don't just look to newspaper headlines for news of the economy and how it might affect your job. Tuning in to the company grapevine or other informal sources of information within your industry can be valuable as well. Rumors of layoffs or deteriorating economic conditions within your firm frequently turn out to be facts.

Yet people continue to ignore the most obvious indicators. The fact that the new product isn't selling, or that new competitors are taking market share from their company doesn't alarm them. "It's not *my* fault," they say. Perhaps not, but it may very well turn out to be their problem.

WHAT'S THE ECONOMIC HEALTH OF MY INDUSTRY/COMPANY?

Summarize the economic status of your company and industry. Is business getting better, staying the same, or getting worse? Are there events on the horizon that could significantly improve or harm the health of your company?

5. You're Not Personally Productive. Even if your company is having a record year, if you are not producing you may lose your job. Sooner or later, the system will no longer be able to carry you. Most corporations share at least one priority today: a determination to increase the productivity and competitiveness of their operations. They demand more from their employees than ever before and do not hesitate to replace people who aren't delivering.

We counseled one man who, for several years, was given absolutely nothing meaningful to do and was paid well into six figures for doing it. He was shocked when he was terminated. We were shocked that it hadn't come sooner.

Companies are devoting a great deal of energy to looking for ways to cut costs today. They are receptive to almost any measure that will give them the slightest competitive advantage. The recent wave of staff reductions is a grim reminder of where they often look.

HOW PRODUCTIVE AM I?

Note recent accomplishments that attest to your personal productivity during the past three to six months. Wherever possible, try to quantify them in dollar terms: how much did they save your company or contribute to your firm's bottom line?

_____

_____

_____

_____

_____

_____

6. You Miss Objectives. Not only must you be productive today, but you must also produce effectively. If you confuse priorities, or if you don't manage your time well, your position will not remain secure.

Many people simply don't function well in the roles that have been assigned to them. They never figure out their jobs. They keep busy, but they don't accomplish the things they were hired to do. They fail to realize that the boss isn't looking for and frequently won't notice those other activities. She thinks, "That guy is always late with his work." He thinks, "Well, she can't possibly be talking about me. Look at all the things I'm doing. I work sixteen hours a day."

Perhaps not for long.

HOW'S MY AIM?

How well do you really understand what's expected of you in your job?
What work-related examples demonstrate that you are on target?
What extraneous activities interfere with getting the job done?

_____

_____

_____

_____

_____

_____

7. You Fail to Change. If you cling to the idea that tomorrow is going to be like today, you run the risk of losing your job. If the bottom line in your career is "I'm going to stay with this company," rather than "I'm going to grow and change with this company," your position probably isn't secure. If your hesitant response to a new plan or idea is "Well, I don't know. We've never done it that way before," you should be alert to potential consequences.

Today, more than ever before, companies are constantly changing and evolving, not only when corporate shake-ups bring in new management teams, but in the normal course of business life as well. If you want to continue to be a part of that life, you must be willing to adapt to change.

These seven indicators don't measure how good or bad you are. Don't assume that failing to change makes you a failure. You may be absolutely right to conclude that a new idea is, in fact, a lousy one. You may have lost your corporate voice raising points that are unpleasant to hear because they are uncomfortably valid.

But no one ever promised that being right would make your

job secure, so you should be aware that something unpleasant may happen if one or more of these danger signs apply to you.

Reasons for Termination

When someone loses a job, his or her employer usually picks one of four reasons to justify the decision: staff cutback, reorganization/merger, poor performance, or "chemistry."

Economic conditions that prompt companies to cut back, suspend, or redirect activities are an obvious reason for many terminations. Corporate response to a deteriorating economic situation has traditionally included staff reductions.

When companies refocus their operations, perhaps through mergers or reorganization or perhaps in response to threats from new competitors, managers may eliminate jobs and terminate employees in the process. Economic considerations need not come into play. If a strategic planning decision does away with a division, for instance, or if a management study shows that certain jobs are duplicated within the organization, people are frequently terminated.

On average, more than 60 percent of the people who enter our firm's career continuation programs do so as the result of cutbacks, mergers, or reorganizations. Throughout the '80s and into the '90s, these have been far and away the most prevalent reasons for termination.

Poor performance is the next most frequent reason for termination. Unsatisfactory performance appraisals, missed objectives or deadlines, low efficiency ratings, and other indicators of substandard performance are included in this category. Poor performance is not necessarily synonymous with incompetence. Bad attitude, poor management or supervision, even antiquated equipment or negative peer pressure can cause performance-related problems that lead to termination. Today, only about 6 percent of terminations are prompted by poor performance. (Staff cutbacks and reductions prompted by mergers or reorganizations undoubtedly lower this percentage rate by filtering out individuals who, ten years ago, might have lost their jobs for performance reasons.)

"Chemistry" refers to a variety of problems that can arise as people interact in a work environment. These include poor communication and differences in personal and professional styles.

When managers say, "He just doesn't seem to be a member of the team anymore," or "I can't communicate with her anymore," or "He always seems to be confused about what we're doing," or "She just doesn't understand the new direction we're taking," they are describing problems of chemistry. About 11 percent of our clients lose their jobs for stated reasons of personal chemistry, although the actual incidence may be higher. By the time an individual is presented the news, the official reason may have been restated in terms of performance: "You haven't been producing as well as you used to."

Bad chemistry can cause legitimate performance problems. If you are a sales manager who says, "We had to let him go because we kept getting bad feedback from our clients about him," you are describing both a chemical and a performance issue. Or, if you are at the other end of the line and your associates no longer consider you a member of their team, you probably won't be able to deal effectively with them, and you certainly won't be used effectively by them. Your performance inevitably suffers.

Questions of chemistry can create situations that are funny, peculiar, or even irrational and grotesque. For example, we counseled one man who lost an important job because of bad breath and body odor. How's that for chemistry? It was also a performance issue. His peers would literally not come close enough to work with him. No one told him the real reason for his termination. Once he changed his personal habits, his considerable competence became clear to prospective employers and he ultimately landed an excellent new job.

Another man was terminated eight months after his wife made an innocent comment to his boss's wife at a cocktail party. Our client's wife talked about how happy she and her husband had been where they last lived at his previous job. The boss's wife convinced the boss that the man wasn't happy at his current job. The man loved his work, in fact, and was performing admirably at it. When he was terminated he was told, "We understand you weren't happy here, anyway."

"Whatever gave you that idea?" the man asked.

"Oh, a lot of people knew it," he was told.

Individuals often create their own chemistry problems. At some point in their careers, for instance, most people discover they aren't going to become president of the company, that they will never become one of the four hundred richest business people in America, that the long black automobiles will never come calling for them. This realization can be devastating, particularly for competitive people who have been taught from day one to win, whatever the game. All of a sudden it appears that everyone else is doing better in life and has a better marriage, smarter children, a nicer house, more money, and a brighter future.

One common response to the situation is to blame the job or the company. Superiors rarely understand what's happening then. "I used to be able to work so well with him," they say, "but lately he's so hostile that I can't even talk to the guy."

Most people work such problems out for themselves. They accept the situation, or they make the move to a more acceptable environment. But others trap themselves in a vicious circle: "I'm never going to make it here," they decide, "but I can't risk something new at this point in my life, so I'll stay here anyway." Soon they are added to the list of people who have burned out at their jobs, and someone else makes the decision for them to move on.

There are additional, less frequently invoked reasons for termination. Ethical misconduct—also called "cause"—includes such acts as breaking laws or violating company policies. Individuals who misrepresent themselves or their work may be fired for cause. Responsible companies typically deal with these situations forcefully, since failure to act may be interpreted by others within the organization as unstated approval of questionable conduct.

Some people lose their jobs because, in the eyes of their superiors, their careers have reached a plateau. They lack the skills, experience, or inclination to progress further with the company. Only about 1 percent of our clients enter Drake Beam Morin programs for this reason.

Some General Steps to Take

These warning signals, reasons for termination, and case histories make the business world seem like a very dangerous place. How can anyone's job remain secure in the middle of such uncertainty? The answer is that no job is ever really secure, even in the best of times. But the question itself misses the point, because there is no need for jobs to be secure. *People* need to be secure. You don't have to depend on your job if you can depend on yourself.

What can you do if you see some of the danger signals striking very close to home? What should you do if one of the reasons for termination seems to have your name written all over it?

First, don't panic.[1] Congratulate yourself for being realistic and objective about your situation. Many people aren't so honest with themselves. Begin to consider alternatives and make plans.

The second step is to review your résumé, not because you may be needing it soon, but because the process is a therapeutic step that helps you begin to take stock of yourself. Writing down the facts of your career forces you to face them. We think you will be surprised and encouraged by seeing just how much and how well you have actually done in the past.

REVIEW YOUR ACCOMPLISHMENTS

Reread your most recent résumé to remind yourself of the things you've achieved in your career. Then write down accomplishments you've made since you last updated the document. Don't try to re-create your résumé just yet. Simply jot down recent "jobs well done" that come to mind.

_____

_____

_____

---

1. If you're reading this book because you just *did* lose your job, you may decide that the suggestion "Don't panic" belongs in a list titled "Things that are easy for *them* to say." But you are reading this book, which shows you've started to take deliberate steps to move forward with your life. That's the opposite of panicking.

_____

_____

_____

   Next, consider your current job by putting together an informal job description. This will require defining your job, something you may not have done in years. You'll see what you should be doing and whether you're actually performing those tasks.

DESCRIBE YOUR JOB

What are your job responsibilities? Which of these do you enjoy, and which aren't as satisfying? Make a list of pros and cons.

_____

_____

_____

_____

_____

_____

   Finally, draw up one additional document. To use an old-fashioned phrase, call it your "career path statement."

CHART YOUR CAREER PATH

Write down as much as you can about what you'd like to be doing at this point in your career. Try to decide where you would like to head. Be specific. Don't shy away from stating the amount of money you want to make or where you would be most happy living. Note what you *really* want, not just what may seem realistic.

_____

_____

_____

_____

_____

_____

_____

_____

   These three writing assignments let you see yourself in the past, present, and future. They show what your skills are, how well you are using them, and whether these skills—and your present job—are leading you in a direction that will reward you tomorrow. Do you perform well enough to stand behind your work? Are you maintaining visibility in your field by participating in business organizations or on industry committees? Are you keeping abreast of trends and staying aware of the direction your business is heading?

   This may also be a good time to think about taking advantage of professional career guidance resources. Many psychologists specialize in career counseling. Or you might contact organizations that administer tests to assess skills and aptitudes. Vocational counselors can work with you to determine where you should head with your career. (There are sharks in the career counseling waters, however, charlatans skilled in separating you from your money. Before you sign on any dotted line, read Chapter 12.)

Should You Quit First?

But what if you have more immediate problems? What if you think that, right here and right now, your job is on the line?

   You have three general options. First, you can choose to leave your job immediately, either by simply resigning or by negotiating your departure. Second, you can try to save the day by working actively to strengthen your position at work. Third, you can continue to work in much the same way you have in the past, realizing, however, that you might be terminated, and preparing to make the most of the situation if that occurs.

When should you quit? If you can absolutely no longer tolerate your job, if your dissatisfaction is causing performance-related problems that threaten to haunt your career in the future, or if unhappiness caused by your job is ruining the rest of your life, then it may be best to walk in to the boss, state that things simply aren't working out, and announce your decision to resign.

There are, of course, drawbacks connected to this plan of action. Does your company pay severance to people who resign? Probably not. How will you support yourself while you look for a new job? Will you have enough time to spend on your job search? Will you have to worry about the mortgage and how to convert your company medical coverage to a private plan?

Also, are you certain the situation is intolerable? Perhaps you simply anticipate being terminated and, rather than face that unpleasant situation, have decided to escape the firing squad by resigning first. If that's true, the job is controlling you; you're not controlling your future. And, even if you are right, what if just before you are fired, your company announces a voluntary separation program (see Chapter 4) that would ease the way to the next stage of your career?

Finally, many individuals—including, perhaps, potential future employers—are convinced that smart people don't leave one job until they have another to take its place. As the saying goes, it *is* easier to find a job if you have a job.

This may be true, but it is also true that finding the right job is generally a full-time occupation. No matter how much you want to change employment, when you're currently employed it can be hard to find time to conduct an intensive job search. You stand the best chance of finding the best job when you can apply all your energy to the task.

Suppose you are asked, "Why aren't you working now?" Your answer can be, "When I realized my former job wouldn't take me in the direction I wanted to go, I decided to look elsewhere. I found that I couldn't carry on an effective search without neglecting my job. I didn't want to shortchange the company, but I did want to get on with my career, so I resigned."

This may work, or it may not. So you owe it to yourself to consider all the risks before deciding to resign. At the very least, make it a rational process. (It goes without saying that the absolute worst thing to do is to get angry one day, decide "I'm not going to take it anymore," insult your boss, and quit. That's not resignation; it's self-destruction.) Even if you have given careful thought to your situation and concluded that resigning is the sensible thing to do, think it through once or twice more. Consider the other options that may be available.

Negotiating Your Way Out of a Job

You might be able to negotiate your way out of your job. There is substantial risk involved, but under the proper conditions, negotiation can produce excellent results. The process involves telling your boss, "I've been giving serious thought to leaving the company, and I'd like to make the move as smooth as possible both for myself and for you." Then discuss whether together you can work out a plan for doing so.

Perhaps he or she can assign special projects to you so that, free from normal routine, you can spend some of your time concentrating on your job search. You might agree to help select and train the person who will replace you so the transition is orderly. The idea makes a great deal of sense because it minimizes trauma and disruption for both the company and you.

After all, if you resign immediately, your boss has a problem. He must find a replacement—never an easy task—and until he does, others in the organization must add your duties to their own.

But don't underestimate the risks. If you try to negotiate your way out of a job, you have to be prepared to resign if the process doesn't work. Your boss's response could be, "Well, yes, let's see what we can work out." But it could also be, "If you're telling me you don't want to work here, then you'd better plan to leave quickly." Or it could even be, "You've obviously made up your mind to resign, so I think it's best for everyone involved to make it effective immediately." You could easily end up with no severance and no benefits.

When one large corporation terminated a group of executives as part of a major reorganization, one man tried to negotiate his way into the group of people who were let go. This man was highly regarded by management and they wanted him to stay, but the cutbacks and general direction the company seemed to be taking troubled him, and he wished to leave. He tried to negotiate his own settlement, but it didn't turn out well.

His superiors worried that agreeing to his request would set a dangerous precedent: other valuable people might be tempted to resign and ask for the same settlement package. They gave the man nothing.

Negotiated resignations and settlements will no doubt become more common in the future, because in many cases they meet the needs of all involved. And, in fact, the voluntary separation programs we will discuss shortly are a current, popular form of negotiated termination. But frequently there is still some resistance to the idea—a feeling that it isn't quite right to "reward" people for quitting the company. This makes it difficult for many employers to agree to such programs.

If you sense that the environment in your organization is receptive, however, and if you have good experience, a good track record, and a solid relationship with your boss, negotiated settlement may well be a good idea. You might even be pleasantly surprised. You give the company a chance to suggest alternatives when you bring up the idea of a negotiated settlement. If they want to, they have the opportunity to make you a counteroffer you can't refuse. But you must also be willing to accept other consequences, which may include resignation.

Strengthening Your Hold

It is more likely that you don't want to leave your job. What if you don't wish to resign? Are there actions you can take to strengthen your hold on your current, apparently tenuous position?

If you sense that things are going badly, talk with your boss.

Ask what steps you can take to manage your job more effectively. Make sure you're not looking to be stroked and coddled, but are really looking for suggestions and are willing to listen to them. If your boss says, "Well, as a matter of fact, you're not doing very well at all," and your response is "How can you say that?" you aren't likely to improve matters.

You might even force the issue. If you ask, "How am I doing?" you give your boss the opportunity to decide, "Oh, why prolong the agony? I might as well finish this unpleasant business right now." (Should that occur, you can at least console yourself with the knowledge that nothing was likely to have reversed the course of events. At least you took an active hand in the process.)

The principal difficulty with trying to work out these problems on your own is that they are often based on "chemistry" issues. If you have trouble communicating with your boss, or if he or she has difficulty communicating with you, chances are slim that the two of you will be able to talk your problems away.

Drake Beam Morin has created and refined a management service to deal with this situation. Directional Counseling is a program that helps companies work with problem performers to avoid having to terminate them. The program requires that a trained consultant work with both the employee who is not performing adequately and with the individual's boss. Two important characteristics make this process different from a single individual's attempt to correct a difficult situation on his or her own.

First, both the boss and the employee are committed to solving the problem. The boss, by investing his time and the company's money, has agreed to participate in the project. The employee takes the program seriously because he has been told in no uncertain terms that his job is in jeopardy. Second, the consultant keeps the process on track. When participants fall into the kind of behavior patterns that caused the problem in the first place, the counselor helps them resolve issues rather than magnify them.

So it may be unrealistic to expect too great a response from personal attempts to salvage your job. This is where the third option makes sense. Continue to do your job. Try to perform as well as you can, so you can stand behind your work. At the same time, arm yourself so if you do lose your job, you'll be prepared to move to a new and more rewarding position. To do this, you'll need to learn the art of getting fired.

CHAPTER 2

The Art of Getting Fired

No one ever taught you how to get fired. You probably haven't had much in the way of practical experience about losing your job. What happens? How will you react? And most importantly, how should you respond to being terminated?

If this were a perfect world, losing a job would be a straightforward matter. Your boss would call you into his office one morning early in the week. He'd get right to the point: "I have bad news. I'm going to have to let you go."

He would give concrete reasons: "As you're undoubtedly aware, the company has spent the past several months assessing the business and determining the areas most likely to keep us profitable in the future. Your position and skills don't fit into that picture. You've done a good job for us, and that makes it extra difficult for me to deliver this news, but that's the situation."

Or she might say, "In the past six months, you've been seriously late with three reports. We have discussed these problems before, and I suggested a number of things you might do to improve your performance. Last week, you were late with another project. When you did turn it in, the work was unsatisfactory. The task had to be reassigned to another member of the department. Now we're seriously behind in our group objectives, and I have no choice but to make a change immediately."

In either scenario, your boss would take no more than five

minutes to describe the chain of events that prompted your termination. Then he would listen. He'd try to get you to talk and would
keep trying until he was convinced you understood his decision
and your position. He wouldn't argue with you, apologize, make
promises he couldn't keep, or attack you personally. He wouldn't
try to get you to agree with his decision. He would simply want
you to accept it as a fact.

Then he would talk about your severance package. He'd say
how much severance you would receive and how it would be
distributed—in regular installments or a lump sum. He would
describe how your other company benefits would be affected: medical coverage and life insurance policies, for example, as well as
profit sharing, pension plans, and other fringe benefits.

He might tell you that office space and secretarial help had
been reserved for you for a specific length of time to help you make
the move to a new job. He might say the company would supply
career continuation counseling during your job search, either one-
on-one or, if you were part of a group cutback, perhaps a series
of group workshops. He'd probably give you a letter describing all
the details of the support package he had just described.

Finally he would identify your next step. He might introduce
you to a career continuation consultant. He'd at least tell you
where to go when you left his office and who to contact at the
company if, later, you had additional questions. He would finish
by suggesting you take time to think about and plan your future
before making any immediate decisions. The meeting would be
businesslike, and the conversation would avoid pontification and
recrimination.

If this were an ideal world, here's what your reaction might
be. "I obviously don't agree with your decision," you might say,
"but it's pretty clear that my most immediate concern is what I'll
need to make the transition to my next job. I feel that I'll need six
to nine months' severance as a bridge to new employment.

"I also think my fringe benefits, including my company car,
should be continued during that period. And I'd like to receive
career continuation assistance. After all, I've spent all my time

working at this job, not trying to find another one, and I admit I'm out of practice when it comes to searching for work.

"This is obviously a shock and a surprise to me," you might add. "It's no secret that the company has been suffering, and I've seen the handwriting on the wall. But I never imagined my name was part of the graffiti. I need some time to think about the situation. I'd like to meet with you again tomorrow to discuss reference statements, my profit-sharing benefits, and anything else that needs to be resolved."

And then you'd leave.

This isn't a perfect world, however, and neither you nor your boss is likely to act quite so coolly or rationally. If you've never received lessons in getting fired, he's probably never been taught how to fire anyone. Unless he's a whip-toting sadist (in which case you can give thanks for being rid of him), he won't enjoy the task. No matter how justified he may feel, he's likely to be uneasy or even frightened. (We have witnessed situations in which the person handling the termination was more distraught than the individual being fired.) Few people like to make enemies, and firing people has never been a surefire way to make friends.

Group layoffs are typically announced at a predetermined time, and the managers responsible for delivering the news have often received training in how to proceed. But if your boss is faced with a single, individual termination, he may delay the confrontation for days or even weeks. As time passes, his anxiety will grow. When he does call you into his office, he may combat this uneasiness by moving toward either of two extremes.

He may decide that the best defense is a good offense. The result can be an insensitive, even brutal termination. Real and imagined sins may be dredged up. Your boss may try to attribute his decision to a majority rule: "No one can get along with you," he might say, or "Your people don't support you anymore." He may try to wring a confession of guilt or admission of failure from you. "You agree that you've done a poor job, don't you?" he may ask, or "You can see I have no alternative, right?" or "You never did like it here, did you?"

There probably won't be much of a discussion, and you may never resolve the real reasons for your termination. Your boss is unsure of himself and terribly ill at ease. He needs to convince himself he's made the right decision, and overkill seems his best strategy.

On the other hand, your boss might wander off in the opposite direction and never get to the point. He may tell himself that he's worried about your reaction to the bad news and is trying to soften the blow, when he's really just trying to make things easy on himself. In this case, you will find yourself in for a particularly surreal conversation.

You'll drink coffee, discuss the weather, and talk about your families. Finally your boss will say, "Well, I don't know how to . . . How have things been going lately?" You'll begin to deliver a progress report, and your boss will make lame attempts to bring the conversation around to the subject of your termination.

He may not succeed, and you may walk out of his office in a state of limbo. "I'm not sure we can continue this way," he may say. "You'd better go talk to Human Resources. Maybe they can find you a job somewhere else in the company." You leave wondering what has happened, and he sits hoping that someone in Human Resources will tell you the real news. You have been fired, but no one has delivered the message. You're in corporate never-never land.

Your boss could even head in both misguided directions, circling the issue awkwardly at first, growing frantic when he discovers things aren't progressing like a business school case study, and then overreacting. If you're able to remain calm and objective in the midst of such a barrage, you might turn this lack of control to your own advantage and negotiate an exceptionally comfortable severance package for yourself.

But you probably won't. Even if your boss is calm, supportive, and on top of the situation, you may not be. As soon as you realize you have lost your job—whatever the reasons—you may be besieged by uncomfortable feelings and emotions. And when the termination interview is finished, your boss gets to go back to his normal life. You don't. You've just been shoved into what appears to be a very uncertain new world.

HOW WOULD I COPE?

Imagine that you are sitting in your office. Your boss enters and announces, "We're going to have to let you go." What do you think your immediate reaction would be? What would you say? How would you respond?

_____

_____

_____

_____

_____

_____

Five Reactions to Termination

Whether you're the only person terminated or one member of a group caught in a major staff reduction, the bottom line tends to be a firm conviction that you have lost control of your life. You feel that you ceased to be in charge of things the moment your job was taken from you. You've lost the structure it provided, and the habits and rules that shaped your life an hour ago do not seem to fit this new and abnormal situation.

You are likely to react in one of five ways. You may be violent or you may be euphoric. You may react by trying to escape or you may respond with total disbelief. Or you may have anticipated the termination and may react accordingly. Let's look at this last reaction first.

Anticipation. This is the most typical reaction to termination. It is likely to occur to anyone who has thought, rightly or not, that he or she might lose a job. (If you're reading this book and currently hold a job, for example, you're dealing with the thought that, however faint or remote an idea it may be, termination isn't beyond the realm of possibility.) If you decide that one or more of the danger signs we discussed previously applies to your situation, and you subsequently lose your job, you'll be likely to have an "anticipated" reaction. You may be surprised and shocked by your termination, but the shock results from having your worst fears confirmed, not from being totally surprised by the decision. You may never have acted on these fears, and you may never even have admitted them openly to yourself. But at one level or another, you recognized them.

When the actual termination does occur, you're somewhat prepared for it. Your reaction is not likely to be too intense. You may say, "I don't think this is all my fault," or "It's too bad we couldn't work together," or "Top management failed, and my department took it in the neck," but you're likely to realize what the situation is and accept it as a real, if unpleasant, fact of life.

Some people anticipate termination to such a degree that they try to escape it before it ever occurs: they avoid their bosses, don't return phone calls, even stay away from their offices for days at a time. When they do get fired, they may be relieved. The pressure is off, and they don't have to hide any longer.

Others are angry, scared, or ashamed. But their feelings are not so intense that they become paralyzed. The common denominator in the anticipation reaction is the relative ease with which the individual accepts his or her fate.

The termination interview is not likely to be extremely emotional, as a result, and the individual is able to concentrate on practical matters related to a severance package and to the future.

Disbelief. You may not anticipate the termination at all, and your reaction may be complete disbelief. You'll feel totally shocked, and you'll say things like, "You can't do this to me," or "I won't allow this," or "This can't be happening to me." You may plead to keep your job, or you may beg for another position somewhere else in the company. You probably won't let yourself be drawn into a real conversation and will answer questions with a simple yes or no.

Or you may not accept the situation at all. You might tell your boss that you really ought to get back to work. You've decided to react by not reacting at all.

This can be a dangerous reaction to losing a job. We worked with one client who had been employed by the same company for twenty years. He rose through the ranks to become a plant manager, knew how to run every piece of equipment on the premises, but never learned how to delegate.

The pager he wore on his belt alerted him to the slightest problem even if he was fifty miles from the plant; he was on call twenty-four hours a day. His subordinates had standing orders to beep him when anything happened.

He ran his plant in this fashion for eight years, until the strain began to show. Serious problems developed at the manufacturing facility. On a Friday afternoon, the company fired him and put him on a plane to Chicago for outplacement counseling.

We had arranged for a meeting on Monday morning, and when he didn't arrive at our office, we called his former employer and learned that he'd been on his own all weekend. We called his hotel and got no answer at his room. When we went to his room and knocked on the door, the only answer was a moan. A bell captain let us in.

He was sitting in a chair with his feet drawn up to his chest in a fetal position. He shook uncontrollably. He hadn't shaved or showered. He thought he was going to die. He had never figured out what had hit him.

He was a capable and talented man, but it took six months of intense counseling before he felt confident enough to go to an interview. He started a new career, became a first-line supervisor, and within two years was back in charge of a large organization.

Escape. You can also react to termination by trying to escape the situation. "I can't stand this," you tell yourself. "I'm getting out of here." You understand what has happened to you, but you don't know what to do and decide that flight is the best option.

You may leave the termination interview before you understand the terms of your support package. You may head to the nearest tavern where, well fortified, you share your troubles with a less-than-adoring public. People have even stormed out of termination interviews and called newspaper reporters—sharing their problems in the most public and, potentially, the most self-destructive manner imaginable.

Euphoria. You might react as if you are delighted to hear the news that you have been fired. You tell your boss that you are positive you can handle the situation. Your boss is overjoyed; you've made a sticky chore easy.

That may present a problem. Euphoric reactions occur to people who are so highly geared to taking directions from their bosses that they agree to be terminated just as they would agree to work overtime.

If you think you've gotten where you are in life by agreeing to everything, why stop now? Keep agreeing, and the boss will take care of you. The trouble with this approach is a misunderstanding of exactly where you've gotten in life.

We counseled one woman who seemed positively overjoyed about her situation. She was excited, outgoing, and an absolute pleasure to work with. It took her two and a half years to find a new job. It took us that long to get her to be realistic about her situation without losing her enthusiasm. Nothing that was offered to her seemed "real," she said, and when she talked to potential employers, she left the impression that she wasn't seriously looking for a job.

Violence. The reaction that terminators and terminees fear most is the violent response: What if I punch him in the mouth? an employee wonders halfway through a termination interview. What if he punches me in the mouth? the boss asks himself. It is actually the least common response to the situation. Almost everyone feels some degree of anger at being terminated, but most people control their emotions; even those who do make threats are less likely to carry them out than to feel sheepish about having made them.

If there is violence during a termination, it is usually verbal. You may scream, holler obscenities, threaten to sue the company, or swear that you will pull it down with you by publicizing damaging news.

Several years ago we decided we would have to terminate one of our managers. (It happens everywhere.) We sat down with him in his office and launched what we thought would be a well-delivered, sensitive termination interview. When he heard the news he began shouting at us, then jumped from his chair, threw open the door of his office, and yelled at his secretary, telling her it was all her fault and condemning her for not supporting him.

Not having the faintest idea what was going on, she was thoroughly stunned. He stormed off to the receptionist, started in on her, and finally barged out of the office.

Later, he tried to make amends. Still later, he asked his former secretary to help him with some typing as he began his job search. "Not on your life," she said.

Five Common Emotions

If you react violently to losing your job, you are venting the anger the situation has provoked. There are other feelings and emotions that are commonly associated with termination. People we counsel tell us that one, several, or frequently all of the following emotions surfaced almost immediately after they learned they had lost their jobs.

Anger. Someone has just taken something very valuable from you—your livelihood—and you feel furious. Who do they think they are? How can the company let your boss cover his failures by taking your job? You've spent years working for them, and this is what you get in return.

Shame. You have lost something valuable, and you have an unpleasant feeling that it's your own fault. How could you do this to yourself? How could you be so dumb that you never saw it coming and never did anything to avoid it? How will you ever face your family and friends? How could you be such a failure?

Fear. A central part of your life's structure has been taken away suddenly, and you don't know what the consequences will be. How will you pay the bills? What about your children's tuition? Will this ruin your marriage? Are your friends going to ridicule you? What will this do to your career? Will you ever find another job? Worst-case scenarios race through your mind.

Sadness. You have lost your job, and that is cause for mourning. You'll never find another to match it. Friends and co-workers will be left behind. Life will never be this good again. It's all downhill from here. This is the end of the world.

Self-Pity. You don't deserve this fate. How could they do this to you? Why, of all people, were you singled out? Why not somebody else? You just did your job, stayed out of office politics, and look at the thanks you got.

These are the most common emotions, but they aren't the only possibilities. We mentioned, for instance, that some people feel relieved when they lose their jobs. If you've been hanging on to a really unpleasant position, and if the pressure has been eating you alive, then it makes sense to feel relieved if you get fired.

As a matter of fact, you have every right to feel any emotion, no matter how strange or ugly it may seem. The question is: what do you do with these feelings?

The Art of Getting Fired

What can you do to improve the situation, or does the art of getting fired mean rolling up your sleeves to help your boss slit your wrists?

There is most definitely something to do, and the key to the process is realizing that, while you cannot control how you feel, you can control how you react. The art of losing a job involves taking control of a very negative incident and turning it into a positive—or at least neutral—situation. You can accomplish this by identifying all your options and measuring each against a single yardstick: what is the best thing you can do for yourself in this situation?

Imagine you are in a termination interview and have just heard the words, "We're going to have to let you go." Pretend that you can stop the world for a few minutes to discuss your options with a trusted adviser.

"So, how do you feel?" he or she asks.

"I'm furious," you reply. "How could they do this to me? I'm going to let that guy have it, tell him just how angry I really feel. I'll blister his ears."

"That's definitely an option," your adviser says, "but what's it going to do for you? Will telling him off get you a better reference when you need one?"

"But I'm really angry," you say. "That guy didn't look out for me. He's a liar. He's dead wrong. I'm going to punch him in the mouth."

"That's certainly an option," your confidant says, "and it might make you feel better, but it also might land you in a police station."

"But I'm mad."

"And you have every right to be," your friend answers. "But if you hand him that anger right now, all you'll do is convince him he made the right decision. He'll say you're acting like a child. So let's assume that's not a great choice.

"Now," your adviser continues, "what else do you feel?"

"I feel really sorry for myself," you say. "I didn't deserve this."

"What can you do about it?"

"I could go over my boss's head and get his boss to give me back my job."

"That's an option," your friend says. "But what would it get you? Don't you think your boss already cleared this with his boss? Didn't Human Resources, and the Legal Department, and who knows what other departments, sign off on this decision, too? What do you gain by trying to hang on by your fingernails? Are you going to get the best possible deal by taking this route?"

You can consider all your options in this way. If you feel ashamed of the situation, you may conclude that running from the room and out of the building is a pretty good idea. Ask how that will help you. If you're not letting yourself feel any emotions yet, you may be pretending it's all a bad dream and nothing's really happened. Will that view improve matters?

This process should begin to warn you away from useless or self-destructive paths of action. But what if you simply can't control your emotions? What if you realize that, whether or not it's a good idea, you're about to explode? What if you're getting ready to cry?

The best thing to do is leave. But don't run away, and don't try to convince yourself nothing is wrong. Tell your boss that his decision has taken you completely by surprise. Say that you need time to think about the situation. Tell him (and remind yourself) that this is a critical issue for you, and say that you need time to consider your options so that you can deal sensibly with them. Make an appointment to see him the following day. (Don't wait much longer than that, however. As time passes, the company loses interest in you and may become more difficult to deal with.)

Unless you feel very sure of yourself, postponing matters for a day makes good sense. You'll have some time to come to terms with your emotions, and you'll be less likely to do or say something that could return to haunt you as you move forward with your life. This is an important life issue, after all, and you ought to have your wits about you.

Be aware, however, that you may not have much freedom of choice if you've been caught in a group reduction. The apparatus put in place by your company to deal with the event may leave little room for flexibility.

If you decide to leave immediately, do just that. Leave immediately. Don't go back to your office. Don't start a conversation with anyone. If someone comes up and says, "You don't look so good. . . . Is everything OK?" answer that something has come up, you have to leave immediately, and you'll tell them about it in the morning. Go home. Avoid liquor. Don't telephone everyone you've ever known. Don't try to contact the president of the company.

If you feel you may really lose control and do something that will hurt you or someone around you, get professional help immediately. Call your doctor or contact a psychologist or psychiatrist. We mention this sort of crisis as a possibility. We are sensitive to it and watch out for it in our business. It's not a situation to fool with, so if you're not sure of yourself, get a professional's opinion.

What if you are in good enough control of both the situation and yourself to continue the dialogue with your former employer immediately?[1]

What you need to take home with you is an understanding of what the company is prepared to do for you. They have undoubtedly figured out the severance package already, and you need to know the details. How much will you be given, and how will it be paid to you? (Chapter 3 discusses why regular checks can often be preferable to a single large payment.)

What will happen to your fringe benefits? Will your medical coverage continue as long as you receive severance pay? What about profit sharing and your company's pension plan? What will become of your other fringe benefits—a life insurance policy, for example, or a company car or club membership?

Will the company provide additional support as you look for a new job? Will they give you an office? Will they answer your telephone? Will they provide secretarial support? Will they pay for career continuation counseling to help you sharpen your job-search skills?

Beyond these practical considerations, you'll also want to learn as accurately as you can exactly what caused your termination. You need to know precisely what happened, not because you might save your job (you're through with that thought by now), but because the information will help you plan for the future. It may not be pleasant: you may be told you drink too much, or you never meet deadlines, or your department really did think you were an animal. But you should ask the question nevertheless.

You may not get a straight answer, particularly if you are being fired for reasons related to personal chemistry. In addition, the company's legal staff may have told your boss what to say and what topics to avoid.

If you don't agree with something in the severance package or you're not sure whether you should agree to one or more of its

---

1. If you nodded agreement as you read the word *former,* give yourself a gold star. You're beginning to realize that you no longer work for the company. You now work for yourself.

clauses, the best thing to do is to say, "I'm not sure about this. I want to take some time to put my thoughts in order. Can we get together tomorrow to finish up?"

If your boss replies, "I'm sorry, but that's all there is, and that's all there's going to be," say, "I understand your position, and the fact that we're at an impasse, but I really need more time to think. So it would be best if we met tomorrow."

Don't say, "Well, that's OK," to something that isn't. But don't be argumentative or defensive, either. Make the best of the situation.

Realize that the period from the time the company tells you you've been terminated to the time you leave the office for good is an extremely delicate interval. It may last ten minutes, or ten minutes plus the next day, or perhaps a much longer period of time. As long as you're there, measure everything you do against its potential effect on your future. How will it influence the search for your next job?

CHAPTER **3**

The First Seventy-two Hours

"Don't get mad, get even" is a popular saying and, if you've just lost your job, a terrible piece of advice. You deserve better counsel: Get mad, but don't get even; get *ahead*.

You have two immediate priorities: dealing with your emotions (getting mad) and answering several practical survival questions. Tackling these issues helps to orient yourself away from the past (and the urge to get even), and toward the future (and the opportunity to get ahead).

During the first seventy-two hours after you have been terminated, you should concentrate on understanding and accepting what happened to you so you can begin to devote your energies to the practical business of finding a new job. What you do and how you react during this three-day period will determine the general ease or difficulty with which you find new employment in the weeks and months ahead.

This is easier said than done, of course. Major concerns surface just when you feel most vulnerable. Being on the street is no longer a cliché but a new and unpleasant fact of life. Your emotions threaten to engulf you: confronting them may seem particularly risky just now. You've been handed a difficult assignment—determining your future. You haven't asked for this assignment, you probably don't know how to proceed, and all of a sudden you may feel very much alone.

35

Incidentally, in the next chapter we discuss early retirement and voluntary separation programs: staff reduction methods in which people who may lose their jobs are given a central role in making the decision. If you've just learned you're eligible for a program of this type, you probably aren't out of a job today, but you probably are feeling a variety of emotions. We suggest that you deal with them before making any decisions about your future.

In either situation, you may be convinced that you and your life are suddenly and totally out of control. To top it off, here are two executives with comfortable jobs (as of this writing, anyway) telling you to take control of stormy emotions and troubling details.

Do Nothing

Our first piece of advice sounds simple, but it probably isn't: Do nothing. Your immediate impulse is likely to be: "I need a job, any job, and I need it right now." This is the vocational equivalent of remounting the horse that just threw you. But with horses—as with determining your future—you can save yourself considerable pain by assessing the damage, figuring out why you got thrown, asking whether some other form of transportation might serve you better for your next ride, and then adapting your plans accordingly before climbing back on.

Resist the temptation to call business associates or contact search firms now. You're not ready to talk to either yet. Getting a new job is a systematic process, and if you do things out of sequence, you penalize yourself. Don't talk to people now about getting a replacement job. You don't know what to say to them yet, and you'll probably scare them off if you try. Later, when they can really help you, you may not be able to call on them if you've spooked them this early in the game.

Dealing with Emotions

The important thing is to start the process and stick with it. Look at your emotions first.

HOW DO I FEEL?

In the space provided and on as many additional pieces of paper as you can fill, write down your emotions—how you feel, *not* what you think. Are you sad? Angry? Furious? Relieved? Scared? Don't edit these comments or examine them as they surface. Just let them spill out in sentences, phrases, single words—however they come to mind.

_____

_____

_____

_____

_____

_____

_____

_____

In the previous chapter we discussed the need to control your feelings during your termination interview, no matter how greatly you may have wanted to scream or moan or strangle your former boss. Once you leave the building, however, what's best for you changes. Now you need to vent your emotions, to get them out of your gut and into the open in a way that's safe for you and the people who are important to you.

What happens if you don't? If you hang on to your emotions, they'll almost certainly trip you up later in the job-search process. In a job interview two months from now, you'll be asked a question about your former employer. Let your bottled-up anger show, and a prospective new boss may wonder whether you'd use the same language to describe him or her in the future. Utter as tame a phrase as "I never could get along with those people," and your words may be transmitted up and down the pipeline with a slightly different twist: "He has trouble getting along with people." Try to hide your fury, and you'll furrow your brow, clench your teeth, and mutter something about a "fine" company. You won't fool anyone.

We know one employer who won't hire anyone who says anything negative, however mild, about a former employer. He might be looking for a great engineer, and he might be convinced you are a great engineer, but if he hears you say, "Gee, they had some problems there," he simply won't consider you for the position.

Don't imagine you can hide your emotions. If you've just lost a job, the fact is written all over your face. Two groups of people normally sit in the reception area of our New York headquarters: representatives of companies interested in our services, and recently terminated individuals who are beginning the career continuation process. To our knowledge, no one has ever confused a member of one group with a member of the other. Losing a job is a powerful shock, and it shows.

Don't think your emotions will go away if you simply ignore them. If you don't do something with them, they'll grow. Refuse to deal with your feelings of self-pity, anger, or failure, and a potential employer may conclude, "She left that job six months ago, and she still hasn't gotten over it. She doesn't sound very flexible or adaptable." Continue to feel ashamed about having been fired, and you'll never appear self-assured or self-confident as you look for employment.

Drake Beam Morin consultants meet many of their clients moments after the individuals have been terminated, so they can begin to discuss the situation immediately. By the time these clients go home at the end of that first difficult day, they have already begun the venting process that helps them identify and resolve their emotions.

There are times, however, when we don't begin to work with people until weeks or even months after their terminations. We find that most have been unsuccessful in their job searches because they have neglected their feelings. They have become rigid and even self-destructive, and have been running in circles or staring into space rather than finding new jobs. Putting them in touch with these feelings, a task that might once have taken three days, may now take three weeks or even three months.

Our advice about dealing with your emotions is simple: The longer you wait, the harder it gets, so do something now. Talk to someone. Tell him or her how you feel, what you think, and what hurts. You need a friendly, supportive, noncompetitive shoulder to lean on.

If you are married, your husband or wife is your most obvious choice, but not the only person—and, in some cases, not the best one—to turn to. Your spouse may feel even more threatened by the loss of your job than you do, and he or she might not be able to provide the calm, understanding assistance you need. In addition, when people are terminated for poor performance, there is often a correlation between trouble at work and trouble at home. Losing a job is not likely to strengthen a weak marriage, and if your relationship is troubled, your spouse may not be able to give much support, and you may not be willing to accept it.

Losing your job doesn't have to ruin your marriage, of course. It can improve the relationship, in fact, if your spouse is willing and able to provide help, and you are willing and able to accept it. Couples frequently tell us they pulled together for the first time in years when one of the partners had to find a new job suddenly.

But if you decide to call on someone other than your husband or wife for emotional support, don't pretend you can keep your termination a secret from your family. You may feel scared and ashamed, and you may be tempted to suffer alone. You could even leave home at the normal time each morning, your pockets stuffed with quarters and your destination a telephone booth from which you plan to conduct a secret job search. That has actually happened and, to our knowledge, has only increased the trauma. The idea of a secret job search is a contradiction in terms.

Let's suppose it does work. You find a wonderful new job to replace the one you lost. You rush home to tell your spouse the good news, and he or she is furious—and rightly so—at being cut out of your life at a critical moment. Your next search could be for a new family.

What other person might you turn to? A close friend often makes a good confidant. People frequently ask members of the clergy for help; even if these individuals have no training as job counselors, they are likely to be supportive. You could get in touch with a professional vocational counselor, or a psychologist or psychiatrist. Don't make the mistake of thinking it's a weakness to seek help. Seeking help is a sign of strength and an indication that you intend to improve your situation and not wallow in it.

Professional credentials can indicate experience or expertise, but they may not be necessary in this case. Your most important consideration should be to find someone willing to listen, draw you out, and support you. You need someone who won't make judgments about how you feel but who will encourage you to blow off steam. He or she should simply be able to keep you talking so that you can air your feelings in a safe environment.

Professional counselors use a number of tactics to help people vent their emotions. They ask open-ended questions to encourage wide-ranging responses rather than *yes* or *no* replies. As a simple example, instead of asking, "Do you feel sad?" they might ask, "How sad are you?"

They use restatement and reflection to draw people out. If you say, "I just got fired," they say something like, "You mean they let you go after all these years?" If you say, "I feel terrible," they might ask, "Well, what does that make you feel like doing?"

If you're having trouble talking about your feelings, they'll ask questions to get you started: "What's the one thing that is uppermost in your mind right now?" "What do you think your first step should be?"

These are simple questions, and they involve no psychological mumbo jumbo. Trained career continuation consultants have a body of experience and knowledge to draw on, and that makes them adept at keeping the venting process on track. But a good listener's most important attributes are compassion and understanding, traits that are rarely the result of training.

There are, on the other hand, counterproductive traits to watch out for in would-be confidants, patterns that trained counselors working with a reputable organization are unlikely to exhibit. Beware, for example, of people who speak in clichés.

Someone tells you, "I know just how you feel." (Oh, no, she doesn't.) Someone says, "It's not all that bad." (How on earth does he know how bad it is? It certainly feels "that bad.") Someone tells you, "No problem, you'll find a job easily." (How can anyone be so sure?)

Be especially alert for people who make judgments about your situation. "Gee, how the devil did you get yourself into this mess?" they may ask. "Don't you think you should have seen it coming?" Even if you *should* have seen it coming, you don't need to be reminded of that fact now. Some people, even close friends, cannot refrain from attacking others regardless of the circumstances. Tell them "Thanks anyway," and find someone else to confide in.

Now is not the time for advice, so be wary of anyone who offers you a list of immediate suggestions: "OK, now the first thing you ought to do is call Frank Jones at Acme. Then you should make an appointment with . . ." The purpose of the venting process is to finish dealing with the past in order to prepare yourself to deal with the future. Don't let someone put his or her cart before your horse. Find a person who is comfortable saying nothing more than "What's on your mind?"

Your role in the venting process is to say whatever *is* on your mind and work to bring your feelings and emotions out into the open. If you feel angry, describe how you feel angry. If you feel stupid for letting all this happen to you, try to say why. If you think it's all your former boss's fault, here is the right time and a safe place to say so. If you think you're a failure because you never went to graduate school, get that off your chest. If the whole mess is a conspiracy, mention that as well.

Don't be sensible. The purpose of this process is not to make sense but to clear the air. You're doing fine if you find yourself saying, "This may sound crazy, but . . ." or "This is totally illogical, but I feel. . . ."

The more feelings that surface, the better. In fact, you should be most concerned if you don't feel anything and sit paralyzed in a sea of failure and dejection. Don't let yourself get mired in this sort of silent self-pity. Talk about it.

How long should the venting process continue? In one sense, it never really ends. Years from now when you are happily and successfully working somewhere else, something may remind you of the day you lost your job. "That still makes me furious," you may think. "I'll never understand how I let that happen." You'll spend a few moments lost in thought, then shake your head and go back to work.

At some point in the venting process, you will see a change in your reactions. It could take three hours, or two days, or five days. But sooner or later you will notice that your thoughts are beginning to shift: from what has happened to what to do next. One moment you are complaining about the raw deal you got, and the next minute you may say, "Yeah, but what am I going to do now?" This is a signal that the healing process is being resolved and you're ready to start dealing with other needs.

Three days of venting is a good target to aim for. By the end of that time, you will probably have exhausted and digested your emotions so that you can live with them. If it takes only a day to reach that point, so much the better. If the process lasts four or five days, that's fine, too. If you're still at it after much more than a week, however, it's time to take a hard look at the situation.

You may simply be procrastinating. If the future looks particularly threatening, you may have decided to maintain the status quo for as long as possible. You don't feel too good right now, but who knows, things could get even worse. Why find out? (The most popular occasion for postponing matters comes later, however, when the time approaches to actually talk to someone about employment. Some people spend weeks working on a two-page résumé, telling themselves that it needs to be perfect. What they are actually doing is postponing the day when they have to put themselves on the line by calling or meeting someone about a job.)

You may find that, rather than confronting your emotions, you are hoarding or burying them, becoming more bitter and less sure of yourself every day. If this happens, find a professional counselor or psychologist to help you unload the dead weight and head in a constructive direction. The process of finding a job is punctuated by ups and downs, highs and lows; if you notice yourself getting stuck anywhere along the way, find someone who can help you get moving again.

At the same time, if you feel ready to move on to other matters, don't conclude that you've seen the last of your emotions, and don't consider it a disaster if unpleasant feelings surface again in the future. Expect more of these normal ups and downs, and you'll be able to deal with them, just as you have now.

There is much that is neither neat nor orderly about the search for a good new job. For the sake of clarity, we have tried to make our discussion move logically from one step to the next, and we have suggested that you will simplify the process by trying your best to stick to a plan. Life isn't always quite so predictable, however.

We recommended, for instance, that you take no action until you've dealt with your emotions, a process that may take three days or more. We also suggested that if you did not discuss your severance package during your termination interview, you should schedule a second meeting for the next day. We obviously owe you another suggestion: how to follow both bits of advice.

You must be your own judge. If you don't feel you can control your emotions so soon, don't meet with your former employer until you can. The longer you wait, the less interested he or she may be in your demands. But calling the boss names or dissolving into tears is likely to help your cause even less.

If, on the other hand, you need more immediate answers to questions and are reasonably certain you can conduct the meeting in a temperate, rational manner, go ahead and schedule it even if you haven't yet resolved your unsettling emotions. Consider your options and do what you think will be best for you.

But your primary concern in the first seventy-two hours should be your emotions. If you haven't begun it already, start the venting process now. Review the exercise you completed on emotions (page 37). Rewrite it or make additions if you feel differently now. Find someone to confide in, and begin to vent your feelings.

Practical Considerations

When you finally shift from emotional matters to practical concerns, your first questions are likely to revolve around one topic: money. How much severance should you receive? How much will you get? How will it be paid to you?

As you look for answers to these questions, think of the severance package as a bridge to a new job. Don't look at it as a way to get back at the company or to even the score with your former employer. That approach eats up time, energy, and, if you alienate people, perhaps money as well.

It may help to think of yourself as a new business. You are the product, and your goal is to market yourself to a new employer. To do this profitably, you'll need to identify your costs, set objectives, and specify the services you can provide. You'll have to develop a sales or marketing plan and put it into action.

To start this new business, you'll need to consider your financing: the severance package. In one sense, you're being given a remarkable opportunity. Your former employer is paying you to work for yourself!

How Much Severance Should You Receive?

Our clients frequently ask us to assess the severance packages they've been given. Have they been offered enough? Should they have asked for more?

There really are no answers to such questions. For one thing, asking them assumes that severance is a right rather than a privilege. In fact, unless your employer has established a formal, quantified policy on severance, or unless you've negotiated such an agreement with the company (perhaps as part of an employment contract), not only is setting severance levels an entirely discretionary decision for a company, but deciding to offer *any* severance is voluntary as well. It's no secret that many American workers who lose jobs receive no severance benefits whatsoever. In one sense, then, because any severance can be considered an extra, optional benefit of employment, whatever an employer offers is "appropriate."

At the same time—particularly with the massive corporate staff reductions and reorganizations of the past decade—offering severance has become institutionalized at many companies, even if it hasn't been made official policy. These corporations have given the matter substantial thought, reached firm decisions, and are unlikely to be willing to make many exceptions to them.

Suppose, for example, that Company X offers voluntary separation to a group of its employees. It creates a severance package which management believes enough workers will accept so that the corporation's staff-reduction goal will be met. Then, a year later, the company decides it must announce an involuntary staff reduction.

Management now faces some difficult decisions. Should it offer the same package it did a year ago, or should it sweeten the deal for involuntary terminations? Suppose a more generous package is created. What happens if, a year from now, the company introduces a second voluntary program? Will employees turn it down, hoping they'll do better by waiting for another round of involuntary terminations?

Remember that many companies now believe restructuring and reorganizing aren't one-time events, but a continuing strategic process determined by changing market and economic realities. Under these conditions, management sets precedents with care. In such an environment, there are probably more productive ways to spend your day than wondering whether your severance amount should be amended.

In some terminations, however, unique circumstances could affect the severance package. For example, a company hires an executive away from another firm. In four or five months, management realizes the decision was a poor one and the relationship is not working. Given most standard severance policies, the terminated executive would receive a meager severance package. But this may not be considered a fair solution because the company made at least as big a mistake in offering the job as the individual did to accept it. The executive now has to start a lengthy job search, for which he is unprepared because the company lured him away from his former employer.

We recall a situation in which a large industrial company decided to bring a fresh outlook to its marketing efforts. The company hired a senior marketing manager whose background was in consumer sales, thinking he might provide the innovative approach. Six months later, everyone realized that their good idea had turned out to be a bad decision. Not that the man wasn't trying: he was doing everything imaginable to make a go of the situation. But members of the company's field sales staff weren't accepting the changes, and neither were the firm's customers.

The idea didn't work, and the executive didn't deserve to be blamed or penalized. The company gave him a severance package that enabled him to concentrate on finding his next job, not on his dwindling bank account.

How Much Severance Will You Receive?

Even among companies with formal severance policies, it's rare to find two organizations that share precisely the same severance formula. But the following components, in varying degrees, usually enter into the decision: age of the individual, position within the firm, salary, and length of service.

Different companies give different weight to each variable. Age may be more important than salary to one employer, while at another company, length of service may carry more weight than position within the firm. At least one large, well-known corporation gives a flat, six-week termination payment to everyone, regardless of age, rank, or serial number. Other companies offer a full year's severance to people who have been with them for less than five years.

So the first thing to do is determine whether your former employer has a formal severance policy. If there is such a policy, you can at least make certain that you fare as well as anyone else at your level. This will be your bottom line, but it doesn't necessarily have to end up being the package you receive. Suppose, for example, you think it will take you six months to find the right job, and your company offers you four months' severance. Is there anything you can do?

You can try to negotiate an open-ended severance agreement.

Consult your former boss. Assure him or her that you are planning and are determined to carry out a serious, full-time employment campaign, but that you may need more time to find a good job than the company's payment plan provides for. Try to work out an agreement that if you haven't found work by the end of the formal support period but have worked hard at the process all along, the company will continue your severance payments for a month or two more.

The only real chance you have of securing such an agreement is to convince your former employer you will devote all your energies to finding a new job. Offer to supply regular progress reports as you carry out your search to demonstrate how seriously you take the task.

If the company will not accept your proposal for an open-ended agreement—and many will not, for fear of setting an expensive precedent—you may be able to arrange an informal agreement with your former boss. When your severance period elapses, it is likely that he or she will have to take some action to have you removed from the payroll. This action can possibly be delayed for several weeks or a month, perhaps by as simple a maneuver as not getting around to completing the necessary paperwork for that length of time. Your personal relationship will obviously influence your boss's willingness to do so—a good argument for the importance of acting calmly throughout the termination process.

Even if your boss does agree to such a plan, however, remember that the situation could change drastically before it is ever put into effect. He or she might be promoted, transferred, or even terminated before your severance period ends and, as a result, not be able to help. Or, four or six months from now, your boss may no longer want to help you.

If you decide to seek either a formal or informal agreement to extend your severance period, you need to act quickly. Your former boss is likely to be somewhat concerned about your future immediately after your termination. Five months later, he or she may not want to be reminded of the incident.

Finally, understand that your options for negotiating an enhanced severance package are likely to be more limited if you are included in a group staff reduction or a voluntary separation program. Strict severance guidelines are typically part of these programs, and at most companies, the fear that making an exception for one employee might start an avalanche of requests from others can make it very difficult to bargain for special benefits. Still, if you think your situation really does represent a special case, you probably won't be risking much to at least raise the subject with your former superiors.

How Should Your Severance Be Disbursed?

With only a few specific exceptions, we advise our clients to ask to be paid in regular installments, so that they continue to receive paychecks. You need to concentrate on the job of finding a job. That is where you should invest your time and energy. The best way to do this is to keep the rest of your life as normal and stress-free as possible. By receiving regular paychecks for the duration of your severance period, or until you begin a new job, you'll have one less new thing to worry about.

If you receive a single, lump-sum payment, by contrast, you have to decide what to do with it. You may have to worry about your tax status. You may begin to focus on the money and not on your primary target, getting a good new job. You may even move too quickly, taking the wrong job because you want to hang onto as much of the lump sum as you can.

In addition, if you receive a single payment, you are likely to be removed from the company's books immediately. That normally removes you from health and insurance plans as well. Instead of putting together a solid job campaign, you find yourself shopping for medical coverage. You have other things to do.

Given the stress associated with losing a job, the chances are probably better than normal that you might invest your money poorly. One man took his lump-sum severance payment and rushed out to buy a business of his own. He had no experience working on his own, however, and he wasn't equipped to run the business. He stampeded himself into the situation because he was terrified of being without a job. He lost the business, he still needed a job, and he had no money to tide him and his family over during the search.

Somewhat paradoxically, making the decision to go into business for yourself is one of the few instances in which accepting a lump sum can make sense. But be very careful here. If, in the past, you have given considerable thought to the idea of working for yourself and have investigated possibilities and alternatives, or if you have been waiting for an opportunity to head off on your own, now may be the time to act. But be skeptical of your motives if the idea of starting your own business first came to mind after you lost your job. It could be a panic reaction. Reject the possibility outright if you entertain it because you think it may be easier to buy a job than to find one.

As you'll see in a later chapter on starting your own business, many of the people who begin Drake Beam Morin workshops devoted to work-for-self careers soon discover they really aren't cut out to be their own bosses. What initially appears to be an ideal situation—working for yourself in an area that's always interested you—may, on closer investigation, not look quite so good. Long hours, a continuing struggle for profitability, even the prospect of loneliness in their own small business, prompt many would-be entrepreneurs to reconsider their plans.

The other situation in which a lump-sum payment makes sense occurs when you consider retirement after losing your job. If you are nearing retirement age and really *want* to retire, then you will probably wish to invest your severance to supplement the financial arrangements you've already made for the future. But think before you act. A 64-year-old who wants to keep working should go out and find work. A 55-year-old who has wanted to retire for the past ten years should investigate his or her chances of turning that dream into a reality.

If you must take your severance in a single payment, see your banker, broker, accountant, tax lawyer, or preferably all four. Get sound, conservative advice. You can't be certain how long it will take to find a new job, so now is not the time to invest in speculative deals. Don't take chances.

And don't expect your former employer to make suggestions about how you should handle your money. Companies have landed in court by giving advice that turned out poorly for individuals who subsequently turned around and sued them.

Remember, because finding the right job should be the focus of all your activity, arranging your financial matters so they don't intrude on the time you devote to your job search should be an immediate priority. If you are offered a lump sum, for example, you might be able to trade it for the kind of open-ended severance agreement described earlier. Suggest to your former employer that you be kept on the payroll for as many pay periods as the lump sum would cover. Then, in exchange for the company's agreement to extend the severance period should the need arise, agree to stop receiving payments once you start a new job, even if you are still owed additional severance. You may convince your former employer that you aren't trying to make money at the company's expense, but that you want and deserve a tool to help take you to your next job.

This tactic may work in another situation, too. Among firms that pay severance in regular installments, some companies stop these payments when an individual takes a new job, while others continue payments for the full severance period. If you find yourself in this latter category, consider negotiating the kind of swap described above.

Other Practical Concerns

You may have other practical matters to resolve in addition to your severance agreement. If you had a company car, can you keep it for a while? If you were given a club membership as part of your employment package, how long can you continue to use it? These questions are not as frivolous as they may sound. Just as you don't want to spend your time worrying about money, you don't want to divert yourself by looking for a new car. If a club membership was valuable to you in your last job, it will continue to be valuable to you and your family in your present situation.

There may be additional financial topics to consider. If you were covered by a pension fund or profit-sharing plan at your last job, you will want to discover whether you are owed any benefits. If so, you will have to decide what to do with them. Once again, professional guidance and a conservative investment approach are probably good ideas at this time.

You should also determine whether your severance package contains any additional benefits that will help you proceed with your job search. Will the company provide career continuation counseling? It will certainly help as you conduct your campaign. Will office space or secretarial help be provided by your former employer?

Consider your family's needs as you sort through these practical and financial questions. Suppose you and your family have spent the past six months planning and anticipating a vacation that is scheduled to start next Saturday. Consider how canceling it might affect them and, as a result, yourself. Unless a financial investigation indicates that you are in dire straits, go ahead and take the vacation. It will reduce stress all around. (But if you haven't scheduled a vacation, don't plan one now. It won't help to evade your current situation.)

Meeting Your Former Employer

After you have considered all these topics, you should determine whether you need to arrange another meeting with your former employer. If you didn't discuss your severance package on the day you were terminated, if you don't understand all its details, or if you think you should try to negotiate a settlement different from that which was offered to you, go ahead and set up the appointment.

You may also find it important psychologically to face the person who fired you and find out why it happened. If your former boss is willing to see you (some companies discourage second meetings), that's a good sign. He or she will probably be supportive concerning your future needs.

On the other hand, if you do understand your termination package and feel you can live with it, then you may not want a second meeting. It could be explosive, and you don't need any more fireworks.

Moving Ahead

Finally, to discover whether you are ready to move to the next stage of the job-search process, ask yourself this question: "What's my problem?"

If you answer, "I just lost my job," you haven't finished dealing with the past. If you say, "I need a new job," you're ready for the future.

CHAPTER 4

Deciding Your Own Fate—Early
Retirement and Voluntary
Separation Programs

So far, we've focused primarily on involuntary terminations, situations in which your company's managers decide who will leave and when they'll go. But with increasing frequency—particularly when corporations decide that large staff reductions are necessary—employees are being asked to participate in the process of determining their own fate.

The voluntary separation program, a new kind of manpower reduction tool, strikes some observers as a humane process that lets individuals play a central role in deciding their own futures. Others view these programs as insidious, thinly disguised weapons that push employees to leave companies while removing the responsibility from its rightful place: management.

In a nutshell, a voluntary separation program involves the company's identifying an eligible group of employees, creating a package of severance benefits, and offering eligible individuals a time period in which to accept the offer. The employees can either leave the organization voluntarily in return for the benefits, or reject the package and stay on the job. The company decides who is eligible, and the eligible individuals decide how to respond.

Eligible employees who turn down the offer do so with the understanding, either explicit or implied, that if the voluntary program fails to achieve its goal (that is, if too many individuals elect to remain with the company), an involuntary termination program may follow. And there, of course, is where the controversy arises. Is voluntary separation a threat or an opportunity?

We'll explain our point of view by starting with some history. In one sense, voluntary separation programs aren't new at all. For years many of the nation's largest corporations have offered similar opportunities to employees in the form of early retirement programs.

Early Retirement Programs

Typically, these companies found their organization charts out of whack: too many employees were lodged somewhere in the ranks of middle management. The individuals had served the company well, but for most of them continued movement up the corporate pyramid was unlikely. There wasn't room, or they lacked the skills, experience, or determination to progress further in the corporation.

At the same time, however, employees who joined the company more recently were ready and eager to see just how far up the ladder they might climb. From the vantage point of senior management, the company's future might depend on these people, who may have brought stronger educational backgrounds and more up-to-date skills to the organization than their older colleagues have.

Two things could happen if these individuals weren't given the opportunity to move their careers ahead rapidly. Either they'd lose the aggressiveness that made them valuable to the company, or they might leave the organization in search of a brighter future.

The challenge for senior management was to break up the human logjam. This involved two substantial obstacles. First, most companies really *don't* prefer to reward long-standing employees who have contributed to the company's success with termination. That's bad public relations and, in addition to being unfair, may send ominous signals to those who remain in the organization. As a result, it might hurt rather than help productivity.

Second, even if management doesn't care at all for its longtime employees, terminating a group made up exclusively of older workers would be a surefire way of attracting the attention of diverse government agencies, law firms, senior citizens' groups, and media outlets.

Enter the early retirement program, an incentive making it attractive for employees at or near retirement age to elect to leave the company voluntarily. Most such programs share similar features.

Typically, employees of certain ages—say fifty-five or older—who have been with the company for a certain length of time—say ten years or more—are offered incentives to retire. Additional years of what's termed "age" may be offered. Let's use five years as an example: in a company where retirement is normally an option at age sixty, a 55-year-old employee would become eligible to retire with benefits. A 65-year-old worker, by extension, would be treated as a 70-year-old in determining retirement benefits.

Years of service—again, let's take five as an example—might also be added, so that the retirement package for someone who has spent twenty years at the company would be determined as if he or she had served twenty-five years.

The exact terms of the early retirement package are tailored to the company's specific situation. If management concludes that the departure of substantially more older employees will be necessary to unclog the promotion arteries, the deal might have to be sweetened. Or if, over the years, management has done a superior job of making the company an ideal place to work, it will probably have to offer greater incentives to prompt individuals to depart.

In addition, decisions on a variety of employment benefits have to be made. Will employees accepting the package continue to receive company health insurance, for example? If so, for how long?

With any early retirement program, eligible employees are given a certain period, called a "window," during which they must decide whether to accept the package or reject the offer and stay on the job.

When the returns are in, the company totals them up to determine whether its goal has been met. If it hasn't, the possibility of a group reduction program may surface.

For a 64-year-old employee who is six months away from retirement, an event he has eagerly anticipated for twenty-five years, being offered such a program is like winning the lottery. But for most employees it is, at the very least, a terribly unsettling event.

What troubles many who become eligible for such packages is the concern that if they elect to turn down the offer and stay on the job, they may find themselves involuntarily terminated in the not-too-distant future, with a much less generous severance package to boot. People worry that, one way or another, companies use these programs to get rid of older employees whose years of service—and higher salaries—cost the company more than hiring new employees at lower salaries.

Is the early retirement program a reward for a job well done or a "take the package or beware" threat? The key is this: if an involuntary termination program follows the early retirement offer, the rules change. No longer can age or length of service be a determining factor for selecting individuals for termination.

That doesn't mean that older employees are safe from involuntary termination. If you're a 60-year-old manager at a company where, following an early retirement program, management decides it must cut staff by an additional 10 percent to remain competitive, you could be included in that staff reduction. But if a disproportionate number of your fellow terminees are also of age sixty or older, then the company may have a class-action suit on its hands. Indeed, such suits have been filed and won by groups of ex-employees who convinced the courts they were terminated on the basis of age.

An Offer You May—or May Not—Be Able to Refuse

Our opinion is that an offer of early retirement should be viewed as a bonus, a valuable opportunity to assume increased control over your life and career. That doesn't mean you should automatically accept the deal; it may not make sense for you. It does mean that you should investigate the opportunity carefully and then, based on a close examination of your own needs, decide whether to accept or reject it.

Remember that, even if you reject the offer, you're only placing yourself back into the ranks with all your colleagues. Unless your company *is* trying to break the law by discriminating against older workers, you face the same risks as your fellow employees. The difference is that you've been offered an option they haven't received.

This is not to say that confronting an early retirement offer is an easy task. For most people it's more likely to be terrifying. In fact, it's not at all rare for individuals to tell us, "I can't make this decision. I simply don't know the right choice. I wish the company would either tell me I have a job or just plain fire me."

Later in this chapter, we'll offer advice for making sense of an early retirement offer so that you can feel with some level of certainty that you've made the right choice. But first we'll introduce early retirement's younger cousin.

Voluntary Separation Programs

By the beginning of the '80s, the early retirement program had begun to evolve into a somewhat different form: the voluntary separation program. As corporations across the nation struggled to find ways to reorganize their operations or lower their overhead to compete more effectively, a new phrase entered the language: the "reduction in force," or "RIF." "I just got 'riffed' " became a common, anguished refrain as massive, involuntary group terminations were announced in one industry after another.

But at some companies where reducing staff was acknowledged as a competitive necessity, management worried that such reductions might have serious consequences. There were concerns about fairness, legality, and the effect of such large cuts on remaining employees.

The people who were *not* terminated, after all, would be the horses on which the reorganized corporation would have to rely in the future. If they were demoralized by the departure of friends and fellow workers, or if they felt threatened that their own names might head some hidden "hit list" for the future, the organization could turn out to be even less competitive than it had been before the changes were made.

Enter the voluntary separation program. A key difference between it and the early retirement program is that the voluntary separation program is most often introduced against a backdrop of corporate reorganization, where the company may be redefining the entire nature and scope of its business. Management may decide that the kind of people it employs today will not be the kind of people it needs tomorrow.

It's not just a question of whether there are too many middle managers in a division. It may be a matter of whether the division itself will have a place in the company of the future. If you're employed in that division, and if your skills or experience don't fit the redefined vision for the future, you may well be included in a group offered voluntary separation.

If you decline the offer, however, you may not remain on an equal footing with the rest of the corporation's employees. There may be no opportunities for you in the reshaped organization, and involuntary termination could follow.

Look, Don't Leap!

Once again, however, this does not mean you should automatically accept an offer for voluntary separation. As with an early retirement offer, you need to learn as much as you can about the specific program and its implications for you and for the company's future plans. You need to learn as much as you can about your own financial, vocational, and emotional or psychological needs. And then you need to use all that knowledge to determine whether the offer makes sense for you.

That's the key: does it make sense for you? Let's create a hypothetical offer and see what it might mean for two hypothetical employees. The Big Deal Corporation announces a voluntary separation program open to all employees over the age of forty-five who have at least ten years of service with the company. The package includes a month's severance pay for each year of service (up to a maximum of thirty months of severance) and one year of continued medical benefits and company life insurance, as well as full profit sharing for the current year and immediate payment of all earned retirement and pension benefits. Eligible employees must announce their intent to accept or reject the offer within three weeks.

Jane Jones is a 47-year-old manager who has been with Big Deal for twelve years. She's moved up through the company relatively quickly and has been given increasingly important and visible assignments. Her performance reviews and salary increases have all been above average or better. She is currently concluding an assignment as head of a project team responsible for getting an important new product to market.

Joe James is a 58-year-old manager who has held his current staff job for six years and has been employed by Big Deal for twenty-six years in all. He is comfortable in his position, genuinely enjoys his work, and, while he feels it would be unrealistic to expect major promotions or new assignments at this stage in his career, he believes that his contributions are valued by his colleagues and superiors.

At first glance, it might appear sensible for Jane Jones to reject the offer of voluntary separation and for Joe James to accept it. Jane looks like a rising star making her way up the corporate ladder from one important post to the next. Senior management certainly wouldn't want to lose her.

Joe James seems competent enough but has apparently reached a plateau in his career. Because a general trend in business is to cut staff positions in favor of line assignments where employees can contribute directly to the company's profits, Joe's position may be shaky. If he refuses the voluntary offer he could be a prime candidate for involuntary termination, should such a program follow the voluntary offer.

But basing a decision on this cursory examination of the situation could be misleading. Suppose Jane Jones sits down and really examines the situation and her own needs. She realizes she's had some concerns about the company over the past year or so. Yes, she's been given good assignments and has been amply rewarded for doing those jobs well, but. . . .

Over the years, Jane has built a range of industry contacts through trade and professional associations. Her sources tell her that one of Big Deal's competitors is about to introduce its own new product. If what I hear is true, Jane thinks, it might be superior to our own new product and even beat us to the market-place. If that's the case, it won't be the first time we've been leapfrogged in recent years.

Jane believes that one reason the company has been beaten to the punch is that it cuts costs in the wrong places. Sales and marketing staffs continue to grow, but product development and manufacturing departments don't keep pace. She's felt the pinch in her own assignments, where she hasn't seen the investment of sufficient resources to get quality products out the door quickly.

If this voluntary separation program turns out to be more of the same, she reasons, I may still be a rising star, but on a smaller and smaller stage. That's not the role I've been shooting for.

Jane recalls a telephone inquiry from an executive search con-sultant a month previously. The prospect of a new job at a new company begins to sound attractive. And, if Big Deal will give her a year's pay to make a move, so much the better! She locates the number and picks up the phone.

Joe James has also been thinking about the voluntary separa-tion offer. His plan has been to retire at age sixty-three, five years hence, when his wife, Jean, will turn sixty and become eligible for retirement and pension benefits at her own job.

If he accepts the offer now, Joe thinks, his twenty-six years of service will earn him more than two years' severance. That won't make up for the five years of employment income he'd factored into his retirement planning, but if he retires immediately, he could cut his expenses and might just be able to swing it.

"But I don't want to retire yet," Joe tells himself. "And I know Jean doesn't either."

Joe talks to a colleague who is involved with manpower plan-ning for the company. "I certainly don't know what's going to come of all this," the man tells him, "and I'm in no position to make any promises, but my guess is that you'd have a good chance of surviving a subsequent involuntary reduction. They're not focusing on your part of the business this time around. They're trying to get a handle on massive costs in the production end."

As Joe drives home that day he thinks, We're not ready to retire yet. And even if I do get fired later on, I'll get some kind of severance. It's not as if we're going to starve, anyway. I'm just not sure the difference is enough to make me jump now. I wonder what Jean will say.

Jane and Joe haven't made up their minds yet, and that's smart. They win no extra points for early decisions, and so they have no good reason to "leap." What they are doing is "looking," and that's smart, too. They're looking at themselves and at the company, gathering the facts to make sensible choices about this major life decision.

How the Company Sees It

If you find yourself eligible for voluntary separation, an extremely valuable first move can be to take a step back and consider your position from the company's point of view. (Valuable, but not easy. Your natural, immediate concern is likely to be, "What on earth am I going to do about this?") Understanding the program from your employer's perspective can help you sift through all the conflicting thoughts, ideas, and emotions that arise and may offer some clues for how to proceed intelligently.

Why does the company offer a voluntary separation program in the first place? Obviously, management sees a critical need to reduce or reorganize its operations. But that doesn't require a voluntary program. The company could achieve its staff-reduction goals entirely through involuntary terminations.

Our experience with dozens of major corporations—leading companies that have called on Drake Beam Morin to help plan and implement large voluntary separation programs—has shown that substantially more is involved. First, these companies typically want to minimize the impact of the staff reduction on their employees, both those who will leave the organization and those who will stay on.

Questions of fairness also enter into the decision. When management at these companies makes the difficult decision to abandon a business, for example, they realize that the gravest consequences will involve the individuals whose skills will suddenly be no longer useful to the company. They also realize that it probably isn't the fault of the people who possess those skills. In recognition of this fact, they offer these individuals an extra benefit: the choice of voluntary separation.

Finally, these companies are also concerned with the legal ramifications of large layoffs. One practical reason for creating voluntary programs is that such offers reduce the likelihood of legal actions relating to issues of wrongful discharge or employment discrimination. When they develop these programs, as a result, they are typically very careful to dot the *i*'s and cross the legal *t*'s.

How You See It

What does all this tell you as an affected employee? First, the company is showing some concern for you. Not as an individual, perhaps, but as an employee who is caught in the middle of a difficult situation. That's the good news. Second, however concerned management may be, it is more concerned about the future of the company and is willing to make unpleasant, expensive decisions to seek assurance that the future holds promise for the corporation.

You haven't been forgotten, but the company comes first. That's the company's point of view, but it shouldn't be yours. You need to come first. So scrutinize the situation and the offer to see how best to react in terms of your needs and your future.

How the Company Proceeds

Having made the decision that a voluntary program is necessary and desirable, the company begins to structure the offer. Who will be eligible, and what will they be offered?

There is no single way to conduct this process, but in a typical situation a task force of senior managers reviews the company's future needs. What skills will the organization require to prosper in the future? What skills do its employees possess today? Where are the gaps between the two, both in terms of future skills that aren't already represented in the company, and in terms of current employees whose skills don't match those future needs?

Based on this investigation, the task force creates a set of criteria defining, as accurately and narrowly as possible, a generic profile of employees whose skills will not be essential to the company in the future.

These become the eligibility criteria for the voluntary separation program. They are forwarded to line managers, whose job is to assess their subordinates in terms of the criteria. This is where individual names enter the process for the first time. If you fit the profile, you are identified as someone who would be eligible for the program. If your skills will be valuable to the company in the years to come, you are not included.

These assessments are reviewed and analyzed at various levels of the corporation, and a final list of employees who will be offered voluntary separation is created. Special conditions may be built into the offers made to some. If you're part of a group finishing up, say, a critical restructuring for the company, and if you'll need another four months to finish your work, you may be offered the package only if you'll agree to delay your departure and acceptance of severance benefits until you complete the project.

As this planning process unfolds, the voluntary separation package is also being determined. A variety of questions about severance, fringe benefits, profit sharing, accumulated retirement benefits, even company cars and accumulated vacation days needs to be resolved. The company must decide whether to offer career continuation services to eligible employees either to help them make a decision or, if they decide to leave the company, to help them determine their future career directions.

This can be a delicate process. Since the voluntary route was presumably chosen to avoid the necessity of involuntary termination programs, management ideally wants just as many people to accept the offer as will be necessary to meet the corporation's staff-reduction goal. At the same time, management's greatest fear is that too many people will accept the package and leave the company.

We recall one case in which a large corporation had this fear realized. Following a series of mergers and acquisitions, the company found itself overwhelmed by duplicated functions and over-populated departments. To address the situation, management offered a generous severance package to a broad spectrum of its employees.

What was never factored into the equation was that the merger process had fundamentally changed the culture of the company and many longtime employees no longer enjoyed working there. The dissatisfaction was not great enough to inspire large numbers to quit the company on their own. But when a generous severance package was offered in an environment of general disenchantment, people leapt at the offer. The company found itself in an embarrassing position: spending to locate new staff while it paid qualified individuals to leave.

When the package has been settled and the eligible employees identified, the program is ready to be made public. Often, a preliminary announcement is the first public mention that a voluntary program will be offered. Soon after that, the plan may be introduced in greater detail in a series of department or division meetings. Eligible employees are advised of the fact in person, either by their superiors or by the company's human resources staff.

To assuage the curiosity and uncertainty of employees who are not eligible for the program, some companies see to it that these people are also told in person that their names haven't been included in the group of eligible employees. However, to paraphrase Yogi Berra, a key point to remember is, "You ain't in until you're in." Until and unless you receive formal announcement of eligibility for a voluntary separation program, you are not part of the eligible group.

Eligible employees are most often given a document that confirms their eligibility and defines and quantifies the precise benefits they will be offered. The document may also explain any additional resources the company will provide to help them reach a decision, and it specifies the date by which they must make their decision.

How You Should Proceed

Suppose it's you walking out of one of these meetings, document in hand and uncertainty in your heart. Or, since the circumstances are so similar from the individual's point of view, what if you've just been offered early retirement? How should you proceed?

First, you need to deal with your feelings. When people first learn they are eligible for a voluntary program, many report that they feel one or more of the following: sadness, happiness, confusion, fear, concern, or even relief. That's understandable, of course, since they're facing an unusual, threatening, and somewhat mystifying situation. But, because they're also faced with an important life choice, it's important that they—or you—understand several things about these feelings.

You owe it to yourself to accept your right to have such feelings, whether they make you feel good or bad. Next, recognize the fact that at this important junction in your career, your feelings can be managed in a way that either hurts or helps you. Finally, you need to take control of your feelings in the most positive way possible.

HOW DO I FEEL NOW?

Return to the HOW DO I FEEL? exercise on page 37. If you haven't completed the exercise already, do so now. Then reread the section on dealing with emotions that follows it. If you did complete the exercise previously, review your comments to see if your feelings have changed at all in the interim.

When you've finished dealing with your feelings and emotions, you need to find out as much as you can about two general subjects: what can or will happen to you, and how you should react to those possibilities.

Let's examine the *what* issue first. By the end of the window period, one of two things is going to happen to you. Either you'll accept the offer and leave the company, or you'll reject it and stay on. It will be helpful to learn as much as you can about what is likely to occur in either event.

What If You Leave?

You need to know in detail precisely what accepting the offer of voluntary separation will mean for you. Exactly how much severance will you receive? How will it be paid: all at once or as a series of paychecks? What about your family's health insurance? Will it stop as soon as you leave the company, or will it be continued? For how long? If your company offers dental insurance, will that continue as well? What about a life insurance policy you've had for years as a condition of your employment?

If you accept the package, what effect will that have on the pension or retirement benefits you've built up over the years? What about profit sharing? If you have a company car, computer, or club membership, how long will you keep them?

What will the company do to help you reach your decision? Will they offer career continuation programs or counseling before you make your choice, so you can get expert advice about your options? Or is this a decision you'll have to make on your own? If such programs are offered, can your spouse attend them with you?

If you're thinking about such career options as starting your own business or retiring, will there be company-sponsored programs to help you think through those possibilities? Will such programs be offered before you must make your decision, or will they take place after the window period and be open only to individuals who have accepted the offer? If there are a number of these programs, can you attend as many as you want, or will you have to pick and choose?

You owe it to yourself to ask and get satisfactory answers to as many of these questions as apply to you. Talk to your boss and to the company's human resources staff. Don't assume that asking questions now will make you a target later on, should an involuntary termination program follow the voluntary effort.

At the same time, don't telegraph your intentions, and don't rush to a decision. Give yourself time to reflect on all the information you're collecting.

WHAT IF I ACCEPT?

If you've been offered early retirement or voluntary separation, use the space provided here, and additional sheets of paper if you need them, to answer as many of the questions just discussed as you can. If you don't know the answers, find out from your superiors or from human resources professionals at work.

_____

_____

_____

_____

_____

_____

_____

_____

As you assemble this body of knowledge, what if you think you should try to negotiate more . . . an extra six months of severance, perhaps? Our experience is that you probably won't have much luck with this tactic.

Management has probably given a great deal of thought to the package it has announced, and will most often avoid making an exception for one individual that could mushroom if other employees ask for and receive the same. If the company has been careful about tailoring the package to meet its program goals, the thought of sweetening the deal and perhaps inviting a situation in which the program becomes oversubscribed is not likely to meet with much approval.

Still, if you genuinely think your situation deserves special attention, you won't lose anything by raising the subject with your boss.

"I'm obviously giving this offer a great deal of thought," you might say. "I honestly don't know which way I'm going to go, and there's one issue that keeps coming up for me.

"You know that I just started the business study I'm working on two months ago, and it's going to take at least another six months to complete. My sense is that it's an important project for the company. What do you think the chances would be for me to agree to stay an additional six months to complete the work, in return for receiving the voluntary package at that time, and having the package based on the salary, service, and benefits I'm due at that point?"

What If You Stay?

If you're persistent enough, you should be able to determine precisely what the voluntary program means to you if you elect to leave the company. It can be a lot more difficult—but no less important—to find out what your situation will be if you choose to remain.

At the end of a voluntary separation program, the company analyzes the results in terms of the firm's redefined needs, to determine the condition of the resulting organization. Holes may have been created in the new organizational structure by individuals who accepted the package and left.

To fill these gaps, the company typically looks first at employees who have stayed on the job but whose positions were eliminated in the reorganization. If their skills match any of the openings, they are offered positions. If they do not possess the essential skills or if there are no openings, they become the object of an involuntary termination program, and they ultimately leave the company that way.

The problem here, of course, is that you don't know who's left and what's left for them until after the voluntary offer expires. So you need to learn as much as you can about the possibilities beforehand.

First, talk to your manager, and perhaps to your manager's manager, and try to determine how much he or she does or doesn't know. You may learn nothing. Managers involved in these programs are often instructed in advance how to conduct themselves when the inevitable questions begin. They may be advised to say nothing more than "I just don't know."

Remember that you're dealing with a *voluntary* program. If managers begin to tell one subordinate, "Don't worry about a thing," while they say to another, "I don't think the future looks too good for you," the company could find itself responding to allegations that the program wasn't voluntary at all. It might be seen as a process of coercion aimed at getting certain employees to leave the company, disguised as a voluntary program to escape legal hurdles to terminating those employees.

At the same time, since your manager is a human being, and perhaps also a personal friend or business mentor to you, he or she may want to share knowledge and impressions of the future, no matter what the company says. You owe it to yourself to allow that conversation to happen.

When it does take place, listen very carefully to what's said and how it's phrased. In addition to the fear that too many people will leave the company, managers throughout the organization also worry that the *wrong* people will depart. A boss who wants you to stay on will probably find some way to tell you, either directly or indirectly.

It might not even require a single spoken word. Your question, "Do you think I ought to take this offer?" might be responded to with an intent stare and a vigorous shake of the head, "No." You'll get the message. (Remember, however, that what your boss wants isn't necessarily what *you* want. He and his whole department, you included, may not be part of the company's future plans.)

When you talk to your boss, you may get a message you don't particularly want to hear. One manager we worked with had this conversation with each of his subordinates: "I honestly don't know what's going to happen," he said, "but there's one thing I am sure of. The company as we've all known it is dead. The new company taking its place is going to be a lot different. It won't be the same place and it won't have the same pace. There will be a lot more asked of people. If you're not going to feel comfortable in that environment, you'd better give a lot of thought to this offer."

Think about the conversation with your boss ahead of time. Many people imagine they can go in and say, "Look, if you promise me exactly this job for exactly that pay, I'll stay. Otherwise I'm leaving." Don't make such stipulations. In the middle of a voluntary program, the company is in no position to make promises. Be wary of managers who promise you things they may not be able to deliver.

Try to find out what your boss knows or thinks about the future of the company and your department or division. Has he or she been given any clues about future plans and goals?

Don't just talk to your superiors. Ask colleagues and your own subordinates what they're hearing about the future.

You may find other clues to your future in a number of places. Consider the eligibility requirements for the program, for example. Our hypothetical example of the Big Deal Corporation, where anyone forty-five or older who's been with the company for more than ten years is eligible, suggests two possibilities. Either the company didn't do its homework to determine more precise requirements, or its unstated goal may be to trim the number of middle-aged and older employees in the organization. Whether or not you fit that profile, it does offer you one more piece of information to store and assess.

What if, on the other hand, the eligibility criteria are a lot better defined? If your voluntary separation program is limited to chemical engineers in the coatings products division, you can reasonably suspect that the company has some pretty detailed plans for your division. And you'd file that away.

Finally, think ahead and try to imagine your future in the company if you do stay on board. The first question that comes to almost everyone's mind is "If I don't leave now but do get terminated later, will I get a better severance package or poorer benefits?"

Our answer is an emphatic "We don't know." If your company has been through similar programs before, you may be able to discern a pattern. But some companies offer voluntary terminees better packages, while others believe in giving better benefits to employees who have been involuntarily terminated. Ideally, we don't think either group should be put at any real disadvantage, but there is too much diversity of thought from one company to another to make valid generalizations.

What if you stay on and don't get terminated? Nothing might change: you could simply continue to do the job you've held all along. Or life could get a lot better, as you become involved in the new opportunities and challenges of a reinvigorated organization.

But consider the other side of the ledger, too. What if you stay on, don't get caught in a future involuntary termination, but end up reassigned to a corner—a job you can't stand and a situation that soon becomes intolerable? In the company's mind, you have a job and therefore nothing to complain about.

You could find that your salary is downgraded. Or your salary might stay the same but your job could be downgraded, a situation with its own problems: you might be stuck in that position because you're already above the pay grade for your job. You receive a paycheck, but nothing else. The only way out may be to leave the company—with no severance at all.

While these things do happen, we don't raise them to scare you but to show how important it is to consider every available thought or piece of information you can discover.

WHAT IF I DECLINE?

If you've been offered early retirement or voluntary separation, use the questions and information just mentioned to list the potential consequences of refusing the offer. Once again, use all sources available to you to create the most accurate picture possible.

_____

_____

_____

_____

When we counsel individuals facing the decision of accepting or rejecting a voluntary offer, our objective is that they make an *informed* decision about their future. To do so, they need to know as much as they can about the situation at hand.

In addition, before they can make that informed decision, they also need to look inside, to investigate themselves and their own needs and make a number of fundamental career decisions.

CHAPTER 5

*Career Decision Making—
Overview and Phase I:
Managing Personal Reactions*

You've lost your job or learned you'll be terminated in the near future. You're eligible for early retirement or have been included in your company's offer of voluntary separation. Or perhaps you're simply uncertain enough about your career, either in how you're feeling about your job or as a result of unsettling signals you're receiving at work, to want to consider a change. At some point you wonder, Will I *ever* find something?

Your concern is natural, but you've asked the wrong question. You will find something. The challenge is to find the right new job, the right new career, or make the right decision about pursuing active retirement. To be successful at this you must catalog and organize your resources, assess your needs and requirements, make serious decisions about yourself and your future, and develop an action plan that helps you move on to the appropriate next stage of your life.

Few people are this methodical. In the rush to hit the ground running when they are confronted by an important career decision, they neglect to choose a destination, or even a direction, before starting their travels. Typically, getting another job as quickly as possible becomes the single goal of the process. Planning doesn't earn a role in the campaign.

Planning, in fact, is the weakest part of most careers, as people slip and slide from one job to the next. Have you, for example, ever taken a full eight-hour day to think about your career?

Now, perhaps for the first time in that career, you have an opportunity to reflect on who you are and what you want from the work portion of your life. By matching your needs and personal interests with your professional skills, you can develop and implement a plan that considers both.

You might end up with a new career. We worked with one man who lost a job directing the sales force of a huge corporation. When he explored his interests, he realized he had always wanted to be a professional athlete. Even without considering his athletic skills, however, there wasn't much chance that he would get that wish. He was forty years old, an unlikely age for rookies in any paying sport.

But forty is not an unlikely age for rookies in the *business* of sports. Our client discovered that the owners of many professional sports franchises do not actually run their teams. They need professional managers to look after their interests. Realizing that he might apply his business experience to his interest in sports, our client ultimately took a management position with a pro hockey team, turning his avocation into his vocation.

Another client, a 60-year-old man who had been the general manager of a technical firm, was a brilliant scientist but a poor manager. Nevertheless, when he started career continuation counseling, he was determined to rush out and land another general manager's post.

We asked whether that was what he really wanted to do with his life. "No," he said, "I'd really like to teach, but it doesn't pay enough."

We got the man to figure out how much income his early retirement package would deliver. Then we had him add in a standard teacher's salary. Finally, we suggested he tack on a conservative figure reflecting the amount he might realistically receive from writing and consulting when he wasn't actually teaching. He learned that he most certainly could afford to do what he had always wanted, and he did.

This highly educated man had never worked out that simple equation on his own. Why? He had simply assumed that no options existed.

We counseled a woman who lost a job working in the market research department of a major consumer corporation. She found that she really wanted to be in a garage. Her father had been an automobile mechanic. When she let herself admit the fact, she realized she had been most satisfied when she had worked by his side. She became one of the happiest mechanics around, when she finally opened her own automotive repair shop.

You might also learn what *not* to do with your life. One of our clients came out of the food industry and was intrigued with the entertainment business. He investigated the field and discovered it was characterized by ups, downs, and a pronounced lack of employment security that seemed to bear little relationship to one's actual performance. He also investigated his own needs, learning that he would be happiest in a much more stable environment. He eventually returned to the food business.

You might decide to stick with your present career. In any event, assessing and planning is important, both to identify the appropriate work environment for yourself and to make certain that a more substantial change wouldn't be in your best interests. Finally, if you decide to remain in your present line of work, you still deserve to plan your future.

At the beginning of this book, we raised the idea—our conviction, really—that individuals, not their employers or anyone else, should be responsible for taking control of, directing, and making effective choices about their own careers. To support this belief, Drake Beam Morin has invested substantial time and energy to develop a range of resources and processes that help people do just that.

Underlying all these resources is a process we call career decision making. Career decision making helps you decide, logically and effectively, where to take your career. Additional tools and resources help you attain your goal by teaching various skills you'll need along the way.

In one sense, most people think about career decisions almost continually. At work, you consider an assignment in terms of how it could advance or hinder your career. At home that evening, you read newspaper ads about franchise opportunities and think how rewarding it might be to go into business for yourself. On Saturday afternoon, you look at your tennis racket or golf clubs and try to figure ways to bring retirement a year or two closer. On Sunday night, you rehearse an argument for a raise or promotion and wonder if you should share it with your boss the next morning.

But however frequently many of us think about the subject, most of us make real decisions about our careers only when conditions force us to act or react. And whether we reach effective decisions is another matter entirely. There are two key dimensions to career decision making: first, actually making a decision—any decision; second, assuring that the decision reached is a good one.

Worrying about Change

There is little mystery why people avoid making decisions concerning their careers. The main worry is change, real or potential, and as we all know, change tends to be threatening. Taking action on your own career, whether you're forced to do so as a result of external factors or whether you motivate yourself to plan for the future, is certain to involve some degree of change.

You may have to alter familiar habits or a comfortable routine. You may fear the general uncertainty of change, or be concerned about unanticipated consequences of your actions. If your decision involves leaving a job you hold today, you may worry about the loss of job security or the financial risks of being unemployed. Considering a career move may kindle feelings of self-doubt. Can you cope with the unknown? Are you really worth anything in the marketplace? Do you have real skills, or have you been fooling people throughout your career? What about losing the sense of status and identity that is often an integral part of employment?

Thoughts or worries of this nature can convince people that

the most appropriate action is inaction. As we see continually in our business, the inertia that results is powerful enough to paralyze individuals who have a real and pressing need to act because they've lost their jobs. Think how easy it can be for people who are not confronted with a career emergency to find other matters to occupy their time.

A Model for Decision Making

There is a way to get around these obstacles, which you'll need to do if you're going to be responsible for your own career. The key to making a career decision is to recognize the sequential phases involved. By breaking down what may seem to be a slippery and unmanageable process into a series of smaller, discrete steps, not only do most of the mystery and self-doubt disappear, but the decision that is ultimately reached also tends to be an effective decision. That is, it serves you and your career well.

To make an effective career decision, you need to do a number of things:

- Clarify and organize your thinking.
- Appraise your strengths and marketability.
- Understand the marketplace.
- Determine your options.
- Weigh your alternatives.
- Develop a set of action steps.

These activities can be consolidated and organized into a four-phase decision-making model, which will be discussed here and in following chapters.

Phase I: Manage Personal Reactions
Phase II: Gather Information
Phase III: Review Options
Phase IV: Develop Action Plans

Phase I: Managing Personal Reactions

Feelings and Emotions. In Chapters 2 and 3 we discussed common reactions to termination and described ways to deal with these emotions. In Chapter 4 we observed that offers of voluntary separation or early retirement often provoke similar feelings. If you haven't yet completed the exercises in those sections, return to read or reread the material, and do so now. If your feelings have changed since you first put them on paper, update your entries. Remember that understanding and managing your feelings and emotions are absolutely essential to making an effective career decision and then acting on that choice efficiently.

Resistance to Change. As we suggested a moment ago, resistance to change is both normal and manageable given the stressful conditions of an imminent career decision. But when you think about it, change is inevitable. If you've been terminated, life has changed and, one way or another, you're going to have to deal with that change. If you've been offered early retirement or voluntary separation, accepting the offer obviously requires contending with change. But even if you refuse the offer, you'll still be confronted with change in the revised or revived organization, and you'll have to deal with it. Finally, even if you face none of these situations, the fact that you're reading this book suggests that you're anticipating or contemplating some type of change in your career.

Organizational Reactions to Change. As you react to your personal feelings at the start of the career decision-making process it's important to realize that there are also likely to be external, organizational reactions to change, especially if you've been included in any form of a group severance program. Most of us work in groups, and groups tend to have lives and identities of their own beyond those of their individual members. Individuals generate information in a group, but they also shape information introduced by others, color it, and emphasize or de-emphasize it in a variety of ways. As a result, the group reaction to an event can be quite different from an individual's reaction to the same situation.

Group reactions to impending career change often include apocalyptic thinking. When one person loses a job, it may seem like the end of the world to that individual, but not to the group in which he or she formerly worked. But if all twenty members of a work group learn that they are about to be terminated, or if five hundred middle managers in a division are confronted with a choice of early retirement, or if twenty-five hundred people in a corporation are offered voluntary separation, the information that travels throughout the organization may well create a group perception that the sky really *is* about to fall.

For the work group, division, or even the corporation, the end may in fact be near. In terms of the group, then, apocalyptic thinking may have some validity. But the fate of the individuals in the group is quite different, so the ability to differentiate between group and individual reactions is valuable. If the situation you're facing seems like the end of the world, think carefully whether that's how *you* really feel (in which case, you have a valid personal reaction to deal with), or whether you've merely absorbed the group reaction and accepted it as your own.

Other common group reactions include the tendency to turn inward, the corporate equivalent of locking the castle gates and pulling up the drawbridge as an enemy approaches. There may be a group sense of denial. The group may actually become more productive, trying to work its collective way out of the threatening situation. The organization may become less adaptable, digging in and focusing unilaterally on its uncertain future. A group sense of guilt may emerge: "If we'd only gotten the product to market on time, none of this would be happening." There may be group feelings of suppressed anger or withdrawal. Communications may suffer.

The key here is to be able to distinguish between your own and the group's reactions to the situation. You have enough to handle without adopting the group's sense of guilt as your own. If you feel angry, that's fine, as long as you cope with it. But don't accept the organization's anger as your own. React to what you're feeling and put those external factors aside.

We've discussed feelings and emotions repeatedly, and we'll refer to them again in subsequent chapters. For one thing, it's hard to overemphasize the importance of recognizing and managing your feelings as you deal with career changes. Secondly, dealing with emotions is not usually a one-time event. A month into your job search you may feel stalled, and the difficult emotions you felt and confronted when you were terminated may resurface with a vengeance. The more you're able to stay attuned to these feelings, the better equipped you'll be to handle them.

But now let's move ahead to the second phase of the career decision-making process and talk about the range and variety of personal information you need to develop to make effective choices about your career.

CHAPTER 6

Career Decision Making—
Phase II: Gathering Information

The more information you possess as you consider a career decision, the more likely you'll be to make an effective choice for
yourself. The data can be divided into two general categories:
internal information, which relates to personal needs, objectives,
and requirements, and which is the subject of this phase of the
process; and external information, which concerns the different
career options available to you, and is the subject of Phase III. By
creating these two sets of data for yourself and examining each in
terms of the other, you'll determine the most appropriate direction
to move in your career, and you'll identify specific action steps you
can take to get there.

Six Categories of Internal Information

You'll want to think about six different categories of information
relating to you as an individual:

Values. What are your ideals and goals? How do your situation and the decisions you might make about it affect the attain-
ment of those ideals and goals?

Financial Factors. What do you have? What do you need? What do you want?

Interests. What are your interests? Which are being expressed currently? Which are not?

Psychological Needs. What are your needs? Which of them are currently being met through your work?

Accomplishments and Skills. What have you done? What do you know how to do? Where can you best sell your skills?

Work Satisfiers and Dissatisfiers. What do you enjoy or dislike about the work you do?

The Role of Values

The place to start gathering information is with an investigation of your personal values, since they have an impact on all other personal factors. Your values, the personal ideals and goals that are ultimately most fundamental and important to you, affect your psychological needs, account for many of your accomplishments and skills, shape your interests, and determine your financial needs and status. In fact, to graphically depict the universe of internal information, we can show those categories surrounded by an all-encompassing set of values.

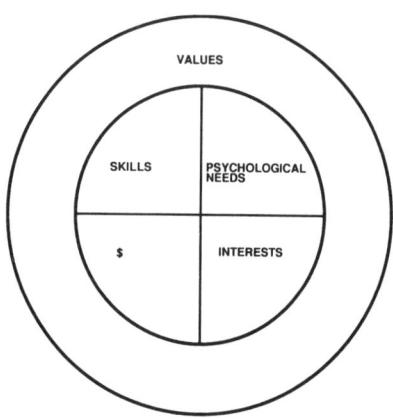

WHAT ARE MY VALUES?

For each of the following areas, answer the question, "What do I want from my life in the next five years?" Include the goals you have for each category.

Personal: _____

_____

Family: _____

_____

Social: _____

_____

Career: _____

_____

Financial: _____

_____

Community: _____

_____

Spiritual: _____

_____

Material: _____

_____

Recreational: _____

_____

Other: _____

_____

WHAT VALUES ARE MOST IMPORTANT TO ME?

Once you've completed your list of values and goals, go back and number them in order of most to least important. List separately your ten most important values.

1. _____

2. _____

3. _____

4. _____

5. _____

6. _____

7. _____

8. _____

9. _____

10. _____

HOW WILL MY SITUATION AFFECT MY GOALS?

Now review your list of goals and circle any items that could be affected, positively or negatively, by the career decision you ultimately reach.

Take a few minutes to review your responses to these exercises, and then turn to the Summary of Insights on page 99 and complete the first entry. As you continue to record your entries in your summary, you'll create a capsule overview of your personal internal information, which you'll subsequently be able to use to make actual career decisions.

Financial Factors

Few individuals facing a career choice need to be reminded of the economic and financial ramifications of the situation. Focusing on three key points can help you deal effectively with these issues. First, you need to understand your current financial status, including the details of any severance package for which you may be eligible. Second, you need a realistic understanding of your future financial needs. Third, you need to create a financial plan and deal with any outstanding money issues.

Since the subject of finances often raises some of the most threatening and volatile issues associated with a sudden career change, we'll deal with these concerns in detail—and offer ideas for managing them—in Chapter 7.

The Importance of Interests

We spend a good deal of our time telling people they deserve to work at tasks they enjoy. Everyone agrees, but we suspect that very few people actually believe us. Perhaps, deep inside, most of us continue to insist that you can't call something work unless it hurts.

Your interests obviously reflect the things you enjoy in life. While it may be unreasonable to expect your work to involve all your life's interests, it is realistic to assess which and how many of those interests either are or could be served in your career.

WHAT ARE MY INTERESTS?

To investigate your interests, imagine that you've just won $10 million dollars in a lottery. You no longer have to worry about earning a living: you can do whatever pleases you.[1]

1. How would I spend $10 million dollars? Be both spontaneous and specific: "I'd buy a yacht," or "I'd buy an advertising agency."

_____

_____

1. The Lottery Exercise is taken from *Career Navigator: The Computer-Powered Job Search System.* Copyright 1987 Drake Beam Morin, Inc., New York, New York. Software developed by Thoughtware, Inc., Plantation, Florida.

2. How would I spend my time? Describe an ideal day or week spent doing something that would be particularly meaningful to you. Be as specific as you can in terms of the actual things you would do and how you would function in this ideal setting.

_____

_____

3. What gifts would make me happiest? Imagine that a mysterious and all-knowing benefactor wants to give you several *nonmaterial* gifts. What would they be? Be specific as you write down anything your imagination offers up: private piano lessons, for example, or acting lessons from Robert Redford.

_____

_____

4. What are your five top interests? Using the answers you've written above, write down your five top interests in the space provided here. Note the implications of your findings for your job or career. For example, are any of your interests so important to you that you should try to incorporate them into your career objectives?

_____

_____

_____

_____

_____

For additional approaches to discovering your interests, refer to Appendix D on page 367.

Finally, record your interests profile by completing the second section of your Summary of Insights.

Psychological Needs

All of us address fundamental psychological needs through our work. We may work to satisfy the need for mastering a task or subject, for example. Many of us work to obtain the approval of others. Our careers may help us meet the needs we feel for status and prestige. We may find work rewarding because it allows us to serve others.

WHAT ARE MY PSYCHOLOGICAL NEEDS?

Study the list that follows. Identify and **circle** any of the needs mentioned here that are or were satisfied by your current or most recent job. Then review the list once more, and **underline** any needs you have that have not been fulfilled by your current or most recent job.

to lead	to be competent	to structure my life
to follow	to influence	to be responsible
to participate	to be dependent	to be alone
to create	to be with people	to be independent
to be sociable	to work hard	to gain approval
to build	to compete	to experience variety
to serve	to cooperate	to reduce boredom
to give me identity	to contribute	to experience stability
to give me status	to be useful	to achieve
to belong	to earn a living	to have fun

Finally, transfer your selections of met and unmet psychological needs to your Summary of Insights.

When you've finished this exercise, spend another few minutes considering ways in which your needs might be met in another job, in another career, or in retirement.

What You've Done: Your Accomplishments

If your values, interests, and psychological needs show why and, often, how you work, your accomplishments demonstrate the things you've actually achieved during your career. Work accomplishments represent evidence of the impact you've made as a result of employing a problem-solving effort. An accomplishment is something that, by your own standards, you know you did well. It is an achievement that brought you a sense of gratification.

In your professional life or business career, you've undoubtedly accomplished many important tasks that have contributed to the organization or organizations you've worked for. What you may not realize is how accurately these accomplishments illustrate your skills, talents, capabilities, and potential for solving new problems in the future. Your accomplishments are the best possible evidence that you know how to work effectively and that you can and do use your skills to good advantage.

As you prepare to make an effective career decision, particularly if that decision may involve a job search, studying and creating an inventory of past accomplishments will provide you with:

- an immediate awareness of things you have done well;
- the information needed to identify your work skills;
- a skills inventory that will help you assess your marketability in similar or diverse industries, functions, and locations.

Identifying Work Accomplishments. Any activity can be accurately termed an accomplishment if it fulfills one or more of the following conditions:

- You accomplished or achieved greater results with the same resources (budget, people, equipment, etc.).
- You accomplished or achieved the same results with fewer resources.
- You improved operations or made things easier or better.
- You resolved a problem or panic situation with little or no increase in time, energy, dollars, or people.
- You accomplished something new and perhaps different.

To probe more deeply into your career accomplishments, ask yourself these questions:

- Did I see a problem, opportunity, or challenge and initiate a solution?

- Did I develop something?
- Did I create or design a new department, program, procedure, plan, service, or product?
- Did I identify a need for a new department, program, procedure, plan, service, or product?
- Did I prepare an original report, paper, or document?
- Did I make a direct or indirect technical contribution?
- Directly or indirectly, did I create or implement an administrative or procedural recommendation?
- Did I participate actively in a major decision related to organizational changes (hiring, terminating, salary, new projects, etc.)?
- Did I implement or participate in a sales, profit-generating, or cost-saving recommendation?

Using PAR Statements to Describe Accomplishments. One way to describe your work accomplishments is to think of the problems (P) you have had to face, the actions (A) you took, and the results (R) of your actions.

Here are two examples showing how to compile PAR statements:

Example 1

Problem	Action	Result
Retail firm unknowingly sold appliances that were not up to standard. Experienced an avalanche of complaints and returns. Clerks, uncertain how to deal with complaints, became upset with customer abuse.	• Called supplier and negotiated return policy • Developed clear procedures for handling customer complaints and returns • Trained clerks to handle irate customers and speed warranty returns	• Rapid decrease (33%) in customer complaints • Minimum loss of customer loyalty • Improved morale and productivity of clerks

Example 2

Problem	Action	Result
High turnover among clerical support staff	Persuaded manager to: • Increase number of personnel by two • Negotiate new benefits package that enhanced job flexibility and enrichment	• Reduced turnover by 50% • Saved more than $20,000 in employment agency fees • Increased support staff productivity

When PAR statements are worded as concisely as possible, they can become strong statements of accomplishment. For example:

- Established "hot line" to handle customer complaints resulting in 33% decrease in product returns.
- Initiated procedures to increase production 20% by reducing turnaround time from five to four days.
- Conducted competitive studies of duplicating equipment, computer work stations, and telephones, saving division $90,000.
- Assisted in setting up overtime reporting systems that consolidated three systems into one.

WHAT ARE MY PRINCIPAL ACCOMPLISHMENTS?

Now it's your turn to create PAR statements for ten work accomplishments spanning your entire career. Place the greatest emphasis on events that occurred in the last five to eight years. First, describe each Problem concisely. Then note what Action you took, what you were responsible for, and how you did it. Next, indicate what happened as a Result of your efforts in terms of:

- dollars saved, new business generated, increased sales or profits;
- improved efficiency, time saved, better procedures;
- reduction in staff needs;

- improved productivity;
- what impact your accomplishment had on the organization.

Whenever possible, quantify your results in numerical or percentage terms. Finally, condense each example into a one-sentence statement of your accomplishment that summarizes the problem, your action, and the results. Write these ten sentences in your Summary of Insights under heading number 4.

1. Problem: _____

_____

Action(s): _____

_____

Result(s): _____

_____

2. Problem: _____

_____

Action(s): _____

_____

Result(s): _____

_____

3. Problem: _____

_____

Action(s): _____

_____

Result(s): _____

_____

4. Problem: _____

_____

Action(s): _____

_____

Result(s): _____

_____

5. Problem: _____

_____

Action(s): _____

_____

Result(s): _____

_____

6. Problem: _____

_____

Action(s): _____

_____

Result(s): _____

_____

7. Problem: _____

_____

Action(s): _____

_____

Result(s): _____

_____

8. Problem: _____

_____

    Action(s): _____

_____

    Result(s): _____

_____

9. Problem: _____

_____

    Action(s): _____

_____

    Result(s): _____

_____

10. Problem: _____

_____

    Action(s): _____

_____

    Result(s): _____

_____

_____

_____

What You Can Do: Your Skills

The work accomplishments you've just described are the result of a combination of the different "success factors" you possess. These include the values, interests, and needs you've identified, as well as the capabilities, experience, and skills you've developed over the years.

Skills are measured by activities in which you have demonstrated competence. They represent the ability to perform problem-solving tasks effectively. Identifying your skills is important for several reasons. The process helps you see your real talents objectively. This revelation is powerful and positive because, in the absence of objective analysis, most people underrate their skills and so underestimate what they might accomplish in the future. If you identify your skills, you are likely to make effective career decisions, to present your talents more proficiently to prospective employers, and, in general, to feel greater confidence as you pursue the career continuation process.

Finally, successful career continuation often depends, in part, on your ability to adapt your skills and talents to new and different work environments. This requires that you be able to identify these skills, learn how to transfer them to new areas, and, perhaps, think about new skills you might acquire to become more successful in the career marketplace.

Types of Skills. The primary mistake most people make when they discuss their skills is that they are too vague. By definition, a skill indicates that you are able to do something in an active sense, and that you do it consistently well. Too often, individuals think they are discussing their skills when they are really talking about job knowledge or imprecise "feelings."

Breaking work skills down into three distinct categories may help avoid this problem.

- *Functional* skills are related to, or acquired within, different organizational functions or units. Examples of functional skill areas include warehousing, accounting, banking and finance, distribution management, electronic data processing, health and education, manufacturing, marketing, and personnel.

- *Technical* skills are acquired through specialized education or work experience. Examples include arithmetic, computer, graphics, mechanical, manual, secretarial, speaking, and writing skills.
- *Administrative/managerial* skills facilitate and enhance administrative and management processes. Examples include analyzing, controlling, creating, delegating, directing others, innovating, leading, motivating, organizing, planning, negotiating, and problem solving.

Identifying Skills by Looking at Accomplishments

Because work accomplishments reflect and reveal important evidence of your skills, reviewing your accomplishments can be very valuable.

Here are several examples of how skills can be derived from accomplishments:

Accomplishment	Skills
Assisted in setting up overtime reporting systems, which consolidated three systems into one.	• Analysis • Problem solving
Initiated procedures to increase production 20% by reducing turnaround time from five to four days.	• Innovating • Organizing • Manufacturing
Conducted competitive studies of duplicating equipment, computer work stations, and telephones, saving division $90,000.	• Analysis • Computer • Cost control
Created a profit and loss statement that eliminated 20% of a less profitable product line.	• Innovating • Analysis • Accounting
Managed laboratory reorganization to eliminate duplication and encourage cooperation, reducing costs by $100,000.	• Directing others • Organizing • Motivating

WHAT ARE MY SKILLS?

In the space provided here, list the accomplishments you identified in the previous exercise, and analyze them to identify the skills they reveal. When you have finished, transfer your list of skills to your Summary of Insights.

Accomplishments _____

_____

_____

_____

_____

_____

_____

_____

_____

_____

Skills _____

_____

_____

_____

_____

_____

_____

_____

_____

_____

_____

Work Satisfiers and Dissatisfiers

Successful individuals, no matter how they are employed, tend to find genuine satisfaction in their work. At the extreme, there are the lucky people who honestly say, "I can't believe I get paid to do this!" Most of us have some feel for the things we like and dislike about our work, but we seldom sort through these feelings and impressions to identify what really satisfies us on the job.

WHAT DO I LIKE AND DISLIKE ABOUT MY WORK?

Using the form here, list some of the more important work activities in which you use your functional, technical, and administrative/managerial skills. Examples might include writing reports, preparing budgets, conducting market analyses, training subordinates, conducting "cold" sales calls, or developing computer programs. Next, for each activity describe the things you find satisfying and dissatisfying.

When you have finished, review your responses and note any common themes or patterns that are repeated. Transfer these to your Summary of Insights under heading number 6.

Activity: _____

Satisfiers	Dissatisfiers
1. _____	1. _____
2. _____	2. _____
3. _____	3. _____
4. _____	4. _____

Activity: _____

Satisfiers	Dissatisfiers
1. _____	1. _____
2. _____	2. _____

Activity:

Satisfiers	Dissatisfiers
3. _____	3. _____
4. _____	4. _____

Activity:

Satisfiers	Dissatisfiers
1. _____	1. _____
2. _____	2. _____
3. _____	3. _____
4. _____	4. _____

Activity:

Satisfiers	Dissatisfiers
1. _____	1. _____
2. _____	2. _____
3. _____	3. _____
4. _____	4. _____

Activity:

Satisfiers	Dissatisfiers
1. _____	1. _____
2. _____	2. _____
3. _____	3. _____
4. _____	4. _____

Activity:

Satisfiers	Dissatisfiers
1. _____	1. _____
2. _____	2. _____
3. _____	3. _____
4. _____	4. _____

SUMMARY OF INSIGHTS

Record your responses to the exercises in this chapter here to create a capsule summary of your personal information.

1. What I *Value* Most:

_____

_____

_____

_____

_____

_____

2. Careers/Activities That *Interest* Me:

_____

_____

_____

_____

_____

_____

3. Psychological *Needs*
   Met/not met by my current job:

_____

_____

_____

_____

_____

_____

   Met/not met in another job or in retirement:

_____

_____

_____

_____

_____

_____

4. Key *Accomplishments:*

_____

_____

_____

_____

_____

_____

_____

_____

_____

_____

5. Key *Skills:*

_____

_____

_____

_____

_____

_____

_____

_____

_____

_____

6. *Satisfiers*	*Dissatisfiers*
1. _____	1. _____
2. _____	2. _____
3. _____	3. _____
4. _____	4. _____
5. _____	5. _____
6. _____	6. _____

By completing this series of exercises devoted to identifying your values, interests, needs, accomplishments, and skills, you've created a comprehensive and detailed picture of yourself in terms of career choices and preferences. The condensed results of these exercises in your Summary of Insights arm you with a useful tool that can serve you throughout the career continuation process.

In the weeks and months ahead, as you consider options, identify alternatives, research opportunities, market yourself to potential employers, and even as you negotiate or accept a job offer, refer back to this document to see how the conditions or opportunities you face compare to this personal career agenda.

Before we turn to the third phase of our career decision-making model—a review of available career options—let's complete our discussion of internal issues by focusing on the financial concerns that often surface during the career continuation process.

CHAPTER 7

Financial Concerns and Information

For many people, financial issues constitute the most terrifying aspect of losing a job or anticipating a major career change. If the psychological and emotional stresses of termination frequently make people angry or sad, fiscal uncertainty often scares them. Since a paycheck is a necessity for most of us, concern about finances is a normal and, in fact, necessary part of the career continuation process.

No matter how you plan to move forward with your life, you'll obviously need to factor financial needs and resources into the decision-making process. But at the same time, you want to avoid the distraction of imagined financial concerns.

We recall one man who rushed home after being terminated and horrified his family by announcing the first move he had planned: selling the house. Panicked, the man had neglected to consider the fact—explained to him a few hours earlier—that his severance package included a full year's salary at his current pay level. Once he calmed down, he realized that fear rather than objective reality had prompted him to contemplate such desperate action.

Many financial concerns are valid, however. Another client, terminated several months before one of his children was scheduled to start college, worried that he wouldn't be able to afford the expense. He thought about telling his daughter she would have to postpone her education.

The man was entitled to six months of severance pay from his former employer, and while he certainly might find a new job in a couple of months, the averages suggested that he could realistically expect a six- to eight-month job search. Assessing the situation, he and his wife concluded that the value of their child's education outweighed the risk of having to pay college bills while unemployed. Deciding that they would be willing to take out a second mortgage on their home as an interim measure if necessary, the couple decided not to change their plans.

As it turned out, the man was successfully reemployed a little more than six months later. With the six months of severance, the family's life-style had suffered only marginally and temporarily. While realizing that the process could have been a great deal more painful, in retrospect the man, his wife, and their daughter obviously agreed they had made a good decision.

The Importance of Financial Planning

We find that most individuals fail to investigate their finances in detail and make plans for the future until they're forced to. It's been our experience, in fact, that many business people don't focus on finances until one of two things occurs: retirement becomes imminent, or they lose a job.

An employer often becomes a surrogate financial adviser, particularly for people who work for a single company for many years. Their retirement income is held in a company pension plan. If they own securities or stock options, these investments are often limited to the company for which they work. Beyond their homes, a substantial part of their net worth is directly connected to their employment. If they're terminated from that employment, their confidence in the company—and, as a result, in their investments—is undermined at best, and perhaps entirely eradicated.

In addition, if they receive a substantial severance payment or pension plan distribution when they leave the company, they're faced with an important challenge: figuring out how to handle or invest the money wisely.

This all suggests that obtaining sound, independent advice concerning your finances should probably be a key priority at this stage in your life. Particularly if you're considering retirement, a second career, entrepreneurial activities, or some other form of self-employment, the value of competent, unbiased professional help in financial planning can be substantial.

If you plan to return to work, you'll want to be reassured that your current financial status will allow you to focus on your job search and not force you to contend with a range of difficult economic issues. Whatever you think your plans might be, if you feel uncertain about whether you'll have sufficient resources to accomplish them, or if you're not sure the income they produce will be enough to sustain you and your family, then you should enlist the help of a reliable professional financial consultant.

If you don't already have a financial adviser, you'll find no shortage of candidates. Many banks and brokerage firms offer financial planning services, and there are large national corporations devoted exclusively to providing financial advice and services to individuals and families. You should proceed with care, of course, because many of these organizations are also devoted to selling you insurance, annuities, and mutual funds.

You want someone who is committed to serving your best interests, not an individual pushing whatever investment offers the highest sales commission that month. Even advisers who charge fees for creating financial plans may produce the bulk of their income by selling investment products. So ask prospective planners how they are compensated. In addition, virtually anyone who can spell the words *financial planner* can claim the title, so you want to identify a competent adviser.

Your accountant or lawyer may be able to refer you to a respected planner. A friend, relative, or business associate who has had a successful, long-term relationship with a planner may be another good referral source. Or you might interview several potential advisers, comparing your impressions of the skills and experience of each before making your choice. However you choose to proceed, remember that just as you've taken responsibility for your career, you—not an adviser—are ultimately responsible for your finances.

Short-Term and Long-Range Financial Issues

If you haven't given much thought to issues of financial planning in the past, a career shift is likely to raise short-term and long-range financial issues you'll need to resolve. To a great extent, these topics will depend on your career plans, so you may find yourself revising your financial plans and projections if your life plans change.

Short-Term Concerns. If leaving a job brings with it a lump sum severance payment or a distribution of retirement funds, you'll need to determine how to deal with this. Should you roll over your pension benefits into a tax-deferred IRA, for instance, or pay taxes and additional tax penalties that may be imposed to gain immediate use of the funds? To reach a sensible conclusion, you and your adviser will want to determine whether you'll need that money today or fifteen years from now.

If you're due a large severance payment, should you ask your former employer to wait until next year to pay it to you? For example, if you anticipate that income tax rates will decrease next year, and if you can afford the wait, you could save money by deferring the income. Or, if you've already earned substantial income this year, and think that next year's income is likely to be substantially lower—either because you intend to retire or because you could be out of work during what might be a lengthy job search—you might also want to postpone the payment. If, on the other hand, you expect tax rates to go up next year, or if you lost your job because your former employer is suffering to the extent that bankruptcy looms as a possibility, you'll probably want to take your severance immediately, if not sooner. You'll need expert professional advice to make such choices confidently.

To reach these decisions, you'll need to conduct a careful analysis of a variety of factors. What are your immediate financial needs? What are all your current sources of available income, and what are the tax implications of each? Can you carry yourself and your family while you search for a new job? If you have a child who is ready for college, what impact will that have? Do you already have a line of home-equity credit or other credit sources you could draw on in an emergency? Might you have to consider the sale of your home?

Your specific situation will affect these decisions. If you're forty years old and confident you'll land a new and better job in a couple of months, you may decide to make no adjustments to your current financial life. If you land that job and need to relocate to start it, you'll need to think about selling your home and moving-related expenses. Suppose you find a buyer but think capital gains taxes will go down next year. Perhaps you can delay the closing until the first of the year, if doing so will create a substantial tax savings.

If, on the other hand, you're sixty-one years old and not certain whether you want to return to work—or not sure just how warm a reception you might receive in the marketplace—you may reach some very conservative conclusions about the immediate steps you should take. Here, too, a trustworthy adviser can help match your plans to your needs.

Long-Range Issues. If you plan to retire, the short-term and long-range issues you're confronted with begin to merge as you investigate your future financial concerns. How should you invest to provide for your retirement? How much will you require to enjoy your golden years? How much risk can you assume and still be comfortable with your investments?

Even people who intend to go right back into the business world often find that their financial perspective shifts dramatically after they lose a job. Individuals whose income has been rising steadily for twenty years can be lulled into thinking that the curve will automatically continue to rise. If their income stops abruptly while their outgo continues at its former pace, they gain a new and sobering view of economic reality. The notion of saving something for a rainy day becomes more pressing, and many people find wisdom in a more conservative approach under these altered circumstances. A competent financial adviser can help them plan for and ultimately achieve those new goals.

Financial Comfort Levels

Whatever short- or long-term financial needs you discover during your investigation into your personal economics, it's important to be comfortable with the decisions you make and the approaches you take. Some of us are born risk takers, and others are not. Neither group is likely to feel comfortable with the financial plans of the other.

To attain an adequate comfort level, no matter what your risk profile, you obviously need to understand the nature of the investments you make. A competent adviser will work with you to develop a plan that meets your personal needs and make sure you understand each element of that plan. If you're not comfortable with the results, you'll probably want to consider a more or less conservative alternative, and perhaps a new adviser.

Practical Preliminaries

To develop the body of financial information you'll require to make effective financial and career decisions, you need to investigate your financial resources and requirements in detail. We'll offer some methods for assembling relevant data, but we won't offer any financial advice; that's neither our business nor one of our business skills.

There are several immediate tasks you can complete to take a preliminary look at your financial situation. Pull together all your important financial documents: bank statements, IRA or Keogh records, insurance policies, certificates of deposit, pension plan statements, records of any securities or other investments you may own, recent tax returns—in short, any material that documents your financial situation and condition.

While you're searching for this information, you may find that this is a good time to pull together and organize other records of your vital statistics as well: family birth certificates, your will, even your marriage license. If you are considering retirement as an option, check with your Social Security office to request a statement of the estimated benefits due you and your spouse.

Because the work sheets that follow have been designed to apply to a broad range of career choices, every category in each exercise may not seem applicable to your situation. At this early stage of the career decision-making process, however, we suggest that you complete as many entries as you can. Suppose that you're sixty-four years old, have been offered early retirement, but have absolutely no intention of accepting. Go ahead and compute your potential retirement finances anyway. You might discover that making part-time consulting the basis of an active retirement represents a perfect career choice.

When many of our clients think about finding a new job, they automatically assume that their new salary will, at the very least, have to equal their previous pay level if they are to maintain their existing life-style. This may not be true.

As the incidence of voluntary separation programs has increased in recent years, for example, many individuals receive substantial pension benefits at relatively early ages. For someone who has worked for one company for a number of years, the financial implications of these "early takeouts" can be dramatic. Conservatively investing $250,000 in proceeds from a pension plan at 5 percent would earn $12,500 annually, for instance. In effect, the individual can take a job paying $12,500 less than a previous position and still enjoy the same income level. If such an option opens the door to a new job that serves the individual's needs and values better than the old position, the psychological or emotional value of the opportunity may match or even outweigh the financial aspects.

In essence, the more thoroughly you analyze and assess your financial data, the more career options you're likely to discover. Even if your investigation confirms that one choice or another doesn't make sense for you, you've given yourself a valuable piece of information. The forms that follow will help you assemble the necessary facts and figures.

INVENTORY OF INSURANCE

Review all your family insurance policies and list them according to the information requested in the headings. Use annual figures in all cases.

Company Name & Policy Number	Type (Life, Home, Auto)	Premium	Coverage	Out-standing Loan	Net Coverage (Coverage [−] Loan = Net Coverage)	Cash Surrender Value (If Applicable)	Comments
Total							

INVENTORY OF NET WORTH

Your Assets

Using your records, list the following information. In all cases where time is a factor, use annual figures.

Cash/Bank Accounts (savings and checking) $_____

Time Deposits/Money Market Funds $_____

Short- and Long-Term Notes (due you) $_____

Stocks, Bonds $_____

Cash Value of Insurance $_____

Precious Metals (gold, silver, coins, etc.) $_____

Vested Company Pension (amount due now
from your company pension plan) $_____

Other Company Savings, Profit Sharing,
or Incentives (due you now) $_____

Severance (compute as lump sum) $_____

Your Residence (current market value) $_____

Other Property (current market value) $_____

Automobiles (current market value) $_____

Furniture/Personal Property (current value) $_____

Collections (stamp, jewelry, art, etc.) $_____

Other Assets $_____

                                    Total Assets $_____

INVENTORY OF NET WORTH

Your Liabilities

Mortgages (what you owe on your home) $_____

Mortgages (what you owe on other real estate holdings) $_____

Loan on Insurance Policy (if applicable) $_____

Tax Liability (Include property taxes; income taxes on city, state, and federal basis; tax on gains from sale of home; stock; and pensions. Do not include payroll deduction taxes.) $_____

Other Liabilities $_____

| | Total Liabilities | $_____ |

Total Assets	$_____	
Minus (—) Total Liabilities	$_____	
Net Worth	$_____	

INVENTORY OF YOUR ANNUAL INCOME

This is a review of your earned income (from salary, commissions, bonuses, and profit sharing) along with your investment income. You should also include the possible sale of assets, particularly if you will be selling your residence. Use annual figures.

	Now	Later (At a Specific Date of Your Choice)
Your Income:		
Salary, Commissions, Bonuses, Consulting Fees	$_____	$_____
Dividends, Interest from Bank Accounts, CDs, Other Investments (including real estate income)	$_____	$_____
Your Retirement Income:		
Vested Pension, Profit Sharing, IRA	$_____	$_____
Annuities/Cash from Life Insurance	$_____	$_____
Social Security (including spouse)	$_____	$_____
Incentives	$_____	$_____
Total Yearly Income:	$_____	$_____

INVENTORY OF YOUR ANNUAL EXPENSES

This is a review of your expenses. Use annual figures.

	Now	Later (At a Specific Date of Your Choice)
Housing: mortgage interest or rent expenses, home improvement, utilities (electricity, gas, water, telephone)	$_____	$_____
Personal Expenses: food, clothing (including dry cleaning, etc.)	_____	_____
Entertainment: hobby, vacation, dining out	_____	_____
Transportation: gas, oil, license, car repair, commuting costs, etc.	_____	_____
Professional Education: books, magazines, memberships, tuition, etc.	_____	_____
Taxes: real estate and income	_____	_____
Insurance: life, health, auto, homeowner, etc.	_____	_____
Uninsured Medical Expenses	_____	_____
Savings: investments, thrift plans, Christmas club, mortgage principal, etc.	_____	_____
Interest Expense: interest on loans, notes, charge accounts, etc.	_____	_____
Total	$_____	$_____
Minus (−) Savings	$_____	$_____
Net Annual Expenses	$_____	$_____

INCOME AND EXPENSE SUMMARY

	Now	Later (At a Specific Date of Your Choice)
Total Annual Income	$_____	$_____
Total Annual Expenses	$_____	$_____
Surplus (Deficit)	$_____	$_____

The Relevance—and Irrelevance—of Finances

When you focus on the details of your finances, it can be easy to think of them as the driving force, or even the sole factor, as you consider plans for the future. Obviously your general financial condition can play an important role in determining the career options that are open to you. And, particularly if you realize that your situation is precarious, you'll have to respond to financial realities. But even if you find yourself in desperate economic straits, you don't have to let the situation take control of your life.

Seek the kind of competent professional financial advice mentioned in this chapter, but don't forget the inner needs and personal values you've already discovered. You might have to adapt your strategy and tactics—taking a job you don't want as a first step toward creating the future that really does suit you, perhaps. If you're fifty-one years old, have been dreaming about retirement for a decade, and can't afford it, you can still create and implement a plan that will keep you pointed toward your goal. If you're sixty-seven and rolling in money but want to continue working, you can figure a way to do it. Consider all your options before you make a career decision.

CHAPTER 8

Career Decision Making—
Phase III: Career Options

You've assessed your skills, experience, and accomplishments, investigated your interests and values, and analyzed your financial resources. Now you're ready to shift your attention to the external aspects of the career continuation process by identifying available employment options. In this chapter, we'll present an overview of the range of career options and offer some general observations about employment opportunities.

Four General Career Options

Depending on your immediate circumstances, as many as four general career options may be open to you.

First, if you've been offered early retirement or voluntary separation—or if you're currently employed and are reading this book because you think you might want to make a change—you can elect to stay where you are.

Second, if you decide, or are forced, to make a change, you can choose to take a job with a new company or organization. Here you have additional options: continuing to work in your current field, entering a new business or functional area, or choosing between part- and full-time employment.

Third, you might elect to work for yourself. Again, you have

116

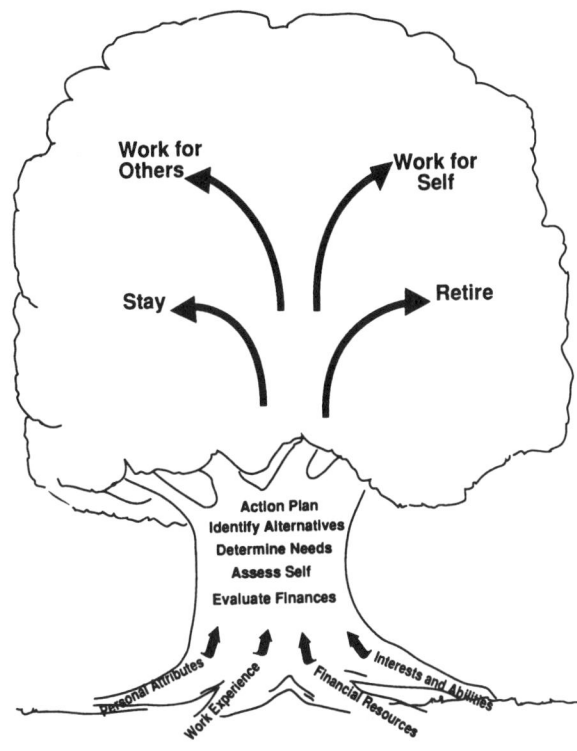

choices: working as a consultant, for instance, or starting your own business. If you start a business, you might decide to invest in a franchise operation, buy an existing business, or build your own operation from scratch.

Finally, you could choose to retire. You face a range of options here as well. For some individuals a traditional retirement remains the preferred choice: a life devoted primarily to family, golf, travel, or some other interest. For more and more people today, retirement has become a mix of activities: one part leisure, one part community or volunteer work, one part consulting or part-time employment, one part financial planning and management, and so forth.

While these are the four most common career continuation options, additional choices also exist. Some people go to school. Others leave the work force without retiring: among younger two-income families, for instance, the urge to start or devote more time to a family may prompt a woman facing a career change to become a housewife or a man to become a househusband.

A few people even end up back at their old companies. Reorganization is rarely an exact science, and sometimes companies lose too many employees, or the wrong people, during such efforts. In a few cases, individuals have accepted voluntary separation offers and subsequently been rehired by the same companies that paid them to leave. (We would emphasize *few,* to discourage anyone from sitting around waiting for a call from a former boss.)

Considering the Percentages

Based on statistics we collect on the people who enter Drake Beam Morin's individual (as opposed to group) outplacement counseling programs, we can offer some general follow-up percentages on the placement status of a cross section of clients:

Placed with new company	74%
Started own business	10%
Started consulting practice	2%
Retired	2%
Left work force	1%
Returned to former company	2%
Other	9%

We should make two observations about these figures. The first and by far the most important point is that these are statistics, and you're not. The fact that 74 percent of this sample accepted jobs with new companies doesn't make that option a better, safer, easier, or more rewarding career direction than starting a consulting business or leaving the work force. The right choice for you depends on your skills, experience, needs, goals, and values.

Second, this is a skewed sample in that it reflects a client population whose average age is forty-four years, a figure that has remained relatively consistent in our individual outplacement counseling business over time. Had these figures been compiled instead from our pre-retirement workshops, the average age would undoubtedly be higher, and the proportion of clients choosing to retire would obviously be greater than 2 percent.

Such averages do offer valuable insights. Given the wave of corporate restructuring that has swept the country, for instance, some reports leave the impression that if you lose a corporate job today, you won't find another because there simply aren't any left. But about three-quarters of our individual outplacement clients do find new jobs at new companies, so the situation is obviously not that desperate. Some of these people enter new industries, and some who have left large companies take positions with small or midsize corporations, but they do not end up serving hamburgers in fast-food restaurants.

Additional statistics support the idea that career continuation is more often a gradual transition than an abrupt and radical shift. Taking this same group of outplacement clients, for example, and comparing their job functions both before entering our programs and after they have moved into new positions underlines this sense of continuity.

	Old Job	New Job
Corporate Staff	12%	11%
Engineering	4%	5%
Finance/Accounting	16%	13%
General Management	23%	21%
Human Resources	5%	4%
Information Systems	5%	5%
Sales/Marketing	16%	20%
Operations	6%	7%
Science	3%	2%
Other	10%	12%

The consistency of these before-and-after figures should not be interpreted as an argument for continuing to do what you've done in the past. The data should reassure you, however, that if you've been in general management and want to continue a career in that field, the experience of others demonstrates that opportunities are available. At the same time, if a more radical career shift makes sense for you, then that's the direction you ought to pursue.

National and Local Industrial Trends

As you begin to assess general employment opportunities, considering a few statistics about U.S. industrial trends may provide a useful benchmark or starting point.[1] Government predictions for the year 2000 indicate a 6 percent unemployment rate nationally. At the same time, total U.S. employment is expected to increase by more than sixteen million jobs.

More than three million of these new jobs are anticipated to be executive, administrative, professional, or technical positions. In 1986, this employment sector accounted for more than 25 percent of the total U.S. work force. By the year 2000, more than thirty-five million Americans—almost 40 percent of projected total employment—are expected to be employed in this area.

Up to the end of the century, the nation's ten fastest growing industries and their average annual rate of change are expected to be:

		Avg. Change
1.	Computer/Data Processing Services	+5.2%
2.	Outpatient Facilities and Health Services	+4.6%
3.	Personnel Supply Services	+4.4%
4.	Health Practitioners	+4.4%
5.	Credit Reporting and Business Services	+4.1%
6.	Legal Services	+3.8%
7.	Nursing and Personal Care	+3.8%
8.	Research/Management/Consulting Services	+3.6%
9.	Residential Care	+3.5%
10.	Miscellaneous Publishing	+3.4%

1. The statistics in this section are drawn from two U.S. Department of Labor publications: "Employment and Earnings: January 1988" and "Projections 2000" (March 1988). Additional government documents are published regularly and can be found in libraries or ordered from the Government Printing Office.

These projections are based on a "moderate growth" scenario for the U.S. economy; such figures often change substantially within the space of a few years. As a result, although it's probably safe to assume that opportunities in the health care field are unlikely to disappear by the year 2000, it might be wise to give careful consideration before launching a career in "Miscellaneous Publishing." Still, the best estimates suggest that there will continue to be ample employment opportunities for skilled and experienced individuals in the future.

In any event, while national statistics may offer insights into general employment trends, what you're really interested in is a single job, not entire industries or macroeconomic projections. Data reflecting business trends in your specific area may prove much more relevant as you consider a career transition.

Local Business Trends

The business climate in the area where you anticipate seeking a job or starting a business will play an obvious role in your career continuation efforts. As you begin to match your skills and interests to actual job descriptions, you may find that local economics attract you to one region or force you to eliminate another market from consideration. Gathering this information helps you begin to focus on a market's relative appeal: is it realistic or overly optimistic to assume that the job you want is likely to be available in the area you've targeted?

Sources of business and economic information vary from one market to another. Good places to begin such searches include chambers of commerce, private industry councils, local libraries (especially business libraries and university reference libraries), state departments of employment, local or regional business magazines, and economic development centers or development associations.

Unless you already have a well-conceived idea of what you plan to do and where you intend to do it, you'll probably be looking for general information at this point. Learning that a multinational corporation plans to locate a major new installation in your area, or discovering that the city's largest employer has decided to relocate its manufacturing operations to Singapore can be valuable whether you're an accountant, manager, dentist, or would-be small business owner.

Researching this type of information also allows you in an entirely nonthreatening way to practice networking, a skill that is virtually certain to become a central part of your career continuation efforts. Networking, which we'll discuss in detail in Chapter 15, involves creating and continually expanding a network of sources and contacts as you conduct your employment campaign. At this stage of your career transition efforts, it's as simple as asking the people you contact at the chamber of commerce for the names of individuals at other organizations to call for additional information about local business conditions.

This not only supports your immediate research efforts, but, equally important, it puts you in touch with people who later on may be able to help you identify and perhaps contact companies and individuals within companies when you begin your marketing campaign. Or, if you decide to start a business of your own, these contacts may be valuable sources for more detailed data and information as you develop a business plan.

WHAT INFORMATION SHOULD I KNOW ABOUT LOCAL BUSINESS CONDITIONS, AND WHERE CAN I FIND IT?

In the space provided here, make notes about general business and economic information that might help you as you begin a job search. Next, list potential local sources for the data. Finally, as you contact organizations, ask for and note additional sources and information.

- Information needs (leave space to fill in information as you develop it)

_____

_____

_____

_____

_____

_____

_____

- Initial sources (include names and telephone numbers of contacts)

_____

_____

_____

_____

_____

_____

- Additional sources and contacts discovered

_____

_____

_____

_____

_____

_____

_____

Investigate *All* Your Career Options

This is not yet the time to make irrevocable decisions about the next stage of your life, although the investigations you've conducted into your strengths, experience, and needs may already have prompted you to lean in one career direction or another. Even if you're convinced that you want to retire, or are certain that now's the time to start a consulting practice, test your convictions by considering all your alternatives. At the very least, you'll make sure that six months or a year from now, you won't find yourself sitting in a new job thinking, "I wonder if I really should have started my own business?"

In subsequent chapters, we'll discuss different options in detail. Here we offer a few general observations about the different choices that may be available to you.

Staying Put

Although people confronted with involuntary termination often find it difficult to believe, making the decision between staying in a job or leaving a company remains a terribly difficult prospect for most people. If you've been offered voluntary separation or early retirement, review Chapter 4. If you're currently employed and contemplating a career change on your own initiative, look back over the sections in Chapter 1 that deal with quitting a job, negotiating your own termination, and strengthening your hold on a tenuous situation.

In either case, reassess both your immediate circumstances and the implications of staying on the job as clearly and dispassionately as you can. If you're convinced you should stay, continue to review your decision by evaluating it in terms of the other options open to you, those which involve leaving your current position. The key is to learn as much as you can about your situation so that you can make an informed decision for yourself.

Working for Others

As we indicated earlier in this chapter, nearly three-quarters of our clients in individual outplacement counseling programs continue their careers by taking positions with new companies. The process they complete is depicted graphically in this Career Transition Model.

No matter what career direction you eventually pursue, you've already completed several phases of this model by assessing your skills, accomplishments, and so forth. If you ultimately decide to continue along the "work for others" path, the nature of your

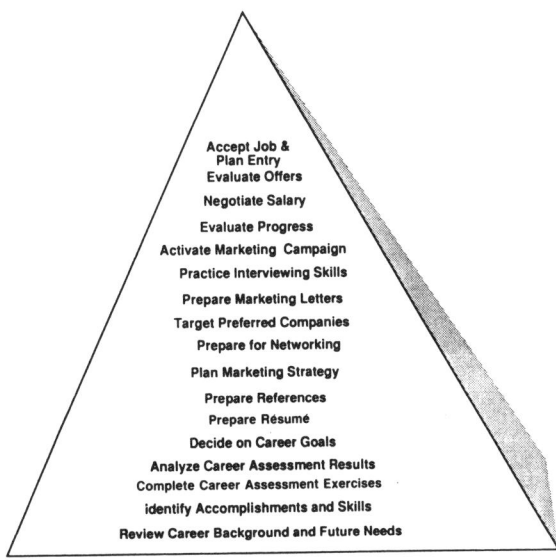

Accept Job &
Plan Entry
Evaluate Offers
Negotiate Salary
Evaluate Progress
Activate Marketing Campaign
Practice Interviewing Skills
Prepare Marketing Letters
Target Preferred Companies
Prepare for Networking
Plan Marketing Strategy
Prepare References
Prepare Résumé
Decide on Career Goals
Analyze Career Assessment Results
Complete Career Assessment Exercises
Identify Accomplishments and Skills
Review Career Background and Future Needs

career transition activities will soon shift, as the emphasis switches to designing and carrying out an effective employment campaign. We'll cover these activities in later chapters.

Some people overlook the idea that working for others does not necessarily mean taking a permanent or even a full-time job. You could find yourself in a position where it makes sense to "take a job to get a job," accepting a less than ideal position because it brings you closer to a job you really desire.

Or, depending on your financial needs and personal goals, you might decide to seek some form of part-time employment, saving a portion of the workweek for family, leisure activities, or a part-time business or consulting practice of your own. Many of the country's largest companies are becoming much more flexible in their employment policies. For example, some corporations either encourage or are experimenting with job sharing programs in which two people each assume responsibility for 50 percent of a single position.

Working for Yourself

In the early '80s the words *entrepreneur* and *entrepreneurial* entered the mainstream of American business language, where they are now firmly lodged. As a result, more and more of our clients are investigating working for themselves or starting their own businesses. As you can see in the diagram below (and as you'll see in Chapters 9 and 10), pursuing a work-for-self career is not a simple task.

Profits
Break Even
Cash Flow
P & L Statement
Select/Train People
Obtain Funding
Make a Plan
Determine Form of Ownership
Develop Marketing Strategy
Check Competition
Define Market
Choose a Field/Research It
Get Professional Assistance
Review Financial Needs/Resources
Self-Assessment

Unfortunately, no test, questionnaire, survey, or formula exists to determine who will be successful and satisfied working for themselves. In fact, the characteristics of a successful business person are much the same whether the individual works for him- or herself or for others. Discovering whether you should work for yourself is a process of careful evaluation. Is your business plan adequate? Can you accept the changes in life-style that such a career may require? How does the range of self-employment options match your own strengths and weaknesses?

One of the most valuable outcomes of the workshops Drake Beam Morin presents for clients considering entrepreneurial activities is that the sessions tend to discourage most participants from pursuing such plans. When people objectively assess the requirements and risks, and when they realize that, at the outset at least, they'll work harder and longer to make less than they have in the past, many realize they are not cut out for such careers.

Dealing with these issues early is critical. We've witnessed more than one individual sink large severance benefits or pension payouts into businesses of their own, only to discover in a matter of months that their actions were ill-advised. In the worst cases, these individuals find themselves back at square one of the career continuation process with their financial resources exhausted.

Still, for individuals who through a diligent, unbiased, and perhaps somewhat skeptical process of analysis discover that self-employment is their best choice, the personal and financial rewards can be substantial. In fact, for these people, such rewards may not be attainable through any other career option. If you're thinking of working for yourself, look hard and look carefully.

Retirement

The subject of retirement may be surrounded by more half-truths and misconceptions than any other issue related to career choices. There is a range of popular assumptions and historical myths about retirement that simply don't hold up:

"I'm in my fifties (or sixties). No one would hire me today."

"It would be great to drop out of the daily rat race!"

"It's too late for this old dog to learn new tricks!"

"If I stopped work, I'd be dead in six months!"

"If I could stop now, rest, and take it easy, I'd live longer and be happier!"

"It would be great to stay home with my wife (husband) and be together all the time!"

"I've worked so hard this year. I'm probably burned out and near the end."

Any of the above might be true for some people, but none may be accurate for you. Some are based on questionable assumptions regarding age and the aging process. Others may overlook the inner needs of individuals and their spouses. In Chapter 11, we'll explore in detail the evolving subject of active retirement. But first, let's consider an increasingly popular career option: self-employment.

CHAPTER 9

Working for Yourself:
A Business of Your Own

"For years I've fought my way up, down, around, and through the corporate trenches. It's time for a real change. I want to be my own boss. Maybe I should start my own business."

Most individuals think such thoughts at some point in their careers. For many it's an exercise in idle daydreaming, but for some it represents the first step in a significant and rewarding career shift. Trouble occurs when people fail to distinguish between the two kinds of urges.

As we'll show in this chapter and in the chapter on consulting careers that follows, starting a business of your own is typically a hard, demanding process. Making it a success is likely to be even more difficult. Unless you have the deep-seated need, relentless determination, and requisite personal and professional qualities to be an entrepreneur, going into business for yourself can turn into a financial and emotional nightmare.

If, on the other hand, you really are an entrepreneur struggling to emerge from the body of a corporate executive, running your own business may represent your best option for a truly satisfying career. Other employment directions simply may not fulfill your personal needs and career objectives.

This chapter won't tell you how to start a business of your own, a topic which at the very least deserves a book of its own. It will describe some of the issues that would-be entrepreneurs typically face as they attempt to transform a business idea into a profitable concern. And it will offer guidelines for determining whether you should actively pursue this career direction.

Are You an Entrepreneur?

How do you know if you're an entrepreneur? As we noted in the last chapter, no one has been able to define a set of personality traits or personal characteristics to accurately predict who will or will not become a successful entrepreneur. Researchers have been able to identify different terms commonly used to describe people who succeed at running their own businesses, however. Such individuals are likely to be called tough, competitive, healthy, competent, confident, hardworking, and socially adroit.

The problem with these descriptions is that they apply equally well to virtually all successful individuals, whether they work in huge corporations or in small businesses of their own design. As a result, because it's generally accepted knowledge that successful corporate types often do not make successful entrepreneurs, these factors probably aren't reliable indicators for assessing innate entrepreneurial ability.

But if we can't predict success, we can approach the question from another angle and investigate some characteristics, not of the successful entrepreneur, but of the entrepreneurial life-style. Only if you honestly conclude that you would be comfortable in a similar setting should you actively investigate developing a business of your own.

First, though, what do *you* think life would be like in such an environment?

HOW WOULD LIFE AS AN INDEPENDENT BUSINESS PERSON DIFFER FROM LIFE IN THE CORPORATE WORLD?

Give this question some thought and write down your observations and comments in the space provided here.

_____

_____

_____

_____

_____

_____

Nine Dimensions of the Business Owner's Life

The life of a business owner differs from the life of a salaried employee in significant respects. As you read through the following comments, ask yourself how you might react to each dimension of entrepreneurial life. At the end of this section, refer back to the exercise you just completed, and make changes or note additional comments that you feel are relevant or appropriate.

Time. People who own and operate businesses frequently say that time requirements account for the greatest difference between life in the corporate world and life in a business world of their own making. No matter how hard you work in a corporate setting, you're likely to work harder and longer in a business of your own. Twelve hours a day (or more), seven days a week, with few vacations, isn't an unlikely work schedule for the operator of a new business during its early years. This leaves little time for family, hobbies, community affairs, church work, softball games, aerobics classes, entertainment, or any other nonbusiness activity.

Accountability. As the head of your own business, you're accountable to no one but yourself, a fact that attracts many would-be entrepreneurs. But, while you don't have to share credit with others, there is also no one else to accept blame. When they find themselves in the relatively common situation that their new business is balanced on a knife edge between survival and failure, many entrepreneurs report that what's most difficult about their predicament is not having another person to commiserate with and consult.

Risk. The category of risk embraces a broad range of situations common to most new businesses. Personal financial risk probably ranks at the top of this list for most people, but other risks are also involved. There is the risk of potential embarrassment should the enterprise fail. Unanticipated legal risks frequently surface in new ventures. Health risks could even accompany the shift from an office environment to a more active and arduous life-style: a new career as a landscape architect, say, or as a marina operator.

Security. Security encompasses many of the real and intangible benefits the corporate world provides: regular paychecks, health benefits, backup support when subordinates miss work, and so forth. In a large company, when you're sick you stay home. The corporate ship steams on, and your sick-day benefits cover your absence. When you work for yourself you may not be able to get sick, because without you there is no business.

Feedback Loop. Large organizations invariably have formal or informal systems for acknowledging a job well done or identifying less than adequate performance. This feedback loop becomes a welcome part of business life, because most of us need an occasional pat on the back. We also need to be told when our performance isn't satisfactory. When you work for yourself, there may be no such loop. If you can't find a way to pat your own back, your spirits may suffer. If you can't figure a way to identify poor performance, your livelihood may suffer.

Sociability. Many people who start their own businesses are surprised to discover how lonely they feel. What's often lacking is the sociability inherent in large organizations. The chat at the water fountain or daily choice of lunch companions, even normal gossip or griping about the company seem insignificant at the time they occur, but often become meaningful in retrospect.

Support. The extensive support structures common in large organizations represent another facet of corporate life that is often taken for granted. Calls are screened, copies are made, memos are typed, trash is collected, light bulbs are changed, and bathrooms are cleaned while we sit at our desks and do *our* jobs. In your own business, however, you're likely to be both the CEO and the janitor. In fact, the range of services and administrative functions requiring your attention has the potential to overwhelm your principal obligation of developing the business itself.

Identity. A sense of identity is another fringe benefit of corporate life that many people overlook. To some extent we are all defined by the work we do. Saying "I'm with IBM" or "I work for Procter & Gamble" answers a lot of questions before they're asked.

We recall one man who left a career with a major national accounting firm and, with his wife, opened a fancy delicatessen at a ski resort. A year later, the couple was back in the city. The problem, they discovered, wasn't the business itself, but their new identities. The abrupt shift from professional to shopkeeper, and the way others reacted to them as a result, didn't match their self-perceptions.

Life-Style. Most people who work in a corporate setting find ways to balance job demands with other values they find important in their private lives. For example, adjustments can often be made at work to accommodate the needs of a family. But when the success or survival of a business depends entirely on one person, that person's commitment to the enterprise may have to take precedence over any and all other personal values. Successful entrepreneurs often have a real love (or perhaps even an obsession) for their businesses. Work becomes their principal commitment. It may have to be that way for the business to avoid becoming part of a grim statistic: the astonishingly high rate of small businesses that fail.

Why Businesses Fail

We've all walked or driven by businesses that have closed their doors for good. In fact, most new businesses fail in their first three years of operation. (In studies completed by different public and private researchers, reported levels for failed start-ups range from just over 50 percent to as high as 80 percent.)

Available evidence repeatedly confirms that the majority of these failures can be attributed to inept management, that is, to the owner's poor business practices. This may not be too surprising when you consider the potential range of "poor business practices."

Many people start businesses for the wrong reasons. They

hope they'll get rich, or become famous, or prove to former employers that they should never have been terminated, or show their friends and relatives that they really can succeed in business. These are escapist reasons for starting a venture, and these people tend to be running away from something, which is hardly a sound basis for a business start-up. Others discover that, day in and day out, they simply can't cope with the characteristics of the entrepreneurial life-style outlined above.

But in addition to internal factors that can affect a would-be entrepreneur's ability to survive, it's important to recognize that external forces can also play an important or even commanding role in determining success or failure.

Six Red Flags

Here are some of the most common causes for small business failures. To the extent that prospective business owners view these conditions as warning signals and remain constantly alert for such symptoms, these red flags may help them avoid potentially fatal decisions regarding new business start-ups.

Lack of Market Potential. Many businesses fail because the market for their products or services is too small or specialized to support them. Thorough and accurate market research and analysis are obvious prerequisites for individuals intent on starting their own businesses. Would-be entrepreneurs need to be especially careful that they aren't planning to enter markets that are contracting or changing so rapidly that they and their new business will not be able to react quickly enough.

Capital Starvation. Survival prospects are particularly grim for undercapitalized businesses, enterprises that lack sufficient cash to carry them through the initial months of operation until the business breaks even or begins to turn a profit. Capital requirements are commonly underestimated as new ventures are planned. The situation often becomes clear only when a trickle of income is met by a river of expenses.

At that point, it may be too late to save the business. Potential lenders or additional investors may shy away from the wounded company. Ironically, these same capital sources might have invested happily during the planning stage of the new enterprise, had the business owner presented them with accurate financial projections that would have avoided the crippling shortfall.

Finally, it's important to note that businesses with adequate initial capitalization can easily become undercapitalized. Poor budgeting and mismanagement of funds have claimed countless new enterprises over the years.

Unanticipated Competition. In their enthusiasm to start a new business, people often underestimate the competitive environment in which they will operate. It obviously isn't enough to know that a market exists for a product or service. Equally important is an accurate analysis of the strengths and weaknesses of existing and potential competition. The "I can do it better" spirit provides valuable inspiration for new entrepreneurs, but only if they really can do things better than entrenched competitors, or if the market is healthy enough to support an additional entry.

Commonly, the appearance of a new competitor in what appears to be a lethargic market turns the environment hostile and aggressive. Existing competitors, sensing a threat, refocus their energies on their businesses and customers. The new competitor is placed at an immediate disadvantage, because he or she typically has to spend substantial time attracting and training staff, establishing supplier relationships, creating marketing programs, and, in general, performing all the tasks required to get the business up and running.

Uncontrolled Growth. As illogical as it seems, there can be such a thing as too much success for a new business. Some new businesses expand too quickly, straining their financial and management structures and damaging the quality of their products or services. If profitability begins to decline in a fast-growing business, lenders tend to run for the hills, while creditors line up at the door.

Therefore, anticipated growth should be planned for early in the process of starting a new business. In addition, astute managers also realize that unless appropriate structures and resources are in place, not all growth opportunities should be pursued aggressively.

Poor Location. Particularly for retail businesses, an advantageous location can be a critical ingredient for commercial success.

Where a retail establishment is located may be just as important as what the store sells. Traffic flow, parking facilities, the character of the neighborhood (and whether it is improving or declining), the identity of other businesses in the area, and a host of other location factors can conspire to make or break a new business.

Disasters. Obviously, not much can be done about "acts of God," although a business owner thinking of locating in a hurricane zone or atop an earthquake fault line might want to factor such information into precautionary insurance plans. It is important for would-be entrepreneurs to realize that even if they develop an outstanding competitive idea, make all the proper decisions, and do all the right things, something totally beyond their control could threaten or even ruin the business. There is no way to assure that a business of your own will be a success: there simply are no guarantees.

Eleven Characteristics of the Successful Entrepreneur

Given this scenario of 50 to 80 percent failure rates, dog-eat-dog competition, and potential earthquakes, who are these superheroes who succeed at building their own businesses? Research into the characteristics of successful entrepreneurs may offer some helpful insights. Studies conducted by David McClelland[1] and by John A. Welsh and Jerry F. White[2] have identified several potential success factors.

Good Health. Successful entrepreneurs tend to be physically resilient. They seem to will themselves free of illness. Some report that symptoms of nagging health conditions they suffered for years, such as back problems or hay fever, disappeared when they started their own businesses. When they do catch the flu or a cold, they ignore their symptoms and keep working.

Successful entrepreneurs are able to work long hours. They

1. David McClelland, et al., cited in *Developing and Training Human Resources in Organizations,* by Kenneth N. Wexley and Gary P. Latham (Glenview, IL: Scott Foresman, 1981), 256 pp.
2. John A. Welsh and Jerry F. White, *The Entrepreneur's Master Planning Guide* (Englewood Cliffs, NJ: Prentice-Hall, 1983), 408 pp.

start with a standard eight-hour day at the store or office and then put in another six to eight hours after their employees have gone home.

Over a four-year period, Drake Beam Morin conducted a series of sixty-four seminars in which distinguished entrepreneurs were invited to relate their experiences and reveal the secrets of their success. Each was asked to list candidly in his or her own words the critical ingredients of making it as an entrepreneur. Entirely independently of one another, each of these individuals mentioned good health as one of the four most important factors for success.

Need to Control and Direct. Entrepreneurs typically do not function well in traditional, structured organizations. They're convinced they can do the job better than anyone else, and they want no one in authority above them telling them otherwise. They thrive on responsibility and accountability. They need the freedom to initiate the actions they believe are necessary. This isn't a need for power, and it especially isn't a need for power over other people. Entrepreneurs are goal-oriented, and achieving one goal usually prompts them to set another.

Before they earn the title "successful entrepreneur," these individuals are often known by another label: "maverick." Many have changed jobs frequently. When asked to describe the circumstances surrounding their decision to start a business, it is surprising how frequently successful entrepreneurs say that they quit a job one morning because they "just knew" they were going to be fired that afternoon.

As their business grows and assumes a more formal management structure, entrepreneurs typically endure a classic, and predictable, management crisis. Their need for control makes it nearly impossible for them to relinquish or delegate authority, and they continue to bypass whatever structured chains of responsibility may have been established.

Self-Confidence. As long as they feel they are in control of things, entrepreneurs tend to be exceptionally self-confident individuals. They tackle problems energetically and directly. They're dogged in the pursuit of the objectives they've set for themselves and their businesses. They work well in crisis situations. They are comfortable working alone. Conversely, when entrepreneurs work on teams or sense that they are not in control of a situation, their self-confidence—along with their involvement and productivity—often suffers.

Sense of Urgency. Inactivity makes entrepreneurs tense, impatient, and uneasy. They tend to display a constant sense of urgency. Particularly when they are building enterprises, they thrive on activity and achievement. They appear tireless in the pursuit of the goals they've set for themselves, and their lives are characterized by a pattern of uninterrupted behavior focused toward those objectives. If they enjoy sports, they are more likely to be interested in games like tennis or golf, where their own brains and skill determine who wins or loses, than in group sports, where they have to wait for others to pass them the ball.

Comprehensive Awareness. Successful entrepreneurs tend to be simultaneously farsighted and aware of important, immediate details. They figure out the effects of single events upon whole undertakings. They maintain a sense of comprehensive awareness as they plan for, make decisions about, and work in specific areas of their businesses. While sustaining a strong overall vision of the enterprise, they devote their energy to the step immediately in front of them. They don't confuse the forest and the trees.

Realistic Approach. Entrepreneurs accept things as they are and deal with them. They may or may not be idealistic, but they are unlikely to be unrealistic. They want to know the status of things. News is neither good nor bad as long as it is timely and accurate. They seek firsthand, personal verification of data, often bypassing organizational structures to get it.

Successful entrepreneurs tend to be persistent in the pursuit of their goals, but they are also realistic enough to change direction when they see that an alternative approach will improve their chances for success.

Superior Conceptual Ability. Entrepreneurs often exhibit the ability to spot critical relationships quickly in the midst of confused and complex situations. They identify problems and begin to work on solutions faster than the people around them. They aren't troubled by apparent ambiguity or uncertainty, because they are able to perceive patterns and order where others do not. This conceptual ability typically applies primarily to objects and functions, and may be less evident when people problems need resolution.

Entrepreneurs tend to be adept at describing their goals and how they intend to attain them. If others identify a fatal flaw associated with these plans, successful entrepreneurs are likely to put forth alternatives immediately with the same clarity and enthusiasm they used to describe their original approach.

Low Status Needs. Successful entrepreneurs like to hear praise for the business they have developed, but are often uncomfortable with praise directed toward them as individuals. Particularly as they are building their businesses, their status needs are often met through the achievements they make rather than by the office they work in or the clothes they wear. Symbols of position seem to hold little relevance for them.

Later, if their entrepreneurial efforts prove successful, they may reward themselves with an exotic automobile or a large new home. But as they establish and build a business—a period in which available assets are likely to be consumed far more rapidly than they can be replenished—they satisfy their status needs through the performance of the business, not through the appearance they present.

Objective Approach to Relationships. Entrepreneurs are more concerned with people's accomplishments than with their feelings. They often avoid becoming involved with others on a personal level, and don't hesitate to sever relationships that might hinder their progress toward their goals. They choose experts rather than friends as their business associates.

As they build a business, and resources are scarce, they devote little time or assets to satisfying people's feelings unless they think such activity is essential for achieving operational effectiveness or efficiency. Their apparent lack of sensitivity often causes turmoil and turnover.

Successful entrepreneurs drive themselves and their organizations relentlessly. They usually feel, and often indicate, that they are mentally ahead of their associates. They are frequently impatient and may lack the tolerance or empathy required to build a tightly knit management team.

This is not to suggest that entrepreneurs should not cultivate good interpersonal skills, even if it constitutes a real challenge for them. Particularly as their businesses expand and adopt more formal management structures, entrepreneurs with good interpersonal skills are likely to outperform those with meager abilities in this area.

Emotional Stability. Entrepreneurs tend to exhibit considerable self-control and handle business anxieties and pressures with relative ease. They are cool and effective in stress situations and are often challenged rather than discouraged by a setback or failure.

Entrepreneurs frequently have strong feelings about events or issues that are important to them, but they are generally able to control their emotional reactions to avoid interfering with the progress of their business. They tend to vent frustration or excess energy through action. When things are going well, for example, many entrepreneurs feel uncomfortable or dissatisfied and stir up the situation to release their pent-up energy. They are rarely content to leave well enough alone.

Attraction to Challenge, Not Risk. Even if they invest all their personal assets in a new venture, successful entrepreneurs do not tend to be high risk takers. They are motivated by challenges in which they perceive the odds to be interesting but not overwhelming. They seldom act until they have assessed the potential risk and feel comfortable with the situation.

Entrepreneurs often appear inactive or seem to be coasting for extended periods of time. They may actually be assessing a situation carefully, waiting to act until they are convinced that the risk associated with the endeavor will be manageable. Finally, other entrepreneurial traits—self-confidence, persistence, realism, and the ability to make sense out of complexity—may allow entrepreneurs to succeed at risk levels that others might find daunting or unmanageable.

Should *You* Pursue a Business of Your Own?

If, following this introduction to entrepreneurial characteristics and potential pitfalls associated with new ventures, you determine that this simply isn't the life for you, you can move on to consider other options without worrying that you've neglected an important career alternative.

But what if you remain intrigued, interested, or compelled by the idea of starting your own business? It's time to put yourself into the picture, and begin to analyze opportunities in greater detail. What is your idea for a new venture? Do you have the necessary personal qualities, business skills, and expertise to make it a success? Even if your business idea is only hazily defined at this time, you can begin the process of examining and refining it so that, at some point down the line, you can make, and be comfortable with, your decision to proceed with or reject the idea.

HOW DO I RATE MYSELF IN RELATION TO MY PROPOSED NEW BUSINESS?

For each category here, rate yourself in terms of your own characteristics and personal habits. Then rate the importance of each quality to the success of your new enterprise.

Category	Personal Level Low High		Importance to Success of Enterprise Low High	
1. Health	1 2 3 4 5		1 2 3 4 5	
2. Vigor	1 2 3 4 5		1 2 3 4 5	
3. Initiative (self-starting enthusiasm)	1 2 3 4 5		1 2 3 4 5	
4. Sense of urgency	1 2 3 4 5		1 2 3 4 5	
5. Responsibility (getting things done)	1 2 3 4 5		1 2 3 4 5	
6. Persistence	1 2 3 4 5		1 2 3 4 5	
7. Self-confidence	1 2 3 4 5		1 2 3 4 5	
8. Technical knowledge	1 2 3 4 5		1 2 3 4 5	

Category	Personal Level					Importance to Success of Enterprise				
	Low			High		Low			High	
9. Stability 1 (coping with stress)	1	2	3	4	5	1	2	3	4	5
10. Stability 2 (reliability)	1	2	3	4	5	1	2	3	4	5
11. Comprehensive awareness	1	2	3	4	5	1	2	3	4	5
12. Leadership	1	2	3	4	5	1	2	3	4	5
13. Creativity	1	2	3	4	5	1	2	3	4	5
14. Analytical ability	1	2	3	4	5	1	2	3	4	5
15. Marital/family status (stability/support)	1	2	3	4	5	1	2	3	4	5
16. Community interests	1	2	3	4	5	1	2	3	4	5
17. Circle of friends (contacts/support)	1	2	3	4	5	1	2	3	4	5
18. Education	1	2	3	4	5	1	2	3	4	5
19. Written communication	1	2	3	4	5	1	2	3	4	5
20. Oral communication	1	2	3	4	5	1	2	3	4	5

If this self-assessment has persuaded you to dispense with the idea of starting a new business from scratch, you may still want to consider another form of self-employment. If this is true, read the discussion of franchise opportunities and purchasing existing businesses later in this chapter, and study Chapter 10 to learn about consulting careers.

If you're still intent on developing a business of your own, however, the exercise has served as the first step in a process of research, analysis, planning, and, ultimately, execution, as you address and resolve the full range of issues involved in launching a new enterprise. The process typically continues until one of three things occurs: you discover an insurmountable barrier that makes further progress unwise or even impossible; you decide that the whole thing just isn't worth the effort; or you develop and actually implement an action plan that turns your idea into a new business.

Creating a Business Plan

A business plan is an essential document for all new ventures. Potential lenders or investors will be unlikely to consider your idea at all unless you furnish them with a detailed business plan. But even if you fund your new enterprise entirely from your own pocket, taking an impromptu approach to starting your new business is as sensible as driving from Helsinki to Bangkok without a road map.

Your business plan will be your road map. If you prepare it carefully, it can guide you from Point X—wherever you are today in your planning—to Point Y—a place we will call "success." Remember, however, that even a perfect business plan can't guarantee you'll reach this destination safely. But a diligently prepared plan should arm you with the best available intelligence for negotiating the difficult road ahead.

It will help you allocate resources and set realistic goals. It will establish standards for measuring the performance of your business. When you have to make a critical decision quickly, you'll probably find the guidelines you need in your business plan.

Six Helpful Tips for Business Plan Preparation

Here are some general guidelines that may prove helpful as you prepare to create a business plan.

Unpredictable Events Will Occur. Perhaps the only thing you can predict accurately about starting your own business is that it will be unpredictable. Real life will never parallel your plans precisely. As you set goals and develop an action plan, then, establish best- and worst-case scenarios. Determine how you would handle either eventuality.

Your Business Plan Must Be Specific. The more specific you make your business plan, the more accurate and useful it will be. Developing a detailed business plan for a restaurant may be useless or even damaging to your chances, for example, if you really intend to enter the fast-food sector of the business.

Keep Your Audience in Mind. Remember that a business plan isn't just a personal, internal document: other people will use and examine it, too. In addition to potential lenders or investors, consultants or advisers you retain may wish to review the document. As a result, your business plan should include not just information about the business, but facts about you as well: your work history and financial resources, for example. In addition, the material it contains must be accurate: you owe a frank portrayal of the situation and your plans not only to outsiders who become involved in your enterprise, but, even more importantly, to yourself as well.

Let Your Business Shape Your Business Plan. The specifics of the business you intend to enter should dictate the form and content of your business plan. Don't assume that you can insert your data into someone else's existing plan and expect to produce a useful document.

Volume Doesn't Equal Quality. In the corporate world, a report is sometimes judged by its weight or thickness. Not so in the art of creating an individual business plan. Keep your business plan lean. Extraneous material won't serve any purpose and may even camouflage potential problems. Remember that lenders, investors, and advisers are likely to judge your business plan—and therefore your competence to run the new business—by your ability to focus on the critical factors that will determine success or failure. Readers forced to wade through sloppy writing and ambiguous thinking may conclude that either your priorities are out of order or your capabilities are limited.

Appearance Counts. If you want people to take you and your new venture seriously, your business plan should be well organized, clean, and professional looking.

Twelve Building Blocks of an Effective Business Plan

While the content of your business plan should be unique, reflecting the special features of your idea and presenting your individual abilities to succeed with the venture, the form your plan takes should follow a tested pattern. By breaking the document down into a series of twelve building blocks, you'll not only include all the necessary items, but you may also avoid feeling overwhelmed by the lengthy process.

1. Select Your Business. To even contemplate starting a business of your own, you obviously need to begin with a good idea. But how do you get one, and how do you know whether it's worth pursuing?

Perhaps the most effective way to identify the business you are best suited for is to consider areas in which you have the most knowledge and the greatest personal interest. Don't automatically exclude hobbies from this investigation. Avocations transformed into vocations have inspired many successful new enterprises.

Whatever field you identify, you'll need to assess and evaluate your own competence in it with candor and perhaps even some healthy skepticism. For instance, we've had people tell us that they feel equipped to open restaurants because, they say, "We eat out all the time." We have to remind them that their experience makes them fully qualified to be customers, not restaurateurs.

In fact, if your idea for a business entered your mind for the first time only *after* you recently lost a job, be a little wary of the urge. There is always the possibility that this new interest is prompted by escapist motives. Be certain your motive isn't "I'll never let anyone fire me again, and I can't get fired if I'm the boss," or "I just can't face going out to search for a job, so I'll make my own."

2. Select and Define Your Business Segment. Once you've identified your business, you need to be certain you'll be entering an appropriate segment of the industry. Let's assume, for example, you've concluded that your experience and lifelong interest in antiques makes that the business for you. You plan to open an antiques store.

But will the market support another store? Perhaps you'll need to limit your business to a specific segment of the antiques market. If you learn that no potential competitors sell Victorian antiques, and if you conclude that a market exists for such collectibles, you may have found your niche. If you discover that antique retailing is a saturated business in your area, you might redefine your plans and choose to wholesale antiques to all those retailers, perhaps, or to start a business devoted to restoring antiques.

In step one, you determine the business you intend to pursue. Here, you apply market research to focus your choice more precisely.

3. Research Your Competition. As in so many aspects of life, knowledge is power when you set out to develop a business. You need to develop a thorough understanding of your competitors, their locations, their pricing practices, the lines of goods they offer, their strengths, and their weaknesses.

Many experts concur that conducting a complete and accurate market analysis is the single most important precursor to the launch of a new business. Not only does the process teach you about the marketplace and your competitors, but it also provides you with valuable knowledge about yourself and your own prospects for success.

4. Define Your Financial Resources and Determine Your Risk Tolerance. Lenders or investors are rarely willing to put up 100 percent of the finances required by a new venture. What will you be able to invest in your new business? Can your emotions sustain this investment level during the venture's uncertain early months?

If you attract outside funding sources for your business, they will expect some degree of control. They may demand to have a say in how much you pay yourself, and they are likely to expect you to make personal sacrifices during the developmental phase of the business. Depending on the size of their investment, they may even expect you to earn back an equity position in the new venture.

The more you invest, the greater your control of the business. At the same time, putting your family's financial future at substantial risk or sentencing yourself to years of economic privation probably isn't a good prescription for business, or personal, success.

5. Create a Marketing Plan. Although this item comes fifth in our chronological list of building blocks, using the market intelligence you've gathered to establish a sound marketing plan for your product or service ranks in importance near the top of a list of building blocks that are absolutely critical for any new venture.

Effective marketing plans typically include two principal elements: a sales or revenue forecast, which is primarily figures, and an action plan or marketing strategy, which explains how you intend to attain your forecast. To create an effective marketing plan, you'll need to make and support a series of decisions about sales and distribution strategies, pricing, advertising, and promotion.

6. Make an Operations Plan. Creating a strong operations plan is another critical element of the business plan. Depending on the business under consideration, it might include sections on geographic location, facilities and their improvement, and production systems, as well as a range of administrative issues. Operations plans also typically include sections devoted to insurance needs, staffing requirements and training, and compensation policies.

7. Work Up a Financial Plan. The financial plan is a third key building block of the complete business plan. A good financial plan includes three categories: financing, financial planning, and financial analysis. Financing refers to plans for assembling the capital needed to launch your new venture. The financial planning section presents operating and capital budgets, as well as cash flow, profit and loss, and balance sheet projections for a three- to five-year period. The financial analysis section incorporates discussions of break-even points and return-on-investment measures that will allow you to assess the performance of your new business.

8. Develop an Organization Plan. As you plan your business, you need to determine whether you want to operate as a sole proprietorship, as a partnership, or as a corporation. Each option presents its own legal and economic advantages and disadvantages, so it will be important for you to consider this issue with care and seek the assistance of a qualified lawyer and accountant.

9. Set Goals. To lay this building block in place in your business plan, you'll establish a series of goals for your business—both for the near term and for several years into the future—for sales, profits, expenditures, inventories, and any other categories that may prove relevant to the success of the venture.

10. Weigh Your Facts. Once you've completed steps one through nine, it's time to step back and carefully evaluate each element. Does the plan make sense as a whole? Can you identify gaps in your planning? Have your efforts raised questions you haven't answered in the plan? Given the amount of capital you anticipate raising, have you made appropriate decisions about your new business? In light of the knowledge you've assembled, do you continue to believe the venture can be successful?

11. Complete Your Plan. Based on the analysis you complete in step ten, you can now pull your plan together into a single cohesive document, review your efforts, and fine-tune the presentation.

12. Take Action. Now, using the finished business plan as your road map, you're ready to establish an action plan and begin to turn your business plan into an operating enterprise.

A Business Plan Outline

The generic outline below presents the structure of a typical business plan. Although it's important to remember that the specifics of your entrepreneurial ideas should dictate the actual form of your business plan, this outline may be useful as a template or point of departure as you work to develop the document.

  I. Summary
 II. Background
III. Business Charter
    A. Description of product/service
    B. Targeted market niche
    C. Potential
IV. Market Analysis
    A. Market characteristics
    B. Customer characteristics
    C. Competitive evaluation
    D. Market potential (trends, sales estimates)
    E. Noncontrollable elements
 V. Marketing Plan
    A. Sales forecast
    B. Sales strategy
    C. Distribution strategy
    D. Pricing
    E. Advertising and promotion
    F. Product/service warranties

VI. Design and Development Plan
   A. Status and next steps
   B. Risks and problems
   C. Projected development costs
VII. Operations and Organization Plan
   A. Ownership/legal form
   B. Location
   C. Facilities
   D. Manufacturing plan
   E. Labor force
   F. Management compensation
   G. Training
   H. Professional support
VIII. Financial Plan
   IX. Critical Risks and Problems
   X. Schedule of Key Events

Where to Go for Help

Listing the elements of a typical business plan in outline form is likely to prompt the would-be entrepreneur to wonder, How am I *ever* going to do all that? That, of course, is the $64 million question, and not just for preparing a business plan, but for actually running and succeeding in your own new business.

Particularly if this is your first new business venture, it's unlikely that you honestly consider yourself a marketing whiz, financial genius, legal eagle, operations expert, master manager, super salesperson, and distribution dynamo, all rolled into one. And yet your new venture is likely to demand some level of expertise in each of these areas.

At the same time, throughout your career you've developed significant skills and experience in a range of disciplines. The first thing to do, then, is to assess these abilities in terms of the requirements of your proposed business. Where you discover weaknesses, you can then decide whether to develop your own skills or seek outside support. Appendix A at the back of this book contains a series of self-assessment instruments for various facets of new business development. Before completing these exercises, you may wish to review the sections in Chapter 6 where you analyzed your skills and accomplishments.

At some point you'll be certain to need outside assistance as you develop your plans and set them in motion. Your attorney and accountant are obvious and immediate resources. If they lack experience in the particular needs of your new venture, they can probably direct you to specialists.

There is certainly no shortage of information related to entrepreneurial activities. Books and publications on starting new businesses are widely available, so that one trip to a good bookstore or library could easily supply you with a month's supply of research materials. Business and university libraries tend to be good sources for economic and financial data. Federal and state business administrations offer reams of reports and other publications. The chamber of commerce can help you investigate the local business climate and may be able to refer you to appropriate consultants or small business experts in your area. Trade associations in the field you plan to enter may have developed materials for individuals seeking to enter their industry.

If you have access to a personal computer and modem, membership in an on-line information service can open an electronic gateway to masses of relevant information. A recent five-minute session we spent browsing through one such service led to reports on International Entrepreneurs, Working from Home, and PR and Marketing, plus a section devoted to government reports, publications, and books on business and the economy.

Finally, established business owners are often willing to help new members of the entrepreneurial fraternity. There tends to be a camaraderie among business owners such that even a potential competitor from down the street—who will happily battle you for every last sales and profit dollar in the future—may just as happily share advice and sources with you today.

Buying a Business or Investing in a Franchise

Each year in the United States, literally millions of existing businesses change hands. The most visible of these are the huge corporate takeovers with multibillion-dollar price tags, but most transactions are completed at or below $250,000, with many businesses being sold substantially under that figure. And the popularity of establishments ranging from fast-food outlets to day-care centers bears testimony to the attractiveness and, under the proper circumstances, profitability of franchise opportunities throughout the country.

Both buying an existing business and investing in a franchise have distinct advantages and disadvantages when compared to new business start-ups. Potential pluses associated with purchasing an established business may include: the venture's track record, which can be analyzed and used to plan for the future; existing customers, staff, suppliers, and facilities; the availability of financing sources that may not be open to businesses which only exist as ideas; reduced risk; existing cash flow. A major advantage of franchising is the support and expertise typically provided by the parent company, which can include everything from finding an appropriate location to hiring and training staff, providing standardized procedures, offering a centralized purchasing function, and even providing some level of start-up financing.

There is often a darker side to such opportunities, however. When you buy a going business, you will generally have to recoup some amount of *goodwill*—that is, the excess of the purchase price over the value of the assets you acquire. If that figure is too high, it may prove difficult or even impossible to ever turn a profit. You might unwittingly purchase a business with a poor reputation. The current owner may be selling out because trouble is anticipated ahead. Finally, you won't be able to create the business yourself; it may not reflect your entrepreneurial vision, and changing its form or image may not be easy.

When you enter into a franchise agreement, your success is dependent, to one degree or another, on the business skills, determination, financial health, even the ethics and honesty of the franchisor. There are many established, reputable companies offering solid franchise opportunities today, but there are probably even more untested franchise operations looking to establish themselves with your hard-earned funds. And, unfortunately, there are also out-and-out crooks roaming the franchise market, intent on separating you from your dollars.

There is also the danger of being lured into the purchase of a franchise or existing business based on the potential profits you think it offers rather than on the fundamentals of the business itself. Remember that in most situations, you're going to be spending your days and nights running the nuts-and-bolts aspects of the venture. You'll certainly want to make profits, but you probably won't want to invest your future in a business you abhor. Given the state of the environment, for example, buying a hazardous waste removal company might represent an opportune financial decision. But, depending on the particulars of the specific business opportunity, it might also mean that for a couple of years you would have to spend your days personally removing hazardous waste.

As with the development and start-up of an entirely new business, careful and rigorous research, analysis, planning, and decision making are important keys to the successful pursuit of other entrepreneurial alternatives. Expert professional advice and support are critical. And the same process of self-assessment you would use to determine whether to start a business from scratch will help determine whether an existing opportunity offers you the best chances for career success and personal happiness.

CHAPTER 10

Working for Yourself:
A Career as a Consultant

Scratch the surface of any large company, and you're likely to uncover a stream of consultants roaming its halls. Whether they descend in teams from large international firms or surface as one-person consulting operations, consultants sometimes seem to flood the American business world.

Their numbers and visibility may be what prompt so many corporate employees to consider starting consulting businesses of their own. And, in fact, consulting can offer attractive career opportunities for many individuals. Consultants get the chance to be on their own, for example, avoiding bosses, red tape, and organizational politics. Starting a consulting business typically requires minimal capital investment and, as a result, often entails less up-front financial risk than other entrepreneurial ventures.

Consultants can control their own time, the number of both hours and days they work, and even the times of the day or night during which they labor. A consulting career offers opportunities for variety and travel. There is no mandatory or traditional retirement age. Finally, given the right circumstances, consulting can provide a handsome annual income, even for individuals who pursue part-time careers as consultants.

At the same time, a career in consulting can also involve major disadvantages. There are already so many consultants, for instance, and barriers to new entrants are so low that competition is likely to be intense. Also, except in large consulting firms, the support and benefits systems common to corporate life are rare. And because consultants remain outside the power structure of the organizations they serve, they lack the authority to impose solutions on others.

Necessary self-discipline may be difficult to develop for former corporate staffers accustomed to the structure and regimen of large companies. Finally, maintaining the distinction between work and leisure time can be hard for new consultants used to a 9-to-5 life-style. Given these issues and a range of additional topics we'll introduce in this chapter, it's clear that investigating a career in consulting demands the same degree of external research and internal analysis required of any radical career shift.

Temporary and Part-Time Consulting Opportunities

Still, we urge you to investigate this employment option carefully, even if you don't see a consulting career in your future. You could be surprised. Perhaps you think you lack a consultant's skills or experience. Examining your work history and career accomplishments might convince you otherwise.

Also, even if you intend to continue your career in a corporate setting, you could discover that working temporarily as a consultant becomes an effective job-search strategy. Not only do consulting engagements provide welcome income, but in the consulting environment you and your clients get on-the-job knowledge of each other. Your performance on a consulting assignment or your ability to identify and articulate additional tasks you might perform could convince a client to offer you a permanent position.

In addition, a common fear among people who make hiring decisions is that they'll make the wrong choice. As a result, some managers actually spend more time looking for reasons to disqualify candidates than focusing on the positive qualifications of individuals. If you're one of the candidates, you obviously face an uphill employment battle in this environment. Gaining the opportunity to work with an organization as a consultant enables the employer to see your strengths and to dispense with concerns about potential weaknesses. The consulting relationship also lets you develop a realistic, insider's perspective of the client company, so that if a full-time job should be offered to you, the danger of making a poor career decision is substantially reduced.

Finally, people frequently discover that working part-time as a consultant makes an ideal career choice. As we'll see in the next chapter, some form of work is often considered an important ingredient of the active retirement favored by many Americans today. Pursuing a limited number of consulting assignments offers one way to fulfill this need. Some full-time corporate employees seek to augment their income by moonlighting—offering their expertise and advice to other companies—becoming, in effect, part-time consultants. It's clear, then, that both the range of consulting opportunities and the identities of consultants themselves are very broad today.

What Is a Consultant?

However vast the range and ranks of consultants may have become, many people still aren't entirely certain what a consulting career involves. What do consultants do?

In the broadest terms, a consultant is an expert adviser brought in from outside an organization to help solve problems in exchange for a fee. To achieve a certain goal, a client pays a consultant for his or her services. These services may include or produce a number of things: a survey, a report, a workshop, a teaching program, a change in organizational procedure or structure, or a meeting for data collection or feedback.

The consulting relationship is temporary, and the consultant is an outsider, not a member of the client organization. Consultants assume two key roles in this setting: they act as experts and as advisers.

Consultants provide expertise in a particular business area. These areas of expertise are probably as broad as the business world itself: from communications and writing to law, accounting, human resources management, data processing, or biotechnology.

A key requirement for a consultant is that he or she be a

proven expert who can satisfy a client's specific needs in a narrowly defined field. Typically, consultants provide highly specialized services their clients cannot obtain within their own organizations.

Consultants are also advisers. They don't have the authority to implement programs or bring about change directly. Instead, they must act through others by obtaining a client's consent regarding a set of recommendations. This lack of direct power distinguishes consultants from managers. Instead of assuming a manager's role—direct involvement in carrying out tasks or programs—consultants analyze situations, pinpoint problems, and propose solutions. In essence, consultants use influence without authority to gain a desired objective.

Consulting Options

Individuals who are considering consulting careers can examine a variety of options for structuring the new business.

Start a One-Person Practice. The most obvious alternative, and perhaps the most common, is to start a one-person practice. The main advantage of this approach is that it allows the individual maximum independence to define and operate his or her business. This can be especially effective when consultants plan to serve narrow market niches, particularly in technical areas.

The principal disadvantage of a one-person practice is that it is likely to be difficult for the consultant to handle broader client assignments. Establishing cooperative arrangements with other consultants may alleviate this problem and can also help avoid the potential loneliness associated with any one-person business.

Start or Join a Partnership. By starting a consulting partnership or joining an established one, the new consultant can focus on a broader market niche than he or she might target alone. The range of contacts and skills available to the partnership is likely to increase as well, and this may enhance both the quality of service and the accuracy of business decisions.

The primary disadvantage of a consulting partnership often involves the difficulty of achieving and maintaining the right blend of skills and personalities. Putting together the wrong skills or the wrong people in a small operation can seriously undermine its chances for long-term success.

Become a Subcontractor. It's also possible to become a "consultant's consultant," supporting other consulting practices by taking on parts of their business. This approach presents opportunities to learn the consulting business and generate references without having to market services directly to clients. At the same time, subcontractors typically earn less than principal contractors, and they usually don't enjoy significant client exposure.

Work for a Consulting Company. Going to work for a consulting company offers the opportunity to begin a hybrid consulting career: the individual works in the consulting field but is a staff employee, receiving a salary and benefits plus the stability and security of employment with an established company. This option enables the would-be consultant to learn about the field and establish a track record in the process. At the same time, however, it obviously doesn't offer autonomy and independence, qualities that make consulting desirable for people interested in work-for-self careers.

Become a Free-lancer. Finally, there is also the related career option of becoming a free-lancer instead of a consultant, acting as another pair of hands for clients rather than performing consulting duties. At the outset, this alternative may demand less specialized expertise than might be required of a consultant. And there may be more free-lance opportunities than consulting assignments available at some times or in certain industries.

The free-lancer is unlikely to assume the role of an adviser, however, and free-lance pay tends to lag behind consulting fees.

The "Typical" Consultant

While the size of consulting firms and the shape of consulting options vary substantially, small firms dominate the industry. According to *The Complete Guide to Consulting Success,*[1] for ex-

1. Howard Shenson, *The Complete Guide to Consulting Success* (Wilmington, Delaware: Enterprise Publishing Company, 1987).

ample, there are more than 72,000 consulting firms in the United States and Canada. Over 70 percent of these firms are staffed by one or two professionals. More than 90 percent of them operate from small offices or private homes.

These "typical" consultants spend less than half their time on actual consulting assignments. More than 25 percent of their workweek is spent on marketing activities, while practice management and professional development activities account for the rest of their work schedule.

Who Hires Consultants—and Why?

It's difficult to think of a business or industry, large or small, that doesn't rely on consultants in one situation or another. A neighborhood retailer retains a consultant to conduct a direct-mail advertising campaign. A giant multinational corporation engages a communications consultant to help polish its image. An individual uses a consultant to assist in the start-up of a small business. A large management consulting firm hires consultants to help select a new telephone system, or to review compensation policies.

A partial list of organizations using consultants includes large corporations, nonprofit organizations, government agencies, schools and colleges, health-care institutions, entertainment companies, advertising agencies, and small businesses.

Why do these organizations turn to consultants so frequently? For one thing, many companies have decided to focus their internal efforts and resources very tightly, "outsourcing" all activities that aren't directly related to their core businesses. A large bank owns or leases substantial real estate assets, for example, including headquarters facilities, branch banks, and back-office operations. Ten years ago, the bank staffed a substantial real estate department to oversee these assets. Today, it relies on consultants to manage the real estate portfolio. In one industry after another, and in all parts of these businesses, similar decisions have created great demand for qualified consultants.

Client organizations retain consultants for a range of additional reasons, as well.

- to identify problems
- to solve problems
- to supply specialized knowledge
- to generate and introduce new ideas
- to "sell" ideas to others
- to identify and pursue growth opportunities
- to teach new procedures or technologies
- to keep up with competitors

Consulting Skills

This brief introduction to consulting indicates that to be effective and successful, consultants must possess two sets of principal skills: technical skills and interpersonal skills.

Effective consultants have expert knowledge in a specific area. Clients are unlikely to be satisfied with consultants who are generalists in one field or another. They typically have all the generalists they need on staff. What they lack is a specialist, someone with profound knowledge of a specific field and an expertise that isn't generally required in the client's day-to-day business activities.

While technical skills are a prerequisite, interpersonal skills are also essential for consultants, both to conduct assignments and to secure additional engagements. As we've seen, the consultant has to persuade clients that his or her problem identification, analysis, and proposed solutions are valid and deserve to be acted upon. In addition, the entire consulting process revolves around the ability to communicate effectively with people at all organizational levels, both to gather information and to reduce anxiety and friction. Finally, consultants must have strong interpersonal skills to get business in the first place by marketing their services energetically and effectively.

Assessing Your Aptitude as a Consultant

To determine whether consulting—whether full-time, part-time, or temporary—holds significant attractions for you, you'll need to assess a range of issues involving your finances, motivation, technical skills, and interpersonal capabilities. For the remainder of this chapter, we'll discuss these subjects in more detail and offer exercises that will help you determine whether working as a consultant might represent an appealing career direction for you.

The Question of Finances

Can you afford to start a consulting practice? On the one hand, the start-up costs of consulting are likely to be substantially lower than the expenses associated with establishing most other types of businesses. As we observed earlier, most of the nation's consulting businesses are one- or two-person operations which are frequently run out of the principals' homes. So at the outset, anyway, you probably wouldn't have to invest in staff or real estate to start a consulting business. You wouldn't need to purchase an inventory of goods, and, perhaps beyond a computer and fax machine, you wouldn't have to buy much in the way of expensive equipment. As a consultant, your "products" would be primarily in your head: your intelligence, skills, and experience.

But until you begin to win consulting assignments, you can't generate any income, and even when you do begin to earn fees, you may have to wait a month or more for reimbursement. So you could encounter initial cash flow problems. Take a few minutes to refer back to Chapter 7 and review the financial information you gathered about your current situation.

WHAT IS MY FINANCIAL PICTURE?

Given your present financial resources, how many months could you afford to invest in a new consulting business before receiving any economic returns? Are there any ways you could trim current expenses to lengthen that period?

_____

_____

_____

_____

As you investigate your finances, remember that simply having the necessary resources doesn't mean you possess the necessary skills and qualities of self-motivation to become a successful consultant. If you lack those other abilities, in fact, cash flow is likely to become a long-term problem. Investing six or twelve months of severance pay only to learn that you really don't want to be a consultant isn't an economically attractive career option.

Key Issues of Motivation

Leaving the steady, regular pattern of the corporate world for a challenging and, at times, frustrating existence as a consultant raises a variety of motivational issues. Your ability to deal with, or better yet to embrace those issues offers important indicators about the desirability of a consulting career for you.

Lack of Structure. For many of us, life has been governed by fixed time schedules since we started nursery school. No such structure shapes the life of a consultant. There is no longer a driving need to be at the office at 8:30 or 9:00 each morning. In most situations, no secretary awaits the consultant's arrival. No subordinates wait for his or her decisions. No superiors expect reports. Even more important, no one watches the consultant's performance on a daily basis.

This unstructured setting is exhilarating for some individuals but debilitating for others. To be a successful consultant, you obviously need to fall into the first category. With no external pressures forcing you to get up in the morning, you need to have the personal drive and self-motivation to get going and stay active.

Past history doesn't always provide an accurate indicator of this internal motivation. If you've spent years dragging yourself from bed off to a job you could barely tolerate, having the chance to "do your own thing" could inspire and reinvigorate you.

Feast or Famine. Corporate life tends to be characterized by a steady stream of tasks and responsibilities. Except in emergency situations, employees do a day's work, go home to their families and outside interests, and return the next day to pick up where they left off. The schedule is less predictable for most consultants, who must endure the peaks and valleys life-style of the self-employed.

With eerie predictability, the period in which you are working away on one or two demanding projects is precisely the time a new client calls with a major assignment demanding immediate attention. You don't want to turn down the new project—you want to earn the fee and retain the client for future work—so you find yourself juggling assignments and working eighteen-hour days for three or four months.

When you successfully complete the final engagement, you collapse for a week to recharge your batteries. Then a second week passes, and a third, and you wonder if you'll ever see another piece of new business. Welcome to the world of feast or famine.

The self-motivation needed to cope with too much work—and too little—is an important quality for consultants. For many, dealing with periods of relative famine is far more difficult than working through an overwhelming work load. At least there's a visible end to too much work, even if it's only a faint light at the end of a long tunnel. But when nothing is cooking in the consultant's pot, the future can seem very grim.

Successful consultants need both the practical energy to stay active, marketing their business and building knowledge to stay on top of their field, and the personal motivation to assure that such activity will continue to create new business.

Willingness to Market. Consultants must sell themselves constantly, particularly as they start their new business. It normally takes several years of determined self-promotion before consultants can relax a bit and assume that they are firmly established in their field. During that time, the self-motivated consultant is constantly out making new contacts, keeping in touch with old contacts, writing letters of introduction to potential clients, and, generally speaking, promoting his or her skills. These efforts continue outside the office environment and beyond normal working hours: the individual in the next seat on an airplane or the person introduced at a dinner party just might be the source of the next consulting assignment.

Even established consultants cannot abandon their marketing activities. As one very successful consultant puts it, "I think of my business as a leaky bucket. My number one priority is to keep pouring new assignments and new clients into the top of it before everything drips out the bottom."

Consultants can't slight their marketing activities even when consulting engagements demand most of their time. A common, and dangerous, syndrome is to market aggressively until a project is landed, and then suspend all sales efforts to work full-time on the new project. The problem with this approach is that the consultant ends up starting over more or less from scratch each time a project is concluded. He or she is likely to encounter lengthy periods of inactivity as contacts are remade and opportunities are identified and pursued. The sporadic result has thinned from the consulting ranks many otherwise capable individuals.

Most corporate executives—even corporate marketing executives—haven't done this sort of personal marketing regularly, and many are uncomfortable with its demands. Given its essential nature, would-be consultants should assess their own marketing motivation carefully before embarking on a consulting career.

Incidentally, the importance of marketing illustrates the folly of pursuing a career as a consultant by individuals who decide, "I just can't face another job search, so I'll be a consultant." Consulting *is* a permanent job search!

The Need to Keep Up. Since consultants are experts by definition, they must continually refresh their expertise in their chosen field to maintain their credentials. In highly technical businesses, this can be a demanding process. But because keeping up is synonymous with staying alive for most consultants, they must be motivated to invest time and effort, without immediate expectations of reward, to keep abreast of new developments.

Many consultants find that they gain intellectual satisfaction from such research. Some are so interested in their field that they have a natural need to stay on top of it. For these individuals, the ability to justify their investigations as a necessary dimension of their work becomes a powerful source of satisfaction.

Lack of Support. Like any small business, a consulting operation typically lacks most of the support systems common to larger organizations. If the fax machine breaks, you don't call an office manager: you take valuable time away from your consulting business to figure out how and where to get the machine repaired and, perhaps, take it there yourself, negotiate how long the repairs will take, return to pick up the machine, and reach into your pocket to pay for it.

Another aspect of the general lack of readily available support involves the give-and-take of information and opinion that is common in large companies. If you're working for yourself, there isn't someone at the next desk to share ideas with, get second opinions from, or ask questions of. A trusted colleague won't be there to pop into your office and suggest you read this article or attend that company-sponsored seminar. You'll need to identify and pursue such opportunities on your own.

Ability to Persuade. As we mentioned earlier, the consultant's role involves giving advice, not ordering people around. More than in almost any other career, success or failure in consulting depends on the ability to persuade people.

In a consulting career, as a result, not only do you have to create coherent proposals, demonstrate superior analytical skills, and offer first-rate solutions to what your clients may have considered insoluble problems, but you must do all these things in a way that shows respect for the sensitivities of clients and their staffs. You may have to sell tough recommendations: making costly investments in new technology, for example, or reorganizing an entire department. In virtually every aspect of your career as a consultant, you'll need to demonstrate excellent skills in interpersonal relations and communications.

ASSESS YOUR MOTIVATIONAL ADJUSTMENT FACTORS

Based on the material just discussed, rate yourself for each of the factors listed here, addressing your personal "fit" with the challenges and frustrations of consulting. When you've completed this exercise, review your responses. Would you have to make substantial changes in your approach to become a consultant? Can you think of ways to make such changes, or do the motivational needs of the consulting life-style simply not mesh with your own?

Adjustment Factor	My Motivation Level				
	Low			High	
Enjoy using influence	1	2	3	4	5
Willing to forgo authority	1	2	3	4	5
Able and willing to do without a support system	1	2	3	4	5
Interested in keeping up with my field	1	2	3	4	5
Able and willing to market myself and my services	1	2	3	4	5
Able to continue working during slack periods	1	2	3	4	5
Energetic: able to work around the clock when necessary	1	2	3	4	5
High tolerance for unstructured work	1	2	3	4	5

Work Satisfiers and Dissatisfiers

Because so many of the perks and benefits of the corporate world are not found in the consulting environment, the need for task-related job satisfaction is particularly important for consultants. In a corporate setting, you might tell yourself, "There's plenty I don't like about the company but, for what they're paying me and the way my pension benefits are piling up, I can put up with it." In a one-man consulting operation, if you aren't satisfied with at least the majority of the tasks you perform, there isn't likely to be much else to be satisfied about.

Review the exercise on work satisfiers and dissatisfiers you completed in Chapter 6. Then, referring to the previous exercise on motivational adjustment factors, see how your patterns of work motivators and satisfiers/dissatisfiers compare with the generic challenges and frustrations that typically confront consultants.

How Serious Is Your Interest?

A final method for assessing the fit between your personal motivators and a career in consulting involves gauging the interest you've already shown and the effort you've invested in your area of technical expertise. Your answers to the following questions may indicate that, consciously or otherwise, you've already made some preliminary moves in the direction of consulting.

- During the past few years, have you read a substantial number of publications and other literature in some area of special interest?
- Do you subscribe to magazines or have you assembled a library of books on the topic?
- Do you associate with people who are already active consultants or authorities in your field of expertise?
- Have you dabbled in this field already, "just to get your feet wet"?
- Have you ever tried consulting on a no-fee basis—as a hobby or avocation?
- Before reading this book, had you ever examined your own strengths and personal traits to see how they might serve you in a consulting career?
- Have you thought seriously about what it would be like to commit two or three years to develop a consulting business?

The Importance of Competence

As we discuss the importance of motivation for consultants, it's important to remember that without technical skills even the most highly motivated individual will make a poor consultant. All the diligence and energy in the world won't save the consultant who consistently displays lack of competence and offers poor solutions to clients' problems.

In the long run, the issue of competence is a function of proven skills and accomplishments, the expertise you've developed throughout your career. That's what you have to sell your clients. But how you sell yourself is important, too, because clients also rely on perceptions to evaluate a consultant's competence.

When we review Drake Beam Morin's knowledge base in this area, we find that clients judge competence based on ten key factors. Four of these factors concern the consultant's perceived professionalism. First, does he or she present a professional appearance? Second, does the consultant take a practical approach to the client's business, presenting proposals that are feasible and offering solutions that can be implemented? Third, does the consultant adopt a broad focus regarding the client's situation, taking the whole organization into account? Or, in solving one problem, does the consultant appear to create others? Fourth, does the consultant seem accountable, meeting commitments on time and within budget, for example, and being prompt for meetings and appointments?

Another set of four factors relating to perceived competence involves interpersonal skills. First, there is the question of rapport: will employees, from top management on down, feel comfortable with this consultant? Second, the issue of communications: can the consultant's explanations and recommendations be understood easily, and are his or her reports coherent and well written? The third factor involves the ability to influence. Will the consultant be able to sell the results or recommendations of a study? Fourth, is the consultant perceived as being trustworthy?

Finally, two additional factors related to finances often influence client perceptions of consultants. First, does the consultant charge reasonable fees, or might billings be inflated? Could another consultant do more for less? Then there is the success factor: will solutions recommended by this consultant actually be implemented, and will real savings or additional profits be generated as a result?

While it's certainly premature to rate your own bottom-line performance as a consultant, it isn't too early to assess yourself in terms of your professional approach and interpersonal skills.

WOULD I BE PERCEIVED AS A COMPETENT CONSULTANT?

Rate yourself as you think you would be perceived by others in the workplace. If you're unsure about a category, enter a best guess rating. Later, you might find it helpful to seek input about these items from people whose judgment, honesty, and constructive intent you trust.

Factors	My Competence Level				
	Low				High
Professional Approach					
Professional appearance	1	2	3	4	5
Practical approach	1	2	3	4	5
Broad focus	1	2	3	4	5
Accountability	1	2	3	4	5
Interpersonal Skills					
Rapport	1	2	3	4	5
Communications	1	2	3	4	5
Ability to influence	1	2	3	4	5
Trustworthiness	1	2	3	4	5

Ultimately, of course, a successful career as a consultant depends on true competence. Perceived competence is important: it can win you business and reinforce your effectiveness as a consultant. But unless you can deliver real expertise, you're likely to have a rocky career as a consultant. To assess your proven competence, turn back to the material and exercises on accomplishments and skills in Chapter 6. Review the information you developed there, and decide whether the self-assessment exercises you've completed subsequently indicate that changes or additions should be made to that original material. Then complete the following exercise.

WHAT ARE MY CONSULTING SKILLS?

Identify the skills and knowledge you possess that would enable you to work effectively in the world of consulting. Your list of work accomplishments, as well as any personal insights you've developed, will help you assemble this information.

_____

_____

_____

_____

_____

_____

_____

_____

At this point in your investigation of professional skills, accomplishments, motivational issues, and other factors affecting a career in consulting, you may be approaching a decision: should you investigate a specific consulting field in greater detail, or does it make sense to move ahead to consider other career options? To test your position, complete the following exercise.

SHOULD I INVESTIGATE CONSULTING IN GREATER DETAIL?

Write brief statements to answer each of the following questions.

1. What areas of expertise could I see myself transferring to a career as a consultant? How much time and effort have I invested in each area?

_____

_____

_____

_____

2. When I visualize myself in the role of a consultant, what do I see myself doing?

_____

_____

_____

_____

3. What skills would I need to strengthen to become an effective consultant?

_____

_____

_____

_____

4. Why do I want to become a consultant?

_____

_____

_____

_____

Defining a Consulting Business

Let's assume that the research and self-assessment you've completed up to this point have convinced you to pursue the idea of a consulting career in greater detail. Now that you have some level of understanding of both the skills and motivation you might bring to consulting, you need to focus on defining your business. In fact, the more specifically you can define this new business, the more likely you'll be to avoid a mistake common to many new consultants.

That mistake might be called the generalist trap, defining one's consulting expertise in general terms. The consultant who has been a corporate general manager or a human resource generalist often forgets that potential clients tend to have very specific problems and seek very specific expertise to solve them. If they do want generalist consultants, they tend to approach large firms with big names.

So you'll need to play to your own strengths—your specific skills and areas of specific technical expertise—as you define a consulting business. If at the start you can establish your competence in one or two narrowly defined fields, later on you may be able to broaden the scope of your assignments.

The Consultant's Business Charter

Because consultants can typically set up shop without undergoing the scrutiny of a bank or outside investors, many fail to define the nature of their business at the outset. Taking the time and investing the effort to complete such an investigation greatly increases chances for success, however. You certainly need to be able to describe your consulting activities in as much detail as necessary to allow potential clients to understand your plans and your strategy for fulfilling them.

Before investing substantial time or capital to get a consulting business off the ground, it may prove useful to address the following series of questions. Your answers will become the first draft of a business charter for your new venture.

WHAT'S MY BUSINESS CHARTER?

Be as specific as you can to answer the following questions.

1. What services will I offer, what kinds of problems will I help solve, and what technical skills will I use to solve them?

_____

_____

2. What types of client organizations will I serve: government agencies, small or large companies, particular industries?

_____

_____

3. Within my targeted client organizations, who (what level, what position) will be my customers? Who needs help with the problems I intend to solve? Who hires consultants to solve them?

_____

_____

_____

_____

4. How will clients learn about my services?

_____

_____

_____

_____

5. Why will customers hire me instead of relying on inside resources or other outside consultants?

_____

_____

_____

_____

6. What's my rationale for thinking I can operate a profitable business solving these kinds of problems?

_____

_____

_____

_____

How to Proceed and Where to Look for Help

As you can see from the Consultant's Action Plan here, creating a business charter is the first in a series of action steps required to start a sound consulting practice. A detailed investigation of the subject is well beyond the scope of this book. If you decide to pursue a career in consulting, where can you go for help?

First, refer to Appendix B, "Resources for Careers in Consulting," located at the end of the book, for a sampling of additional information sources. Go out and talk to established consultants, particularly those operating in your technical field or a related area. (The section on networking in Chapter 15 will show you ways to identify and approach these individuals.) Ask them what it was like to get started in the business, what sort of skills and experience they found most valuable, and what, if they had it to do all over again, they would do differently to get started today.

CONSULTANT'S ACTION PLAN

Business Charter	Marketing Research	Marketing Strategy	Fee Setting/ Revenue Forecasting	Financial Plan	Managing Your Business
• Statement finalized	• Market segments identified • Prospective clients identified • Competitors evaluated • Interviews completed	• Network identified • Other consultants contacted • Business cards/ brochures printed • Marketing letters prepared • Other promotion activities • Directory listings • Newsletters • Direct mailing • Professional memberships • Lectures/seminars	• Structure and amount of fees set • Revenue forecast developed	• Record-keeping system installed • Start-up requirements determined • Personal living expenses budgeted • Financing available • Cash flow projected • Profit and loss estimated	• Attorney selected • Accountant selected • Bank/banker selected • Insurance in place • Legal form of organization decided • Legal forms/ contracts approved • Office space ready • Support staff on board

CHAPTER 11

Active Retirement

Retirement, traditionally perceived as an ending, is more often considered a continuation or a new beginning today. Historically, retirement signaled a slow withdrawal from life. Finished with their formal careers, people viewed retirement as the end of their working (and, consequently, their productive) lives. Their focus shifted to sedentary forms of leisure based on the premise that retirees were too old to be active. For many senior Americans, retirement came to be seen as a penalty for growing old.

That picture has changed dramatically. Although some retirement stereotypes still linger, retirement is much more likely to be viewed as a mixture of leisure, work, and learning today. Retirees often report a new sense of freedom from restraints formerly imposed by others. Far from feeling punished, many interpret retirement as a reward for years of hard work and sacrifice.

Several factors explain this changed approach to retirement. First, life expectancy figures have risen significantly in the United States. In 1920 the average life span was fifty-four years. By the end of the 1980s, average life expectancy had reached nearly seventy-five years. While people are living longer, they are also retiring earlier. In 1930, two-thirds of men aged sixty and above remained in the work force. Fifty years later, the percentage had dropped to one-third. Government estimates indicate that by the year 2000, only 25 percent of men aged sixty and over will be working. And the entrance of women into the workplace has accelerated explosively in the past two decades, with most women also retiring before they reach the age of 60.

Also, company pension programs tend to be much more liberal today than they were forty or fifty years ago. The rise of early retirement programs at major companies has swelled the ranks of retirees. Finally, increased opportunities for second careers and alternative employment options have led many potential retirees to leave companies. The overall result has been the rise of a population of younger retirees who enjoy better health, possess greater financial resources, and have broader retirement options than in previous generations. This group is unlikely to find fulfillment in sun hats and shuffleboard.

Old and New Life Planning Models

Perhaps the clearest way to characterize recent changes in retirement thinking is to consider them in terms of traditional and contemporary life planning models. Until the 1950s, and perhaps into the '60s, many Americans tended to view life as a three-stage linear progression. First came education, then work, then leisure. One phase was completed before the next began.

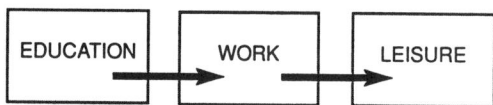

More recently, this generic model has taken on many variations. Today, people are much more likely to view life as a fluid, interconnected process. The major elements of work, education, and leisure remain the same, but they no longer represent mutually exclusive life stages. At different times, most individuals focus primarily on one phase: education during their early years, work during their middle years, and leisure during their later years. But all three elements are likely to be interwoven throughout every stage of life.

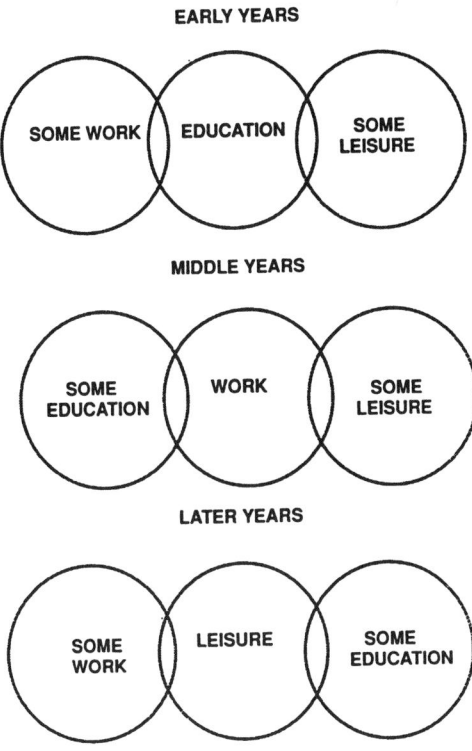

EARLY YEARS

SOME WORK | EDUCATION | SOME LEISURE

MIDDLE YEARS

SOME EDUCATION | WORK | SOME LEISURE

LATER YEARS

SOME WORK | LEISURE | SOME EDUCATION

It isn't difficult to observe this new life view in action among retired people. The nation's colleges and universities are no longer exclusive preserves of the young, for example, as older citizens have swelled student populations and turned continuing education into a growth industry. Anticipating shortages of trained and motivated employees in coming years, large corporations are actively recruiting retired people, creating part-time and shared jobs that match the schedules and priorities of these individuals. Other groups, Elderhostel organizations, for example, blend leisure and education, creating learning programs for older Americans and setting them on university campuses.

"Six Months after He Retired . . ."

Yet even in the face of so much evidence supporting new views of retirement, old myths persist. Consider, for example, perhaps the oldest retirement story of all, the one about the man (it's always a man) who retires at the end of a long career and shortly thereafter suddenly dies (often by dropping dead in the middle of the street). The moral, of course, is that a job keeps us alive, that once the heart realizes the rest of the body has stopped going to the office, it stops too.

Now we face the risk of new myths surfacing. Perhaps soon we'll have to contend with the idea that, given the range of new retirement opportunities, if we don't take part-time jobs or courses in ancient history, we're retirement "failures."

The Transition from Career to Retirement

There is a serious side to all this. No matter how many new options are open today, most people aren't sure how they will react to retirement, how they'll spend their time, or whether they will enjoy their new lives. There is no single response to such questions, since individual reactions to retirement are almost always based on previous life experiences.

For example, if we oversimplify the world for purposes of illustration, we can divide postcareer individuals into three groups: people who have been primarily work centered during their lives; those who have mixed career and personal interests in about a fifty-fifty ratio; and those who have built their lives mostly around home and hobbies.

"The Ending." Individuals in each group are likely to react differently to the transition from career to retirement. In his book *Transitions,*[1] William Bridges describes this "ending" phase as a major life transition. Retirement is the period in which people end one stage in their lives, not only physically, but more importantly (and often with greater difficulty) emotionally, and prepare to move on to another.

1. Bridges, William, *Transitions* (New York: Addison-Wesley, 1980).

People who have the hardest time dealing with this ending period are those who have focused most intensively on work throughout their lives. They may go through a grieving process for the part of their life that has died. Sadness may be mixed with anger and feelings of loss, despair, and finality, and it may not be easy to let the past go and get on with the present and future.

At the other end of the spectrum, people who have always focused most of their energy on family and hobbies sometimes make the transition even before they formally retire, moving their hearts and minds to the off-the-job activities they find so valuable and enjoyable: family life, church, hobbies and sports, travel, or a weekend home or cabin, perhaps. These people find the shift to retired life easy: they can't wait to end the previous chapter and get on with their lives.

Most people fall somewhere between the two extremes, having divided their lives between work commitments and other interests. Ending a career involves some pain and requires readjustment, but these individuals are ready to confront the demands imposed by the transition to retired life.

The "Neutral Zone." Almost everyone requires time to make the change to retired life, as new and old feelings ebb and flow. But at some point, people accept the reality of change, even if they have feelings of emptiness because they've left the past behind but haven't yet found something to take its place.

Bridges calls this period the "Neutral Zone." During it, people often spend time alone, reviewing and recalling the past. Feelings of depression and confusion may surface. It is not a time of high energy or creativity, and not the moment for charging ahead into new ventures.

It can be a very valuable interlude, however. Using the Neutral Zone to resolve the sense of loss and think about what you want to do in the next twenty or thirty years, searching for insights about your values and inner needs, can be a rewarding process in its own right and can form the foundation of a rewarding retirement as well.

The "New Beginning." Sooner or later people feel ready to make a new start, a signal that they've reached what Bridges calls the "New Beginning" phase of transition. They start to develop a picture, however sketchy at first, of how the next chapter in their lives will look. (Notice that it's the *next chapter,* not the rest of their lives. Change is never complete. People continue to make transitions throughout their lives, and there's no reason to expect that retirement signals an end to change.)

When people get the internal signal that they've reached this stage in the transition, they often feel new energy and clarity of thought regarding how to proceed with their lives. They still take backward glances, but less frequently, as new activities and re-defined relationships absorb most of their energy.

If you elect retirement as the next stage in your life, perhaps this three-stage model will help smooth the transition from full-time employee to independent individual doing the things you have always dreamed about.

Should You Retire?

Before you start thinking about how you'll react to retirement, you obviously need to reach a far more fundamental decision: should you retire in the first place? The new freedoms associated with retirement choices and options have actually made it more difficult for many people to answer this question. It wasn't too long ago, after all, that you simply didn't have much choice: when you reached retirement age, you retired. How you fared following that event may have been another matter entirely, but the decision was more or less made for you.

Our advice concerning retirement decisions mirrors our view of other career or life choices. We suggest that you develop as much information about yourself and your options as possible, and then use the data to reach an informed decision that, given your needs and your situation, reflects and serves your own best interests. Compare retirement with other choices available to you: returning to work with another company, for example, or starting a business or consulting practice of your own. What are the pluses and minuses of each option? Seek the advice of colleagues, friends, and family. But don't expect anyone else to make the decision for you.

Retirement Issues

As you consider the retirement option, you'll probably need to think about five broad categories of questions.

Use of Time. Work consumes roughly 50 percent of the waking hours of most individuals. If you no longer have a nine-to-five job, what will you do with those hours to satisfy your needs, exercise your talents, and engage your interests?

Relationships. Long-term relationships are built on negotiated rules and responsibilities, and on shared and private activities and experiences. These qualities develop over time. What aspects of your relationships might have to be renegotiated as a result of your decision to retire?

Self-Identity. To one degree or another, most of us identify ourselves by the work we do and the organizations we work for. If you retire, how will you answer the question, "What do you do?"

Health. Poor health forces some people to retire. At the same time, health may actually improve in retirement as individuals devote more time and attention to diet, exercise, and other leisure activities. How might your health affect your retirement? How might retirement affect your health?

Financial, Legal, and Estate Issues. Although we've listed them last, these issues are of substantial interest and critical importance to individuals considering retirement. Do you have questions or concerns in these areas?

Your Vision of Retirement

To develop a picture of your own views on retiring at this stage in your life, complete the following exercise.

HOW DO I FEEL ABOUT RETIREMENT?

As you answer the questions here, don't try to think too much or be overly analytical. Simply record your initial immediate, honest impressions.

1. To me, retirement means:

_____

_____

2. What I need right now is:

_____

_____

3. My main concern now is:

_____

_____

4. Financially, I am:

_____

_____

5. My future is:

_____

_____

6. I always hoped I:

_____

_____

7. Looking back, I:

_____

_____

8. My only regret is:

_____

_____

9. My family:

_____

_____

10. I'm happiest about:

_____

_____

Visualizing Your Retirement

What do you see when you picture yourself as a retiree during the next few years? What do you see yourself doing on an average day? How do you look and feel? Who are your companions? What activities do you pursue?

_____

_____

_____

_____

_____

_____

_____

_____

_____

_____

Defining Needs, Developing Plans, and Choosing Activities

Even if the retirement picture you've painted above is hazy and imprecise, it probably represents your current gut feelings on the topic and, as such, offers a valid starting point for investigating the subject in greater detail and beginning to form plans.

Like any major life transition, the shift to retirement is likely to be smoothest and retired life to be most enjoyable and rewarding if the process is based on careful planning. The earlier this process begins the better, particularly in terms of financial plans, but also regarding the nature and potential characteristics of retired life. In fact, however difficult it may be for most people in their twenties, thirties, and forties to give much thought to retirement, starting to make long-range plans today may be the only way to assure a comfortable retirement tomorrow.

Retirement planning involves defining needs, developing plans to meet those needs, and then choosing activities that are consistent with both needs and plans. If you've worked your way through this book from the beginning, you've already completed many activities designed to help you articulate your needs. For the most part, however, the exercises you've completed thus far have focused on career-related topics. If you are now considering retirement, it will be useful to devote additional thought to values and needs as they affect you in other aspects of your life.

To consider the subject of needs in the context of retirement, we will explore two general groups: security needs and what we might call inner needs.

Security Needs

Because security needs and a range of issues associated with finances top the list of immediate concerns for most individuals who are anticipating retirement, we'll consider them first. Your current financial position—as measured by such items as net worth and expected future income, and including information on medical coverage and life insurance—offers obvious and important indicators about your ability to retire and the form your retirement is likely to take.

If you have a retirement pension or other income sources that will carry you for the rest of your life at a standard of living you find acceptable, you can shift your planning activities to personal needs. In any event, you'll certainly want to reassure yourself and your family that retirement won't be a continuing saga of financial scrapes and worries.

Start by reviewing Chapter 7. If you haven't completed the exercises in that section of the book, take the time to do so now. Give special attention to material related to income and outgo. Even low rates of inflation can eat away at fixed incomes, so realistic planning in this area is crucial. At other stages in life, it may be possible to underestimate current financial needs without suffering dire consequences: regular salary increases, promotions, or new jobs can raise pay levels periodically, allowing income to catch up with expenses. In retirement, cash flow is more likely to remain constant, so projections need to be accurate.

Retirement finances obviously affect—and are determined by—retirement activities, so financial planning for retirement is an interactive process. You might begin by assessing your finances and then, based on your personal needs, apply that information to choose the range of activities you intend to pursue. During the process, perhaps you and your spouse realize that you want entertainment, in the form of frequent nights out at restaurants and theaters, to be a central part of your retired life. When you estimate the cost of such activities, you find that the income you've projected won't support them. You can either scale back your activities or revise your financial picture, perhaps by choosing to augment your income through part-time work. That decision, in turn, will prompt you to rearrange your activities.

Younger retirees may need to factor in education costs for a child about to enter college. Some individuals may have to include substantial allowances for medical expenses that may be required for a spouse who is in poor health. The planning process should continue until wishes and finances are matched as effectively as possible.

For many people, the approach of retirement also raises the first signals that it is time to think seriously about estate planning. If you and your spouse do not have wills, you should obviously prepare them. If you do have a will, you should review it with your attorney and discuss its provisions with your accountant or other financial advisers to make sure it protects the interests of your spouse and heirs, minimizes estate taxes, and remains consistent with your wishes about how your estate should be distributed.

Inner Needs

As you assess financial needs and resources, you also need to investigate your inner needs and values to begin to determine what you want to do with your retirement. This assessment will help you identify priorities, set reasonable goals, and make sound decisions about the future. You may discover ways to build on existing talents and interests to further enhance your retirement years.

Begin by going back to Chapter 6 and reviewing the exercises you completed on your values, interests, needs, accomplishments, skills, and satisfiers and dissatisfiers. Remember, when you dealt with these topics earlier you may have approached them from an exclusively work-oriented perspective. This time, expand your horizons and make additional comments as appropriate. Consider the things you do on weekends, at home during the evening, with family or friends, out in the community, at church, and so forth. Think about subjects you've never pursued but have always felt interested in or drawn to. Throughout this process of reevaluation, look for and note common themes or patterns that run through your responses. As a summary, complete the following exercise.

WHAT ARE MY SECURITY AND INNER NEEDS, AND GIVEN MY RESOURCES, HOW WILL MY RETIREMENT LIFE MEET THEM?

Consider the review of values, interests, needs, accomplishments, skills, and satisfiers/dissatisfiers that you have just completed. Based on the themes and patterns you identified, what conclusions can you draw regarding your retirement needs and resources?

_____

_____

_____

_____

_____

_____

_____

Retirement Options

Your review of financial issues and inner needs should help you focus on the broad outlines of your retirement. If you consider your options in terms of the three-part perspective introduced earlier—leisure, work, and learning—you can begin to design the framework of a rewarding retirement. Later you can fit specific activities into this framework.

First, are you totally indifferent to any of these three general areas? If, for example, you're convinced that you've had enough work to last a lifetime and your finances allow it, then you'll be able to remove work options from your list of potential retirement activities. (But for reasons we'll introduce shortly, don't be too quick to jump to any conclusions. Consider all your options.)

As we discussed earlier, most Americans focus the greatest part of their energies on leisure activities during retirement, devoting lesser amounts of time to work and educational activities. There are no rules, of course, and the categories often overlap.

For example, individuals who are convinced they'll never "work" again—that is, never take formal jobs and draw regular paychecks—may well spend twenty hours a week or more working in volunteer positions for religious or community organizations but considering these hours leisure time. Others might conclude that 100 percent of their work, leisure, and learning needs could be fulfilled by pursuing a full-time course load at a college or university, or by opening an antiques shop.

We'll assume, however, that no matter what form it takes, some portion of your life in retirement will be devoted to leisure activities, and that the percentage will probably be greater than it has been at any time since you started your working career, and perhaps even since you began your formal education.

Many people visualize spending all their retirement time taking it easy: playing golf or tennis, fishing, socializing, traveling— doing whatever they please whenever the urge strikes. The image is certainly appealing, particularly at the end of a stress-filled career marked by deadlines and demands.

The move from tough job to instant leisure tends to be the most difficult transition of all, however. After so many years of so much activity, it's hard to slow down or stop. Boredom and restlessness set in. Spending the entire day around the house can create unexpected friction between spouses. For these reasons, many retirees feel a need for alternative activities, particularly in the form of a second career.

Working in Retirement: Second Careers

One way or another, many retirees continue to work. Some create second careers by drawing on the most enjoyable features of their first careers. Others head off in completely new directions, taking entirely different jobs in novel settings.

Interestingly enough, these individuals do not tend to be motivated primarily by the needs for prestige, status, or money that may have fueled their first careers. Finances often enter the picture, of course. But most working retirees indicate that they sought employment because they missed the social side of the work environment or the challenges and accomplishments associated with work itself.

Financial Considerations. If dollar issues don't rule the decision to return to work, important financial questions do surface, the most common being, "Does it pay to work in retirement?" Added to the income you'll receive from Social Security, a pension, or other retirement investments, additional income might push you into a higher tax bracket, canceling the economic attractiveness of your job in the process. And, until you reach age seventy, the greater your wages, the smaller your Social Security check.

You'll obviously want to consult your financial advisers to develop an accurate picture of the effects a paying job might have on your finances. But be careful before making a decision based solely on economics. Consider noneconomic factors as well: the challenge a job might provide, the social relationships it may offer, and the structure continued employment could bring to your life.

Typical Second Careers. By definition, retired people can't work full-time and still be considered retired. Some retirees can't be bothered with definitions, however, particularly those individuals who use retirement as an opportunity to start businesses of their own. But to a substantial degree, given their other interests, retirees tend to pursue employment in less than full-time settings.

Many join the swelling ranks of temporary workers, either working on temporary assignments for a single company (often a former employer), or signing on with a temporary agency and accepting assignments with a range of companies. Nearly 90 percent of the country's large companies use temporary employees today, often to increase staffing flexibility. Many temporary assignments are not for a single day or a few days, but become long-term, quasi-permanent positions.

And, while originally the "temp" business was primarily a source of clerical workers, the fastest growing segments of the industry today are devoted to supplying companies with individuals skilled in professional and technical areas. As such, the field offers broad new opportunities to retired corporate employees.

Temporary work can be attractive for retirees. The flexibility can be ideal, for example, since the individual decides when and if he or she will work. People seeking permanent part-time employment often locate such jobs through temporary assignments. Many agencies provide training, and some large national temporary firms even offer benefits, which a retiree could conceivably retain while working for an agency in California during the winter and in Massachusetts during the summer.

Part-time employment is another option for retired workers. Part-time jobs offer the stability of regular hours, income, and relatively well-defined duties, characteristics that may be attractive to individuals who want greater structure in their retired lives than temporary employment might provide.

Traditionally, though, and particularly in large companies, part-time opportunities have been restricted to low-level jobs with limited pay and benefits. That perception is changing at many companies, as management experiments with job sharing—where two workers split one job—and other nontraditional forms of employment.

Seasonal employment attracts many retired workers, particularly those who spend parts of the year in different geographic locales. Some individuals find that the best way to satisfy their work needs is to work full-time for several months and then devote all their time to other activities for several months.

Finally, if additional income isn't an objective, innumerable opportunities—most of them part-time—exist as nonpaying jobs. Volunteer positions can help retirees avoid the shock of an instant transition to full-time leisure, enabling them to make valuable contributions to society in the process. As a volunteer, you have the greatest control of both the number of hours you work and your work schedule. You may learn a marketable skill, and could conceivably be offered a paying position with the organization. Volunteer work also offers rewarding opportunities for becoming part of a new group and establishing new relationships.

WHAT'S MY IDEAL JOB OBJECTIVE?

Drawing on your review of values, needs, skills, interests, satisfiers and dissatisfiers, and factoring in conclusions you may have reached about different employment options, complete the following statements.

1. My top interests are:

_____

_____

2. My top skills are:

_____

_____

3. My top values are:

_____

_____

4. My top satisfiers/dissatisfiers are:

_____

_____

5. I want to work because:

_____

_____

6. I want to work:
   A. Where (geographic location and type of environment):

_____

_____

   B. When:

_____

_____

   C. Doing what:

_____

_____

_____

D. Other important employment considerations:

_____

_____

Perceived Attributes of Older Workers. Wanting to work is one thing for a retired individual. Finding a job is another. If you haven't been in the employment market in recent years, you're likely to find it more competitive than you remember. If you spent your career with a single employer, your job-search skills are likely to be rusty or even nonexistent. Subsequent chapters will introduce you to or reacquaint you with a range of important topics and issues.

One distinctive aspect of the retiree's employment search is how he or she is perceived in the marketplace. Attitudes toward retired workers who wish to remain in the work force are changing. As retirement itself becomes less defined by the old "withdrawal from life" image, retirees are less likely to be seen as frail creatures possessing diminished capabilities.

In fact, studies indicate that perceived attributes of older workers currently include: stability, reliability, good basic skills, maturity, conscientiousness, safety orientation (fewer accidents), loyalty, flexibility, and well-developed "people skills."

For employers, particularly those in service industries who are struggling to find employees with just such qualities, retired people are beginning to look like a very valuable segment of the population. A decade ago, we typically counseled older workers to concentrate their searches on small and midsize companies. Large corporations just weren't interested. That situation has changed, and some of the nation's largest companies are actively recruiting older workers. At first, long conditioned to expect subtle or blatant age discrimination, many older workers found it difficult to take these organizations seriously. Today, however, it no longer makes sense to categorically avoid any employment sector.

Educational Opportunities

Many retirees discover that acquiring new knowledge or developing credentials in a new field is both satisfying and rewarding. People who detested school when they were younger—perhaps because earlier in their lives, education was a stressful experience associated with becoming a success or landing the right job—often find that learning for the sake of learning becomes an entirely different proposition. Many who have never had the opportunity to finish their education gain a gratifying sense of fulfillment or completion by returning to school.

A range of educational opportunities awaits these individuals. Some enroll as full-time students. Others attend evening classes in a single subject. Still others select special courses targeted to particular occupations—second careers as real estate brokers or financial planners, for example. In addition, workshops and seminars in almost any imaginable field are available in most areas.

Colleges and universities welcome and often depend on the fees and tuition of older Americans. As a result, they are providing expanded services for this class of students. Many institutions have created special advisers to attend to older students, and others offer special courses addressing the interests of this group. Older Americans should certainly not feel out of place on campus today.

Choosing Retirement Activities

As people retire earlier, in better health, and with more disposable income, leisure options open to them have grown exponentially. The range of activities, from travel, hobbies, and sports, to cultural and recreational activities, is virtually unlimited.

Given the diversity of retirement options and the variety of choices within each option, selecting your retirement activities may not be easy. To narrow the field, ask yourself the following questions:

- Which activities interest me most?
- What activities will I do alone, and which will involve other people?

- How much time will I devote to each activity?
- What are the financial requirements of each activity I choose to pursue?
- What can I do today to prepare for these activities?

As you answer these questions, don't try to anticipate needs and interests too far into the future. Remember that change is constant, and your retirement picture will almost certainly change in the years ahead. For now, complete the following exercises to focus your thinking on the first year of your retirement.

If you are married, you and your spouse should do each exercise individually and then compare responses, looking for areas of compatibility or possible conflict.

WHAT RETIREMENT ACTIVITIES DO I PLAN TO PURSUE?

Examine the chart that follows to start your thinking about how you will use your retirement time. Add activities and rearrange them as desired to make the discovery process more effective for you.

Rate each activity with an *A, B,* or *C* to indicate how interesting you would find it:

A = Exciting
B = Moderately interesting
C = Not interesting

When you rate an activity *A,* make a note of the general interests, needs, and values it satisfies.

For each *A* or *B* rating, note with a check mark whether you are "Doing It Now," or "Want to Prepare."

Rate each interesting activity in terms of significant cost factors:

1 = No significant costs
2 = Can fit within budget
3 = Expensive

Which activities meet your need to be by yourself or to socialize with others? Check the appropriate column.

Finally, in the Planned Action column, indicate with a check mark if a substantial action plan will be required to get going on this activity.

PLANNING RETIREMENT ACTIVITIES

Activity	Interest Level (Rate A, B, C)	Self-Assessment — Interests, Needs, Values It Meets	Doing It Now?	Want to Prepare?	Cost Factors (Rate 1, 2, 3)	Do It Alone?	With Others?	Planned Action
Self-Development								
Reading, study								
Seminars, lectures								
Correspondence courses								
On-campus courses								
Write (books, articles)								
Use library								
Self-Maintenance								
Golf								
Tennis								
Bicycling								
Swimming								
Jogging, running								
Walking, hiking								
Other sport								

Activity	Interest Level (Rate A, B, C)	Self-Assessment Interests, Needs, Values It Meets	Doing It Now?	Want to Prepare?	Cost Factors (Rate 1, 2, 3)	Do It Alone?	With Others?	Planned Action
Service Activities								
Civic groups____								
Church/synagogue activities____								
Service clubs____								
Volunteer work____								
Business and Work								
Managing investments____								
Running business____								
Consulting____								
Part-time work____								
Seasonal work____								
Temporary work____								
Household Upkeep								
Yard work____								
Improvement projects____								

Activity	Interest Level (Rate A, B, C)	Self-Assessment Interests, Needs, Values It Meets	Doing It Now?	Want to Prepare?	Cost Factors (Rate 1, 2, 3)	Do It Alone?	With Others?	Planned Action
Fixing meals								
Shopping								
Housekeeping								
Bills, taxes, desk work								
Social Activities								
Large gatherings								
Small groups								
Entertain at home								
Family gatherings								
Call on friends								
Phone visiting								
Holiday celebrations								
Other								
Hobbies/Pastimes								
Arts, crafts								
Collecting								

Activity	Interest Level (Rate A, B, C)	Self-Assessment Interests, Needs, Values It Meets	Doing It Now?	Want to Prepare?	Cost Factors (Rate 1, 2, 3)	Do It Alone?	With Others?	Planned Action
Building things___								
Gardening___								
Other								
Recreation								
TV, radio___								
Movies, theater, concerts___								
Dine out with spouse/friends___								
Read for fun___								
Museums, art shows___								
Play cards, games___								
Listen to/play music___								
Travel/Vacation								
Cruise, tours___								
Elderhostel___								

Activity	Interest Level (Rate A, B, C)	Self-Assessment						
		Interests, Needs, Values It Meets	Doing It Now?	Want to Prepare?	Cost Factors (Rate 1, 2, 3)	Do It Alone?	With Others?	Planned Action
Motor home trips____								
Visit family____								
Other____								

WHAT IS MY ACTION PLAN?

Review the activities you selected in the previous exercise, and choose those you will possibly pursue during the first year of your retirement. Now you can make tentative or actual commitments to take necessary action steps.

Activity	When I want to do it	What action steps I will take/The start date	Time I will allocate
Self-development:			
Self-maintenance:			
Service activities:			

Activity	When I want to do it	What action steps I will take/The start date	Time I will allocate
Business and work:			
Household upkeep:			
Social activities:			
Hobbies/pastimes:			
Recreation:			
Travel/vacation:			

HOW WOULD I DESCRIBE MY FIRST YEAR IN RETIREMENT?

Finally, to pull together all the thoughts you've developed about retirement, use the sentence starters below to write a brief description of your first year of retirement as you now imagine it.

1. I will be living in (location, environment):

_____

2. The most important new activities I will be involved in will be:

_____

3. My principal travel plans for the first year will be:

_____

4. My biggest capital outlay for the first year will be:

_____

5. The biggest change I anticipate in my relationships will be:

_____

6. My principal health and fitness activities will be:

_____

7. My biggest concerns about this plan are:

_____

8. The parts of this plan I'm most comfortable with are:

_____

9. During this first year, the major decisions I will need to make for the following year are:

_____

10. (If applicable) The parts of this plan on which my spouse/partner disagree are:

_____

Where to Look for Additional Help and Resources

This chapter offers only a brief overview of relevant retirement issues. We don't even mention such important topics as housing: should you keep your current home, move to another part of the country, think about a retirement community, and so forth? A list of useful resources for additional research and planning is contained in Appendix C at the end of this book.

Finally, as you review your thinking about retirement, the following guiding thoughts, which we've collected at Drake Beam Morin during our years of working with people considering retirement, may prove helpful.

Nine Thoughts about Retirement

1. The most successful retirees focus on three issues: planning, planning, and planning!
2. A successful retirement is largely within the control of the individual and is typically based on goal-oriented, self-directed behavior.
3. People must assess their own needs, talents, and interests to make wise retirement plans and decisions.
4. Retirement presents opportunities to earn income in an increasing variety of ways.
5. Retirement is a stage in life, not a new life. People have important needs that do not disappear when they retire.
6. Analyzing the past and present reveals important clues to future satisfaction.
7. Managing the gift of time provided by retirement requires time management skills different from those used in other stages of life.
8. Some people manage retirement much more effectively than earlier phases of their lives.
9. *Workless* does not mean *worthless.*

CHAPTER 12

Career Decision Making—
Phase IV: Action Plans

Throughout this book, you've been gathering information and insights about yourself. Until now, you've evaluated different career and life options independently of one another. Now it's time to synthesize, analyze, and set priorities, weighing your options systematically to produce a plan for targeting your efforts as you move on to the next phase in your life.

First, you'll want to define your alternatives. Then, you'll need to evaluate them from two perspectives: in terms of your own preferences, and through probability analysis. The latter will help you identify what might go wrong and what might go right with each alternative; you can then consider ways to reduce the likelihood of the former and increase your chances for the latter. Finally, you can start to create a personal action plan: a list of next steps to help you achieve the goals you've identified.

WHAT ARE MY ALTERNATIVES?

Define as precisely as you can, based on the information you've developed, the nature of each career option open to you. What alternatives do you see within each career scenario?

1. Stay in my present position (if appropriate):

_____

_____

2. Work for others:

_____

_____

3. Work for myself:

_____

_____

4. Retirement plus—
   Leisure:

_____

_____

   Work:

_____

_____

   Learning:

_____

_____

WHAT ARE MY PERSONAL PREFERENCES?

Now review the alternatives you've defined, and select the three options *(A, B,* and *C)* that are most attractive to you. Next to each option, jot down as many reasons as you can why it interests you.

Alternative	Why?
A. _____	_____
	_____
	_____
B. _____	_____
	_____
	_____
C. _____	_____
	_____
	_____

WHAT ARE THE RISKS AND BENEFITS ASSOCIATED WITH MY PREFERENCES?

Note potential risks that might be associated with each preferred alternative listed. Rank these risks in terms of high to low probability. Then write down ideas about actions you might take to reduce risks. Repeat this procedure for the benefits you can identify for each alternative, noting ideas for increasing those benefits.

Risks

What could go wrong?	Probability (high, medium, low)	How to reduce or avoid
A. _____
_____
_____
_____
_____
_____

Risks

What could go wrong?	Probability (high, medium, low)	How to reduce or avoid

B. _____

_____

_____

_____

_____

_____

C. _____

_____

_____

_____

_____

_____

Benefits

What could go right?	Probability (high, medium, low)	How to increase

A. _____

_____

_____

_____

_____

_____

Benefits

What could go right?	Probability (high, medium, low)	How to increase

B. _____

_____

_____

_____

_____

_____

C. _____

_____

_____

_____

_____

Reaching Your Decision

Now you've reached the decision point. Given the substantial effort you've invested in exploring different career options, considering each in terms of your personal needs and values, it's quite likely that one alternative now seems inherently more attractive to you than the others. Because it comes as the result of a comprehensive process of research and self-examination, you can trust your decision and begin to take steps to achieve your new career objectives.

Having made a choice you're comfortable with, you're ready to begin the action phase of career continuation.

MY DECISION

_____

_____

WHAT'S MY ACTION PLAN?

Given the career direction you've identified as most attractive and appropriate for you, what immediate next steps can you identify? List them according to this chart, specifying starting and completion dates. Note potential obstacles that might require special action or attention. As additional tasks come to mind in the future, return to this list and add them.

Task	Starting Date	Obstacles	Completion Date
1._____	_____	_____	_____
_____		_____	
2._____	_____	_____	_____
_____		_____	
3._____	_____	_____	_____
_____		_____	
4._____	_____	_____	_____
_____		_____	
5._____	_____	_____	_____
_____		_____	
6._____	_____	_____	_____
_____		_____	

Task	Starting Date	Obstacles	Completion Date
7._____	_____	_____	_____
_____		_____	
8._____	_____	_____	_____
_____		_____	

Coping with Indecision

What if you're still torn between choices? What if you can't decide between, say, working for someone else versus starting a consulting practice of your own? How can you resolve your dilemma?

You may need additional information about your options. Refer to the appendixes at the end of this book for additional information resources. Study the section on networking in Chapter 15, and then practice those skills by locating and contacting individuals in your community who can provide additional information and insights.

What if *no* option seems attractive? If you think back to the discussion of transitions in the previous chapter on active retirement, you might realize that you're stuck in the "Ending" or "Neutral Zone." Perhaps you could benefit from some form of professional counseling to get you ready for your "New Beginning."

Vocational Testing. Taking a battery of vocational and aptitude tests and discussing the results with a competent counselor may supply valuable objective data about job-related strengths and weaknesses, define areas in which you might profit from further development, and give additional clues about career directions that mesh with your skills and interests. Although you've addressed these issues in the self-assessment exercises you've completed in this book, gaining an experienced counselor's perspective of your situation may help you identify pertinent issues you've overlooked or misinterpreted.

We urge our clients to take advantage of the vocational review process. Most spend four to six hours taking a series of tests and discussing the results with one of our staff psychologists. Almost all find that the process helps them define new career opportunities. Most refer back to their test conclusions often as they complete the career continuation process.

Such tests frequently confirm feelings you've had about your interests. They may help you avoid repeating past mistakes and point you toward a better career climate in the future. They often help to crystallize vague thoughts about the future.

Finding a Qualified Counselor. Before you begin the testing process, of course, you need to make certain that the counselor who administers and interprets the tests is competent and trustworthy. Unfortunately, anyone can call him- or herself a "career guidance counselor."

Personal referrals are perhaps the best way to locate a good counselor. Business schools or graduate schools of psychology may offer referral services. Your family doctor may know a skilled vocational counselor. The director of personnel or human resources management at your former company might be able to offer advice. If you know a psychologist or psychiatrist, ask this person for suggestions.

It may help to look for professional credentials and seek a board-certified, Ph.D. psychologist. But make sure the individual is a specialist in counseling or industrial psychology, not in linguistics or some other specialty not directly related to your needs.

Next Steps

Subsequent chapters in this book deal with the specific concerns of individuals who decide to resume their careers by continuing to work for others. Even if you've reached a different decision about your own future, we hope you'll keep reading. A great deal of the information, particularly the sections on networking and communications skills and styles, will undoubtedly be helpful and useful to you no matter what direction your future takes.

CHAPTER 13

Working for Others— Targeting Your Search

If you've decided to seek a new job with a new company, you've narrowed the scope of your career continuation efforts considerably. But you still need to focus your efforts even more closely. Precisely what new job will you seek, for example, and where will you seek it?

As we noted in Chapter 8, most of our clients reestablish themselves in positions similar to their previous jobs with organizations similar to their previous companies. They find it easier to locate a job in a field in which they have a track record and easier, as well, to maintain or improve their income in fields where they have established a reputation.

This makes perfect sense, as long as their investigations into skills and interests point them in that direction. In any event, by investigating other options, they get the satisfaction of having considered alternatives and found them less intriguing than their own profession. They also learn what makes a job satisfying for them.

As you prepare to embark on the search for a new job, you owe it to yourself to consider new opportunities too, even if the process only ends up reinforcing your decision to keep doing what you've been doing.

Some people choose a career at an early age, pursuing it with enthusiasm and satisfaction for a lifetime. But it's much more common for people to select a general field of education, stumble into a first job without much planning or foresight, and then continue along that track throughout their careers. If they're lucky, the requirements of their jobs coincide with their abilities and desires. All too frequently, however, their work does not have a great deal to do with their skills and interests.

Even people who plan their careers with care find that needs and interests can change during the course of a working lifetime. Some people adapt: dentists become real estate developers; real estate developers become teachers; teachers become stockbrokers. But many people never choose new career paths to fit changing personal needs. Ten, twenty, or thirty years into their careers, they discover that they no longer enjoy going to work. Perhaps the job has grown too stressful. Perhaps it has become boring and repetitive. Maybe a career has taken the individual in a direction he or she does not enjoy. Perhaps the field itself is no longer expanding and, as a result, offers limited future opportunity for personal and professional growth.

Targeting

Right now, you can determine whether you're on the career track that suits you best. By looking at the parts of your work that have brought you real satisfaction, you can pinpoint the kinds of challenges and the type of working environment that are most likely to make you happy and successful in the future.

You've already done most of the homework for this exercise in self-understanding. The patterns and themes that have shown up in the assessments of your interests, skills, values, and accomplishments will point to the qualities you find most enjoyable and satisfying. People tend to perform best doing the things they like most.

Turn back to Chapter 6 and the list of satisfiers and dissatisfiers you created. Looking at all the positives and negatives you identified, make a mental summary of experiences that make a job satisfying to you and items that make a position unattractive.

But don't just look to the past for inspiration about the future. You may possess additional skills and interests you haven't called upon recently. Your interests may prompt you to learn new skills. You may want to enter an entirely new field.

WHAT'S MY DREAM JOB?

Describe your dream job as completely and as specifically as you can. What pluses and minuses do you think might be associated with it? Let your imagination roam as you consider the possibilities. Be a little outlandish. Don't put a damper on your thoughts.

_____

_____

_____

_____

_____

_____

_____

_____

HOW PRACTICAL IS MY DREAM?

Now that you've fantasized about your ideal job, examine the practicality of your dreams. If the position would be in an entirely new field, could you establish credibility for yourself? If potential compensation associated with your dream job would be substantially less than what you are used to, could you adapt? For each hurdle you identify, try to determine a way to resolve the problem.

_____

_____

_____

If the practical questions you identified above don't shake your faith in the idea of a radical career change, investigate the new field in detail. Put together all the information you can assemble. Check brokerage firms for research reports on industries or companies in the field. Talk to people who work in the business. Locate recent articles on the industry in business magazines and journals. Attend conferences and conventions related to the new area of interest. As you learn more, you'll move closer to an educated decision about whether you should become involved in it. If you decide to make a dramatic career shift, the information you've assembled will prepare you to speak intelligently with potential employers and may convince them that you're both serious about making the change and sufficiently skilled to do so.

Several years ago, we worked with a man who had lost a senior-level position in consumer marketing. He looked around and decided that cable television would be just the place for him. At the time, we weren't convinced. Too many people, it seemed, appeared to think that salvation lurked somewhere in cable TV. We wondered whether our client, given his background, should contemplate such a move seriously.

But he was persistent, studying the industry in remarkable detail. He read everything he could find on the subject, talked to everyone he could contact, and gave a great deal of careful thought to the industry. He was fascinated by the opportunities and possibilities he discovered. He ended up by completing an exceptionally thorough market study of the cable business that convinced him (and us, finally) that he should enter the industry. Today he occupies a senior position in cable TV.

When he concluded his job search, the man told us that the targeting phase of the career continuation process had clearly been the most valuable ingredient of his employment campaign. Without it, he said, he doubted whether he would have made the decision to head off in such a new direction, and he wondered whether he would have been taken seriously when he searched for a position in the field.

Your investigation of a new career may have different results, of course. You might conclude that you shouldn't make a radical change, at least not just yet. You could convince yourself to start planning, training, and saving to switch careers at a later date. Perhaps you're one job away from your dream job.

Or you may discover that you really don't want to change careers, even if you didn't enjoy your most recent job. You might learn that something in your personal life makes it difficult for you to enjoy your work. The industry you worked in, not the duties you performed, may disagree with you. The work environment at a particular company may have been the problem. Any of these issues is an important discovery. If something tripped you up in the past, it's likely to snare you in the future unless you change either your own habits or the conditions that caused the difficulty.

In any event, the important thing to do is to create a target. Repeat the exercises in this section for each new area you wish to investigate, until you identify an occupation that is right in the bull's-eye.

But what if no well-defined areas or industries come to mind? Try to narrow the field by asking yourself a series of questions to help limit your search. First, what kind of organization do you think you would like to work for? Consider variables like these:

- Profit or nonprofit?
- Retail or wholesale?
- Industrial or consumer?
- Manufacturing, processing, distributing, or service?
- Domestic or international?
- Federal, state, or local government?
- Church?

- Public or private company?
- Centralized or decentralized?
- Large, medium, or small organization?

Second, do you have strong geographical preferences? Are any locations totally unacceptable to you?

Third, what sort of working climate appeals to you? Do you prefer a relaxed environment, or do you need constant activity or a crisis atmosphere to stay interested and productive?

Include your family in this question-and-answer exercise. Get agreement on such matters as geographic location, work patterns, and travel requirements. Don't assume that your spouse will be ready to follow you blindly. What are your children's needs?

Be honest with yourself as you answer these questions. Some of our clients lose jobs because they think they thrive on an aggressive environment but actually can't handle the stress and, worst of all, don't really enjoy the pressure. But if you really *are* an aggressive individual, admit it and look for a job where the trait will be welcome. Or, if you care about family life, realize that this need must enter your planning process. A twenty-four-hour-a-day job simply won't work for you.

A Weighted Approach to Targeting

The chart that follows represents a systematic, numerically weighted approach to targeting. Using it, you can identify what is important to you in a job and, later in your job search as you consider particular fields or companies, you can determine how well they match your needs.

CAREER TARGETING GRID

Consider the criteria on the chart, and refer to column 1 at this time (the Job Option columns will be discussed in Chapter 18). Rank each item on a scale of 1 (least important to you) to 10 (most important). If, as you pursue your job search, you discover that your needs are changing, refer to this chart again and make appropriate changes.

Criteria	My Needs	Job Option A	Job Option B	Job Option C
Career/Professional Factors				
Accountability				
Adequacy of staff				
Title				
Promotion/personal growth potential				
Decision-making authority				
Company Factors				
Size of company				
Company/ industry history characteristics				
Management style (participative, autocratic, etc.)				
Personal Factors				
Compensation base				
Bonus/profit sharing/stock options				

Criteria	My Needs	Job Option A	Job Option B	Job Option C
Benefits (pension, disability, life insurance, vacation)				
Perks (car, country club, etc.)				
Geographic location				
Travel requirements				
Commuting requirements				
Special expenses (commuting fares, taxes, relocation, etc.)				
Total Scores				

When you've completed column 1, you'll have a handy set of guidelines that will help you plan your search. As you investigate job options, you can be especially observant for the criteria that are most important to you. Rank the criteria for each new job option similarly, from 1 to 10, using the columns to the right. Totaling these columns will give you quantitative figures to compare.

The chart will also help you focus your search. If, for example, you gave geographic location a *10,* indicating that where you work is very important to you, you'll have narrowed your search significantly.

Targeting is invaluable to the job-search process, but only if you approach it properly. Some people act as if hitting the bull's-eye involves grabbing a gun, facing a wall, closing their eyes, pulling the trigger, and then painting concentric circles around the resulting hole. That's not the kind of targeting we're talking about. Don't let yourself be picked by a job. Don't automatically assume that because you've done something in the past or because it's a popular occupation today, or because everyone says there's a future in it, you must convince yourself that it is the position for you. Approach the question from the opposite direction. Discover what's important to you, and then find a job that fills those requirements.

CHAPTER 14

Working for Others— Résumés and References

More talk and less sense are devoted to résumés than to any other topic in many job searches. There is no shortage of experts on the subject and no lack of conflicting opinions about the proper form and actual usefulness of these documents. Some people insist that the résumé is the key to finding a job. Others argue that writing a résumé is unnecessary and perhaps counterproductive.

Less and less attention is being given to references today. It's still likely that you'll be asked to provide them during your job search, but because of legal concerns your former employer may have a policy against giving references, and even the company doing the asking may no longer provide them for its own ex-employees.

Résumés and references continue to be valuable tools in most job searches. The thing to do is attend to both without lingering over either, and then get on with your employment campaign.

The Importance of Résumés

People who discount the importance of résumés say that they are commonplace and ordinary, that they make one person indistinguishable from the next, and that if someone is really unique, he or she won't need a résumé to get a job. People who argue that résumés are the most important piece in the job-hunting puzzle are likely to feel that job searches begin and end with the distribution of hundreds of résumés to hundreds of companies. The trouble with both arguments is that neither addresses the real purpose of the résumé. It is a supplementary tool, a personal advertising brochure that lets you communicate with a number of audiences. It doesn't take the place of a marketing strategy; it supports one.

If, for instance, your search plan includes working through executive search firms, they will want to see your résumé. If you answer newspaper advertisements, you'll need to send copies of your résumé along. When you start to build a network of personal contacts, you'll need to distribute résumés to most of the people you meet along the way. If you send out a mailing to companies, you'll usually include a copy of your résumé. In the next chapter, we'll discuss each of these marketing strategies and recommend that you include all of them in your job search. You'll need a good résumé to pursue them effectively.

Résumés serve other purposes, too. They organize your career by selecting and presenting events clearly and concisely. This pays dividends. Without having gone through the process of creating a résumé, some of us might sit in interviews and say, "Let's see, in '79 I was with Monsanto. No, that was in '78. I joined Allied in '73, and in '75 they moved me to San Jose, so by '77 I was probably. . . ."

A résumé also lets you emphasize the things you think are important about you. You create a format of your own choosing and, at many interviews (particularly when you are speaking to an inexperienced interviewer) this format becomes the agenda for the discussion. That's a clear advantage for you: you've predetermined the interview's structure.

Whenever one person mentions your name to someone else, the first question is likely to be "Can I see a résumé?" You need a résumé at any career level. In fact, the further up you move in business, the more important your résumé becomes. This surprises some people who assume that, at the highest levels, the search process is a person-to-person verbal event. On the contrary, even if a CEO interviews you for a job as president of a company, he or she will have to discuss or describe you throughout the organization: up the line with the board of directors; across the line with other senior executives, who may be scattered across the country or around the world; and often down the line as well, with some of the people you would manage if you took the job. A memo attached to your résumé will probably be used to communicate with many of these individuals. That should please you, as you'll be represented by statements you've made about yourself.

The only real problem with résumés is that too many people spend too much time working on them. The task simply isn't complex enough to warrant the obsessive attention it often receives. You should be able to march swiftly through the preparation of your résumé, since you've already done most of the work by cataloging your skills and accomplishments. You'll just need to organize and distill this information, choosing your most important career accomplishments and listing them clearly and concisely.

Don't turn résumé writing into a delay tactic. Don't spend weeks revising and rewriting. Don't decide that you need to create a separate résumé for each employment opportunity you investigate. Cover letters, which we'll discuss later, will tailor your generic résumé to specific situations.

Make sure that you write your own résumé. You're the one who will have to live with it. Avoid résumé-writing services, which normally end up being expensive printers. If someone else does the job for you, your résumé won't be a part of you; you'll have to sound like it.

If you don't think you write well enough to prepare a good résumé, get a friend with better writing skills to review what you've done. But remember that *everyone* is an "expert" on résumés, so anyone is likely to tell you to move this or delete that. Don't take the bait. Let your own best judgment rule. And once you're satisfied with the results, don't be too quick to reinvent the document unless you discover a major omission or glaring error.

Résumé Formats

Most résumés follow either a chronological or a functional format. The chronological variety describes your career in reverse chronological order, starting with your most recent job and working back through earlier positions. It discusses your employment history concisely and straightforwardly, tying your skills and accomplishments to the companies you've worked for and positions you've held.

We recommend that most people write chronological résumés. Individuals who read résumés normally consider a number of these documents at one time. They appreciate résumés that show them quickly and clearly what an individual has done and where he or she has done it. They may not be patient: rather than search for information, they may simply discard one résumé and proceed to the next. For this reason, you need to get your message across quickly and forcefully. The chronological résumé is usually the most direct means to that end.

There are situations in which a chronological résumé may not deliver the message you want to send. Here, a functional résumé may work best. This format plays down your actual employment history and stresses a summary of functions you've performed during your career. If your work history is somewhat erratic—if you've held several jobs in a relatively short time span, for instance, or if there's a considerable gap between positions—you may not want to draw attention to this fact. Or suppose you intend to make a radical career change: the companies you've worked for and the titles you've held probably won't apply directly to your new career objective. You'll want to downplay them and emphasize skills and accomplishments that support your new goal. If your actual work experience is so limited that a chronological résumé might not represent your abilities accurately, you won't want to use one. If you intend to return to a previous occupation, you'll want to stress the experience you have in that field rather than raise questions about why you left it and now want to return.

In situations like these, where the accessibility of the chronological résumé—normally its major selling point—hinders rather than advances your cause, think about drafting a functional résumé. But weigh the fact that some people simply don't like to read functional résumés. If you can, use the chronological format.

Take the time to study the sample résumés that follow. Each is well planned and well written. Each speaks in terms of responsibilities and accomplishments. Each strikes a good balance between stressing the needs and goals of the writer and addressing the likely priorities of potential readers.

These samples demonstrate how to use short phrases and sentences to get your message across quickly. They use action verbs and simple language, and avoid long, indecipherable paragraphs. Topics and subtopics are carefully arranged in outline form, and bullets or other symbols are used to set items off. Enough blank space is left on the pages so that readers aren't overwhelmed with type.

When you write your résumé, remember that simple is usually elegant. Don't get fancy with design elements, unless you're looking for work as an art director. You may lack the skills, or a reader may lack a sense of aesthetic appreciation. Don't let anyone think, Anyone who has to resort to these tactics must really be in deep trouble.

Chronological Format

DONALD JOHNSON
5 Colonial Way
Westville, Connecticut 06516
(203) 555-6789

Seeking a position in the insurance industry as Regional Director/Sales Manager/Company General Agent or District Manager. Qualified by extensive experience in selling and promoting the entire range of financial services products. In-depth knowledge of the business. Solid record of achievement. Ambitious. Get along well with people.

GENERAL LIFE INSURANCE CO., Hartford, CT
<u>Financial Services Specialist</u>   **1986–1990**

Worked with 12 multi-line agents and 30 independent brokers to promote the firm's financial services. During 1989 generated:

- $10 million in annuity revenues
- $5 million in mutual fund revenues
- $200,000 in life insurance premiums
- $120,000 in health insurance premiums

- Ranked in 6th place out of 250 Financial Services Specialists nationwide for total production and percentage of quota.

JAMES WHITNEY COMPANIES, Boston, MA
<u>Sales Manager</u>   **1975–1986**

- Raised sales productivity to increase the office's ranking in the region from 75th to 20th place.
- Recruited three sales reps, training and directing them to achieve President's Club and Honor Club status.
- Developed a marketing strategy to cross-sell products to include property and casualty insurance and financial services.
- Repeatedly achieved Honors Club for Sales Managers.

<u>Insurance Agent</u>   **1970–1974**

- Member of the Honor Club during two years for achieving top 15% rank in generating sales.

INTEGRATED LIFE INSURANCE CO., New York, NY
<u>Insurance Agent</u>   **1967–1970**

- Entered the sales training program and exceeded the sales quota in each year of service.

EDUCATION

B.A., Economics, New York University, 1973.

PERSONAL

Member, National Association of Life Underwriters, 1983–present.
U.S. Army, E-4, Communications Specialist, Vietnam Era Veteran,
  Honorable Discharge, 1967.
Married; two children.
Interests include personal computers, reading, and music.

Employment Objective

The first sentence of the preceding chronological résumé sets forth
the individual's employment objective. Because the first question
most résumé readers ask themselves is "What is this person looking for?", a clear employment goal is generally the most effective
way to begin a résumé. Here are some other examples of succinctly
worded objectives:

- Chief executive officer of a small manufacturing company
- Senior operating officer in the petrochemical industry
- Product manager with a pharmaceutical organization
- Manager of human resources for a medium-sized company
  or head of compensation for a large company
- Chief financial officer

Make your objective as specific as you can. If you know precisely what you want and will settle for nothing else, write down
that goal. If, as in this résumé, you have several closely related
objectives, include them, but only if they are logically related to
one another. If they are not related, you should either write separate résumés or mention no objective (see the second sample résumé).

Background Summary

The next element in the résumé is typically a short background
summary, a sentence or two (or several phrases, as in the preceding
example) which offer readers a quick overview of the individual's
strengths or qualifications. This capsule summary should lead the
reader to the more detailed explanation of jobs and responsibilities
that follows.

Business Experience

Next comes the body of the résumé, a detailed description of the writer's business experience. Sensibly enough, this résumé begins with the most recent place of employment, but we still see résumés that lead with an individual's earliest job. We can only speculate how many such documents have been tossed away by readers who wondered how someone could list "Senior Vice President—Marketing" as an objective when the most prominent job on the résumé is "Assistant Account Executive." If your résumé isn't absolutely clear and logical, people will be likely to dismiss it outright.

Some people fall into a related trap by putting their second-to-most-recent job first in their résumés. This raises a crimson flag among readers, who assume that something terrible must have occurred at the most recent job. If there is no way for you to emphasize your last job, consider a functional résumé.

Note that the preceding résumé follows a standard pattern, listing company names first and then adding job titles and dates of employment. Résumés can, of course, be tailored differently. If you've held high positions at small companies, you may wish to stress titles and then name employers. If you think that the company's identity pulls more weight than your job title, put the firm's name on top. It goes without saying that, once you choose a pattern, you should stick to it throughout the résumé.

This writer has chosen his accomplishments well. Wherever possible, each has a definite result, which is quantified. These accomplishments support the "Solid record of achievement" phrase in his summary statement. His résumé, which could be reproduced on a single sheet of 8½-by-11 paper, creates an effective portrait of a career spanning more than twenty years.

Additional Information

At the end of this résumé, the writer mentions his education and touches on other personal information. We believe such data should be kept to a minimum. Describe your education, perhaps including management or technical seminars you may have attended. List memberships in organizations that relate to your field of work. If you think something you've done outside your career is a real asset, mention it.

If this man's résumé were substantially longer, we might suggest that he leave off his service record, since it probably won't be critical to his job search. Stating that he is married with two children suggests stability, so that's fine. Including a few outside interests suggests that he's a well-rounded individual.

Listing too many outside activities can be counterproductive, however. Potential employers may wonder whether an individual will find enough spare time to do his or her job. If you hold an important post with a community or nonprofit organization, go ahead and mention it. It supports the fact that you're a solid citizen. Just don't let anyone get the idea that you spend your days planning what you'll do when you leave work.

In general, the simpler you keep the additional information included in your résumé, the better. Don't include the phrase, "Health: Excellent." It's more or less meaningless: how many times have you seen "Health: Poor" on a résumé? If you're sixty-three years old and ready for a new business challenge, don't list your age. Wait for a face-to-face encounter to dispel age stereotypes and replace them with a demonstration of your experience and energy.

There are no salary details in this résumé, because it is much too early to offer unsolicited details on that subject. If you discuss pay now, you may knock yourself out of contention for jobs later on. Suppose you write a low salary figure on your résumé. A potential employer decides that you can't possibly be qualified for the higher paying job she needs to fill. If you quote a high figure, on the other hand, someone could decide without asking that you wouldn't be interested in a job that pays somewhat less. You should be the only one to reach that decision. If something doesn't serve a real purpose in your résumé, it shouldn't be there.

Additional Sample Résumés

Look at the following sample résumé, also in the chronological format. Its writer doesn't include a job objective, but begins with a background summary that provides a general picture of her business experience. This probably means she is willing to consider a variety of possibilities related to her skills and experience. Writing down an objective might unnecessarily limit the scope of her search. Here, by contrast, a potential employer gets the opportunity to read something into the summary, perhaps fitting the writer's abilities to the company's needs.

Chronological Format

Joan Blackwell
9000 Park Avenue
Riverdale, New Jersey 07457

Home: (201) 555-1212
Office: (212) 555-2121

SUMMARY

Operations-oriented Chief Financial Officer with significant career progression over 19 years in domestic and international operations of consumer products and pharmaceutical companies. Strengths include: CPA with broad financial experience in public accounting, manufacturing operations, cost accounting, planning/financial analysis, and license negotiations.

EXPERIENCE

PELHAM GROUP, p.l.c.   **1977–Present**

Vice President, Finance, Pelham Labs   **1989–Present**
U.S. Pharmaceutical Division, Raleigh, NC

Chief Financial Officer for pharmaceutical operation with sales of $600 million. Supervise staff of 125 with responsibility for accounting, MIS, telecommunications, credit/collections, budgeting, financial analysis, strategic planning, and cash management.

- Served on the Senior Executive Committee which planned and directed the postmerger integration of the U.S. operations of PharmaCorp with Pelham. A 19% reduction in combined headcount resulted through reducing the field sales force.

- Restructured and consolidated financial operations yielding 30% staff reduction.
- Created financial model for sales management implementation to evaluate pricing alternatives affecting 15,000 independent and chain drugstores in the face of severe competitive pricing pressure.

Vice President, Finance—Western Division   **1984–1989**
Pharmaceutical Division, New Brunswick, NJ

Chief Financial Officer for International Division with sales of $160 million. Operations included subsidiaries in Canada and Latin America.

- Developed product sourcing and pricing strategies for Mexican subsidiary resulting in incremental profitability of $1 million annually.
- Initiated foreign exchange program for Venezuelan subsidiary, featuring stop/loss orders, generating profits of $950,000 during 1988–89.
- Served on inventory reduction team implementing JIT/TQC program which reduced inventory coverage from 21 weeks to 12.
- Negotiated raw material supply agreements in Canada to utilize excess capacity and produce annual profits of $250,000.

Vice President, Finance—Western Division   **1981–1984**
Consumer Products Division, Princeton, NJ

Chief Financial Officer for toiletry, cosmetics, fragrance, and household products business with sales of $140 million. Operations included subsidiaries in Latin America and Canada.

- Identified and screened acquisition candidates in South America leading to the eventual acquisition of a prominent Brazilian household products company.
- Integrated the financial activities of a major acquisition with 13 subsidiaries in Canada and South America.
- Converted manual headquarters accounting and budgeting functions to computerized, PC-based systems.

Controller—Western Division   **1977–1981**
Consumer Products Division, Princeton, NJ

Chief Financial Officer for Latin American Division with sales of $40 million.

- Was assigned interim responsibility to manage subsidiary in Venezuela; converted an operating loss to profits of $700,000 in 18 months.

JONES WHITMAN, INC.   **1973–1977**

Asst. Corporate Controller—Sterling Beverage   **1975–1977**

Supervised staff of 23 with responsibility for accounting, taxation, policy development, consolidations, payroll and financial analysis of $160 million subsidiary.

Manager, Corporate Planning and Financial Analysis   **1974–1975**
The Thompson Company, New York, NY

Responsible for corporate budgeting, planning, and financial analysis of $50 million subsidiary.

Manager, Cost Accounting   **1973–1974**
The Thompson Company, Des Moines, IA

Developed standard costs, annual and long-range manufacturing budgets, cost reduction programs, and the ongoing analysis of operations.

Manager, General Accounting   **1973**
The Thompson Company, Des Moines, IA

HASKINS & HASKINS CERTIFIED PUBLIC ACCOUNTANTS 1969–1972
Des Moines, IA

Senior Auditor	1972
In-Charge Auditor	1971
Staff Auditor	1969–1970

EDUCATION

B.B.A., Finance, University of Wisconsin	1969
Haskins & Haskins Accelerated Accounting Program	1970
Certified Public Accountant	1971

ASSOCIATIONS

American Institute of Certified Public Accountants	1972–Present

PERSONAL

Married with two children
Fluent Spanish speaker

Notice that the writer doesn't list everything she has done during her career. The farther back she goes, the less specific she is until, in referring to her earliest accounting experience, she simply names the company and lists her job titles. Potential employers are normally interested in recent, major accomplishments, so there is rarely a need to go into detail about early, relatively junior positions. As it stands, this résumé describes a career marked by orderly growth and regularly increasing responsibility.

The résumé also includes an excellent summary statement. Here are some additional examples of summary statements that capsulize work experience in other careers.

- More than 16 years of progressive experience in the manufacture of precision mechanical and electronic instrumentation. A broad and highly successful record in the introduction of new products and cost control programs. Strong background in organization in a fast-growing company.

- A seasoned general manager with a 21-year record of problem solving and profitable management. Successful at all levels of retail marketing management, from store manager to full profit responsibility for an 80-store chain.

To create a summary statement for your résumé, find the points that should be stressed by looking back through your lists of skills and accomplishments. Make sure that everything you include in the summary is supported by precise accomplishments in the body of your résumé, however. If your summary statement makes you sound like a hero of modern business, but your accomplishments are somewhat less than heroic, guess how you'll be judged.

Here, a third example of a good chronological résumé shows that you don't need the experience of a captain of industry to create a good résumé.

Chronological Format

TRACY JOHNSON
14 Middletown Road
Winthrop, Michigan 48010
(616) 123-4567

OBJECTIVE:

An administrative position offering responsibility and opportunity for advancement to management level.

EXPERIENCE:

1987–Present:

XYZ CORPORATION   **Administrative Assistant to Vice President, Marketing**

Prepared résumés and mailings (both company and executive search firms) for terminated executives as part of company's career continuation program.

Monitored computer operations dealing with career continuation activities and special corporate events.

Coordinated special projects (training seminars, presentations, workshops).

1983–1987:

SIMPSON PUBLISHING **Administrative Assistant to Vice President, Director of Marketing (1985–1987)**

Arranged editorial meetings and coordinated activities of Sales Promotion, Advertising, Art, Publicity, and Rack Departments, working as liaison between my boss and heads of these departments.

Researched newspapers and industry journals for articles on Simpson books. Kept records of competition ratings and a daily sales record on status of current best sells. Maintained daily scheduling of project phases as much as six months in advance to meet upcoming publication deadlines.

Handled correspondence for and with various authors.

Helped organize authors' parties for upcoming books and worked with motion picture companies for movie/television tie-ins.

Personal Secretary to Vice President, Treasurer (1983–1985)

Scheduled meetings and appointments and handled correspondence.

Kept logs of bids from various real estate brokers, furniture suppliers, etc., in preparation for relocation of offices.

Typed financial budgets, quarterly reports; prepared special reports for parent company.

1981–1983:

QUINDATA Marketing Service Representative

Demonstrated personal computer systems for salesmen and potential customers and conducted special office seminars.

Instructed purchasers in computer operations following sale. Worked closely with sales force to learn customer requirements, then created and administered personalized training programs based on specific applications.

When not engaged in customer service activities, managed the office, logged service calls, and solicited new accounts.

Attended manufacturers' seminars to become familiar with new equipment.

EDUCATION:

Michigan State University B.A. Degree in Business
To be completed June 1991.

Associate Degree in Applied Sciences, 1981.

The two following sample résumés present good examples of the alternative, functional format.

Functional Format

MURRAY JAMES
10225 Coastal Boulevard
San Francisco, California 94199
(415) 555-9876

SUMMARY

Seeking a position as a marketing and executive sales representative for a leading firm. Qualified by 11 years' experience in marketing, sales, and promotion of institutions, images, and products. High energy and sensitive to client needs. Excellent communication skills. Record of innovative approaches to increasing sales and revenues.

ACCOMPLISHMENTS

- Communicated research information to sales personnel through daily broadcasts, symposia, and publication (circulation: 10,000).
- Gathered information for sales support.
- Conducted briefings and orientations for new personnel following the acquisition of a new subsidiary.
- Prepared a series of instructional articles that resulted in a 20% reduction in errors on order placement.
- Prepared an educational column for *Industry Week* that was hailed by investors for its helpful content.
- Recruited securities analysts, foreign exchange dealers, and exchange representatives for a symposium creating visibility for the respective participants.
- Achieved recognition from brokers for directing business to them.
- Cited as the "most read" author in a weekly publication, *Financial Markets.*

WORK HISTORY

SHARPTON SECURITIES, INC., San Jose, CA   1979–1990
Vice President—Sales

PRECIOUS METALS LTD., Seattle, WA   1978–1979
Customer Representative

EDUCATION

B.A., Oregon State University, 1977

PERSONAL INFORMATION

NFA Series 3 License
Campaign Coordinator, United Way Campaign

FUNCTIONAL FORMAT

TERRY P. BATES

29 Stonewall Lane   Home: (202) 555-4920
Washington, DC 20099   Office: (202) 555-0294

SUMMARY

Over 19 years of increasing responsibility in areas of Project Management, Strategic and Short-Range Planning, MIS, New Product Planning, and Operations/Budget Controls.

MAJOR ACCOMPLISHMENTS

Strategic Planning

Structured MBO programs resulting in elimination or reduction of several low-priority programs and intensification of effort for three highly promising program leads.

Working closely with senior management, developed standards and implemented MIS/EIS systems to monitor and analyze short- and long-range plan performance.

Modeled a new product "success grid" which highlighted the organization's inability to meet long-range goals; this led to an intensified program of licensing and acquisition.

Identified long-range space/manpower limitations, resulting in the construction of a new $2.6 million facility to house needed increase of technical staff.

As member of four-member Systems Review Board, played an instrumental role in establishing and implementing divisional long-range systems strategy.

Several duplicate projects were eliminated, and investment returns were optimized through priority allocations of capital and MIS budgets.

Information Systems

Directed the development of a computerized, priority-based planning and control system for a multimillion-dollar worldwide corporation. System provides realistic scheduling, identification of manpower/facilities bottlenecks, and serves as basis for tactical decisions.

Developed a departmental MIS which surfaced inefficient use of limited resources, thus avoiding $1.5 million of noncontributing expense.

Directed the development of an automated regulatory tracking system which improved, by fivefold, compliance with government regulatory agency demands for research information.

Worked with software companies to evaluate and customize commercially available programs for specialized applications, thus avoiding the necessity of in-house development of major systems.

New Product Planning

Assumed responsibility for the planning and control of more than 40 new product introductions, several representing investments of up to $15 million.

Steered an important new product through regulatory submission process on time and with maximum quality, avoiding a potential loss of $7 million in sales.

Formed eight project coordination teams of multidiscipline functions, resulting in improved quality and timeliness of technical programs.

Operations/Budget Control

Responsible for a $750,000 departmental budget including 18 professional employees.

Made recommendations on "risk spending" investments which increased new product sales potential by approximately $9 million.

Designed and implemented new product budget controls providing readily available cost information for variance analyses as well as documentation to support joint venture allocation expense.

WORK HISTORY

1978–Present	Henry Morris Corporation
	1988—Director, Operations Planning
	1984—Associate Director, Project Planning
	1980—Manager, New Product Planning
	1978—New Product Coordinator
1974–1978	Seldon Products, Inc.
	Assistant Director, Product Development
1970–1974	Merrimack Products, Inc.
	Pilot Plant Supervisor

EDUCATION

M.B.A. (Executive Program)   American University, 1981
B.S., Chemical Engineering   Purdue University, 1970

The preceding résumé illustrates a structural element that is both an important component of all good résumés and an area in which functional résumés can be particularly effective: it covers all pertinent bases. Without even reading it, a potential employer could learn at a glance that the individual has had extensive experience in four major business areas. In addition, a reader interested in this person's achievements in only one functional area wouldn't have to sift through separate job descriptions to search for relevant details.

In the functional résumé no less than in the chronological résumé, you not only need to back up what you say, you also must demonstrate that you have solid experience in the main areas of responsibility demanded by the kind of position you're looking for.

The "Look" of Your Résumé

As you draft your own résumé, try to limit its length to two typewritten pages. (Proportional fonts available in many word processing programs can fit substantially more than two standard typed pages of information into a two-page word-processed document.) At the same time, don't cram so many words onto two pages that there is no white space in your résumé.

If you've had a great deal of exceptional experience, you may expand the document to three or even four pages. But make sure everything you include really earns its place. Don't make a reader wade through repetitive or extraneous material. Don't assume that a long résumé is a good résumé.

The key to brevity is to write a draft résumé and then mercilessly pare away everything that doesn't absolutely need to be included. If you can think of one word that will take the place of two others, use it. Short words are often stronger than long words, and they take up less space. Check your grammar, punctuation, and spelling. The editing process can transform a meandering four-page résumé into a tight, action-oriented model of clarity.

Unless you have access to a computer and a good printer, it's worthwhile to have the master copy of your résumé typed or word processed professionally so that you can make copies from a crisp original. You'll need about five hundred copies, so the best course is typically to have them offset-printed. You might decide to use a copying machine for the first fifty copies or so, just in case an early reader spots a glaring error. Choose a quality grade of paper, and make it apparent that you took the time to produce a business-like résumé.

References and Reference Statements

It wasn't too long ago that the final line of most résumés read, "References available upon request." Such language is uncommon today, primarily because companies have grown increasingly reluctant to provide references for former employees, or even to discuss them in any detail when they are contacted by potential new employers.

Employers worry about legal repercussions, should something be said that cannot be proved. For example, if a company spokesperson tells a potential employer that you were fired, when technically you were asked to resign and did so, the company might find itself on shaky legal footing. If someone says, "Well, he did seem to be a little past his prime the last year or so," a company could be slapped with an age discrimination suit. As freedom of information legislation has allowed individuals access to statements that are made about them, companies have sealed their organizational lips. As one observer noted: "If your policies won't stand up in court, you will."

Many companies will only verify that an individual did in fact work for them and provide the dates of employment. Some may share the job title or titles for positions held, as well. Most companies will no longer say anything more, at least officially.

If you left your most recent employer on less than amicable terms, such policies can obviously work to your advantage. At the same time, if you left on excellent terms, you can at least investigate whether a reference might be forthcoming. If you know there is a company policy against references, you might ask your previous boss to provide an informal reference. If you had a strong relationship and remain on good terms, so that you would be trusted not to turn any of the remarks against the company, he or she might agree. A boss who regrets the fact that you were swept up in a large staff cut, for example, might go out of the way to help.

You can also ask former colleagues or even subordinates to serve as references. Or you can go outside your last company, asking a satisfied client, supplier, consultant, or virtually anyone with whom you've enjoyed a strong professional relationship in the past.

We suggest drafting your own reference statement, bearing in mind that you may have to alter it or create different versions acceptable to various individuals who agree to speak for you. You'd be surprised how frequently the things people have written about themselves in reference statements turn out to be the same things others say about them.

Begin your reference statement by telling in a paragraph or two how the reference knows you. What was your working relationship? Next, describe your key skills and accomplishments. Mention personal traits next. Finally, describe why you left or plan to leave your job. Think this through, because you'll have to live with it. And keep it brief: you, not one of your references, should be the only one to get involved in a detailed discussion of the subject.

If you left because of a staff reduction or reorganization, it's simplest to say that. That's what you want to do: keep things simple. If you were terminated for some other reason, it may be best to adopt some variation of the "we agreed to disagree" theme: "He didn't feel that the company's plans matched his own, and we agreed that his best option would be to search out an opportunity closer to his own needs and objectives."

Make the statement clear and straightforward. Don't try to make yourself sound like a saint or savior. Don't try to prove that your termination represents a major error on the company's part.

When you've completed the statement, review it with the two or three individuals who've agreed to act as references. Be willing to compromise. Suppose you can reach agreement with your former boss on this statement:

> He was an effective manager in the field of communications. He managed a staff of 25 professionals, and he reported directly to me. He did this job for four years. He left the company when, in a major reorganization, we decided to rely on outside consultants to provide most of our communication needs.

That isn't the most inspiring reference of all time, but you ought to be able to live with it. Given the hesitancy of people to even offer references today, it's a serviceable description of your situation.

As we noted earlier, even if companies won't provide references, they may still ask for them. People making hiring decisions want to be reassured that they aren't making a mistake by considering your application for employment, and hearing good things— or even bland statements—about you provides a measure of reassurance. So even a neutral reference probably won't hurt your chances, unless the potential employer talks to four individuals who all make you sound like a drone.

In the past, individuals who left their jobs on terrible terms with their bosses had to worry that these former superiors might try to ruin their chances for a new job if a potential employer called. Given today's litigious climate, however, such action is unlikely on the part of any but the most intemperate, or perhaps suicidal, individual.

If you suspect such treatment, and if you're convinced that a prospective employer will talk to that individual, you might say, "I should explain that my former boss and I had a number of disagreements. He stuck to his guns, I stuck to mine, and neither of us kept our thoughts a secret from the other." If your former boss then says, "We fought tooth and nail," all he's done is confirm what you've already said. On the other hand, if you say, "We got along just fine," and your former boss says, "We fought tooth and nail," then you're in trouble.

This situation is less and less likely to occur today, however, so it makes no sense to overreact or overanticipate. You could even find that a boss you detested does you a favor. Suppose that, in an involuntary staff reduction, he rubbed his hands in glee after making your name number one on the list of terminees. Suppose that you were given severance for six months or until you took a new job, whichever came first. What might your boss say if a prospective employer calls in three months? Perhaps something along the lines of "Well, we had to trim staff, and John had to be included in the group. But, you know, from what you say about your company, I think he might do exceptionally well in the position you've described."

CHAPTER 15

Marketing Strategy

Now you're ready to go public with your job search. It's time to arrange interviews that will lead to firm job offers. To do this, you'll need to develop a marketing strategy: tactics and priorities that determine what search activities you'll pursue and the emphasis each will receive.

Our clients use four techniques to find new jobs.

- Personal contacts account for 70 percent of the positions they take.
- Executive search firms or placement agencies lead them to 15 percent of their new jobs.
- Direct mailings produce 10 percent.
- Published openings account for 5 percent.

The key to a successful marketing strategy is to touch all bases by pursuing each search avenue. The fact that personal contacts produce seven of every ten new jobs for our clients does not mean that you should devote all your time to this tactic. Remember that 30 percent of these new jobs still come from other sources. You only need one job; don't limit your horizons by arbitrarily excluding any legitimate search technique.

But don't devote too much time to tactics that obviously don't deserve the effort, either. Many people feel uncomfortable asking for assistance or approaching relative strangers for help. Typically, they resist building personal contact networks and retreat to what they think is safer ground, spending most of their time answering advertisements or mailing out résumés. They avoid the face-to-face contact that worries them, but they also insulate themselves from most job opportunities.

Let the search technique's effectiveness determine the amount of time you devote to it. Assume that you'll spend thirty-five hours a week actually working at your search. Based on the experience of our clients, we recommend devoting about 70 percent of that time—twenty-five hours—to creating and expanding a network of personal contacts. Spend five hours or so working with search firms or employment agencies. Devote three or four hours each week to creating a direct mailing for targeted companies. Answer Help Wanted ads for an hour or two.

You'll have to fine-tune your own schedule. If you don't have substantial business experience yet, for example, you may find initially that you don't have enough contacts to spend 70 percent of your time on your network. Should that occur, you can devote relatively more hours to other tactics—answering ads or contacting placement agencies, for example—until the expansion that is a natural part of the networking process makes it possible to spend additional time developing these critical contacts. If you're looking for and have the credentials for a position near the top of the business world, you'll probably find it useful to spend more than 15 percent of your time working with executive search firms, since they concentrate on this end of the employment spectrum.

If you've decided to make a radical career change, you may discover that the skills and accomplishments described in your résumé don't quite meet the requirements of positions that really interest you. Because you won't match their expectations precisely, there is a greater than normal likelihood that résumé readers will screen you out before you get a chance to explain your new plans. In such a situation, we suggest that you devote proportionally more time to the face-to-face encounters that typify the networking process. Such meetings will give you a chance to articulate your new goals and sell your abilities in a manner that simply can't be accomplished in a résumé.

But in general, don't give away any options. You want to generate as many interviews as you can: we find an average of eight interviews is required to land one job offer. Ideally, you should have two or even three offers to consider when it comes time to make a final decision about your next job. If you end your job search enjoying this embarrassment of riches, it will probably come as the result of having set up sixteen to twenty-four initial employment interviews along the way.

Published Openings

Answering Help Wanted advertisements is a time-honored and, many insist, singularly ineffective way to find a job. It is true that only about 5 percent of the jobs our clients take come through this channel. But it's also true that these ads make 5 percent of those clients 100 percent employed!

If you rely exclusively on the employment sections of newspapers and industry publications, you'll certainly have put all your eggs into a very flimsy basket. But if you think of the effort as only one part of your search, you might be pleasantly surprised. People really do find jobs through the *New York Times,* the *Washington Post, Advertising Age, Chemical Week,* and any of a number of other consumer and trade publications.

Responding to an ad can seem like dropping your résumé into a bottomless pit, particularly when the ad is identified only with a box number. Many such ads don't describe real jobs. Search firms place them to build files of résumés in particular fields. Other agencies try to drum up business by approaching major employers with unsolicited mailings of stacks of résumés. To keep this scattershot maneuver going, they need to replenish their stock of résumés continually. Companies may decide to test the employment waters by placing ads to determine the availability of talent and assess industry salary levels for particular jobs. Blind ads are relatively inexpensive research tools for them.

But box-number advertisements can also describe real job opportunities. The hiring company may wish to remove someone from its staff without telegraphing the decision until a successor has been identified. Or would-be employers may simply seek protection from having to acknowledge the hundreds of inquiries a single ad can produce.

In general, if a company does name itself, you can assume that an opening does exist (although there's no guarantee that it will be filled by someone responding to the ad), and that you can expect at least a form letter thanking you for your interest. You may not get this response for months, but most companies regard thank-you notes as a cheap form of good public relations. Other companies include this sentence in their ads, however: "Only individuals selected for further consideration will be contacted." The moral is clear: don't haunt your mailbox waiting for news about ads you've answered.

Since there is no infallible method for determining an ad's legitimacy, we think you should go ahead and answer any that seem interesting to you. There is little to lose and, potentially, a great deal to gain by taking a few minutes to send off a résumé and short cover letter.

Even when advertisements describe legitimate job openings, the odds of getting past the initial screening process remain low. A single ad may draw four hundred or five hundred responses, and even the conscientious reader of résumés may no longer be concentrating by the time he or she reaches number 302. If that's your résumé, it may not receive the attention it deserves.

Responses are typically put into one of three categories. The first group consists of excellent possibilities, résumés of individuals who appear to meet or surpass the job's predetermined specifications. The second group holds the résumés of possible choices, people who probably meet the job requirements but who, for one reason or another (which may be subjective), don't seem quite as qualified as members of the first group. Résumés that land in the third category come from people who do not seem qualified for the position. They are likely to be discarded. Your objective is to see to it that your response lands in the first pile.

While your résumé is probably not a perfect match for any advertisement, you can write a good cover letter to tie your résumé to the job you're investigating. When you locate an ad that interests you, study it to isolate three or four key requirements it stresses. Mention each in your cover letter, tailoring a skill or accomplishment from your résumé to the specific job. Even if you've emphasized the key items in your résumé itself, restate them in the cover letter. Help the reader simplify the screening process by making it unnecessary to dig into your résumé to determine whether you fit the job specifications. A good cover letter can convince people you do.

Consider this ad as an example.

REGIONAL SALES MANAGER

Leading plastics manufacturer seeks successful sales executive to head its $16 million Southwest region. Ideal candidate will be a results-oriented achiever with an impressive track record in industrial plastic sales and at least four years of successful sales supervision. Must have demonstrated training ability. Position requires 40% travel. Send résumé with salary requirements.

Here, the key requirements appear to be:

- A track record in industrial plastics sales
- Four years of sales supervision
- Demonstrated training ability

You would refer to each of these in your cover letter, and you would also consider the tone of the ad as you prepare your response. Words like *successful, results-oriented, achiever,* and *impressive* tell you how to shape your answer to the ad. Your cover letter might begin:

As the attached résumé indicates, I am a successful sales manager whose commitment to bottom-line results has been demonstrated during eight years of aggressive sales experience with Lucid, Inc., a $15 million manufacturer of industrial plastics products. For the past five years, I have supervised a nine-member sales force and managed the company's sales training programs. Last year, my staff and I increased sales by 14% over the previous year.

Respond to both the substance and tone of the ad. You can almost play it back to the people who devised it.

Don't prescreen yourself. If, to continue with the same sample, you have had only two and a half years of sales management experience, go ahead and answer the ad, but don't quantify your experience in your cover letter. Or, if the job really interests you, don't exclude yourself from the running because you're not sure you're as "fast-track" or "results-oriented" a candidate as the company seems to be seeking.

If everyone were as aggressive as personnel ad writers apparently want them to be, newspaper employment sections would have to be printed on stainless steel pages. When employers are defining job openings, they tend to call up a somewhat limited list of modifiers to describe their requirements. Once the talk stops and the decision making begins, they hire people with whom they feel comfortable.

You want the company to get in touch with you. If it does, you'll have plenty of time to decide whether its style matches your own, and you'll have much better evidence to work from than a single advertisement. If, however, an ad identifies the company, and you know from experience that it's not the kind of organization you want to work for, then don't respond. You're not looking for just any job. You're interested in the right job.

Our sample ad asks for "salary requirements." In most cases, we advise our clients not to mention money, even if salary information is requested. Salary level is often used as a screening device, and it can knock you out of the game before you get a chance to sit down for an interview with the company. If your credentials look right, you'll probably interest a prospective employer even if you haven't said how much you earn or would like to earn. But if your skills seem appropriate and you mention a salary level somewhat above a limit the company may have set, you could be dismissed from further consideration. In a face-to-face interview, you might be able to convince the employer you're actually worth the amount you seek, or you might negotiate your compensation level.

If your salary history or requirements seem too low to a prospective employer, the company could conclude that you don't have sufficient experience to handle the job. Worse still, someone might assume that you've been less than truthful about your qualifications.

There are some situations in which you should mention salary. You might decide to do some screening of your own. If you're seeking $125,000 a year and won't consider anything less, for example, you might mention that fact tactfully in your cover letter. Understand, however, that this may substantially limit the number of responses you receive. Finally, if a company is so determined to learn your salary that its ad includes the line: "Responses lacking salary information will not be considered," then you'll most likely have to mention a figure to stand any chance of getting a response.

Generally speaking, however, don't offer salary information unless the ad demands the data in no uncertain terms. But don't let anyone think you left the information out because you didn't read the ad carefully. In your cover letter, include a sentence like "Before providing a meaningful and sensible salary figure, I will have to discuss the responsibilities and opportunities presented by this position in greater detail."

When you finish a cover letter, think for a moment before you clip it to your résumé and mail both away. The majority of responses to employment ads hit the recruiter's desk two or three days after the ad has run. One way to avoid being on the bottom of that pile is to wait a day or two (but not much longer) before sending in your materials. Your résumé will land on a somewhat cleaner desk, where it may stand a slightly better chance of receiving a thorough examination. Some people have used overnight courier services to respond to ads, hoping to beat the rush of mail. If an opening seems ideal to you, you might want to make that investment, but the tactic could obviously become very expensive very quickly.

If you haven't heard anything at the end of two weeks, but feel strongly that the job may really be made for you, write again, emphasizing the fact that, because the position seems so well suited to your abilities and needs, you thought you should at least send along another résumé. Your first response might never have reached its destination, or it might have been misplaced as it was being routed from one company official to another. Take nothing for granted.

If someone's name is included in an ad, you might give the person a call. If the advertisement states, "No calls, please," wait a couple of weeks before phoning. Tell the individual that although your résumé apparently didn't meet the requirements of the advertised position, you remain interested in the company and would like to arrange a short meeting to discuss the firm. Our experience has been that company representatives respond very positively to this level of interest and energy.

In one instance, a man we counseled answered a newspaper ad for a job he thought was totally in line with his career goals. Two weeks passed and no word came back to him. Even though he realized the ad could have been placed by someone stockpiling résumés, it interested him so greatly that he sent off another résumé and a second cover letter. He received a telephone call a few days later and learned that one of the screening criteria for the position was a test of persistence. Only people who responded twice were considered for the job. Our client went in for an interview and landed the job, which, interestingly enough, was a counseling position with a church organization.

Company Mailings

When you considered your skills, needs, and values to define goals during the career decision-making process, you created a relatively precise picture of an ideal job or, perhaps, of several interesting career possibilities. One way to contact the companies and organizations in fields that survived this winnowing process is to create a direct-mail package—a cover letter and résumé, or a single document that combines the two—and send it to an appropriate individual at each targeted firm.

Our clients often mail these packages to at least one hundred companies. Typically they receive two or three solid invitations to employment interviews as a result. These interviews, in turn, lead to about 10 percent of the jobs our clients accept.

There's no escaping the fact that distributing a company mailing, like answering a Want Ad, is a low-yield endeavor. But if you're determined to take the time to find the right job for yourself, you shouldn't dismiss opportunities that 10 percent of the time have found other people their "right" jobs. Don't assume that you're wasting time or making work for yourself by pursuing this tactic.

The cover letter that accompanies your résumé in a mailing should be short, informal, and persuasive. Try to emphasize quickly and in an interesting manner who you are and what you have to offer. If there is something unique about your background or abilities, mention it. Don't restate your résumé, since you'll enclose it with your letter. Try to raise a few highlights that will attract a reader's interest. Be sure to tell how the person you are writing to can contact you. (You'd be amazed how many people forget this!) You may also indicate that you will follow up your letter with a telephone call. If you do, be sure you actually make the call.

Consider the two sample letters that follow.

Company Letter

32 Center Street
Northport, CA 91999
February 21, 1991

Mr. Amos Tucker
Senior Vice President
Mid Central Industries
100 Fifth Street
Wichita, Kansas 67676

Dear Mr. Tucker:

I am an international executive for a major consumer products company, with general management experience (headquarters and overseas) and a strong marketing background.

Recently, I proposed and carried out the decentralization of our Canadian subsidiary, which I managed for the past two years. In effect, this action eliminated my own position as Director and General Manager. Because the alternative positions offered me are inconsistent with my career goals, I have decided to seek employment elsewhere. My management is aware of this decision.

My objective is to obtain a senior position in line or staff management, preferably with a multinational firm, and I am willing to relocate.

If my résumé matches any of your current openings, I would be pleased to meet with you. I'll call you in a few days to see if you're interested in setting up an interview. You can contact me at (805) 555-1111.

Sincerely,

John C. Sloan

JCS/cu
enc.

Company Letter with Reference

3 Owens Road
Midland, OH 45148
August 3, 1990

Mr. James C. Cavelli
Director of Personnel
Insatco, Ltd.
100 Broad Street
Dover, Delaware 19901

Dear Mr. Cavelli:

I recently mentioned to John Jones, a friend at Simpson Industries, that I do not find sufficient challenge in my present position. He told me of Insatco's growth record and possible interest in seasoned executives with international experience, and also suggested that I contact you.

Briefly, my qualifications comprise 20 years of progressively responsible experience, including six years of bottom line P&L responsibility and 12 years of line and staff marketing management. In terms of depth and diversity, I have:

- Prepared successful marketing and business plans, both single- and multicountry, focusing on market penetration, profitability, and effective resource allocation.

- Prepared and directed successful marketing campaigns at foreign subsidiary and headquarters levels.

- Assessed and negotiated acquisition, licensing, and joint venture agreements.

I would very much appreciate an exploratory meeting to determine how my qualifications might match some of your current or planned management needs, in either domestic or international areas. I will call you to see if we can arrange such a meeting. I can be reached at (614) 555-1234.

Sincerely,

Anthony Bracer

AB/cu
enc.

While the first sample letter is an acceptable, workmanlike note that describes the overall background of its writer, the second is clearly a superior effort. It begins with a reference, the name of an individual known to both the writer and the recipient, who now have one thing in common: they both know John Jones. As we'll see when we discuss personal contact networks, this kind of reference point lowers barriers and opens doors to interviews.

The second letter also offers specific details about the writer's career accomplishments. A reader won't have to wade through a résumé to make an initial assessment of this writer's business qualifications. If the points highlighted in the letter catch the reader's interest, the natural inclination will be to turn to the résumé for additional information.

The second letter also shows that the writer has done enough homework to realize that this company might be an ideal place for him to seek employment. The reader learns that the writer has taken the time to determine what he does well, what he would like to do next, and where he thinks he might do it. The writer is approaching this company from a very positive reference point; he isn't trying to shape himself to the company's needs but is demonstrating that he and the company may share similar needs. This individual isn't *asking;* he's *offering.*

Even if you can enlist the power of a personal computer's mail-merge and customization capabilities, it's unlikely that you'll tailor letters this specifically for each of a hundred target companies. But you might create personalized packages like this for a few prime targets: companies you think might be particularly appropriate for you.

Marketing Letters

The goal of any company mailing is to get and hold the attention of an appropriate decision maker at the target firm, in the hope that he or she will grant you an interview. But because the mailing is unsolicited, this is not normally an easy task. Some observers feel that sending out a résumé that hasn't been asked for only inspires its recipient to forward it in either of two undesirable directions: to the personnel department or toward the wastebasket.

To avoid this fate, some of our clients prefer to create and distribute marketing letters, single documents that combine the strong points of both cover letter and résumé in one piece of effective business correspondence. The thinking behind a marketing letter is that it gives the writer a better than average chance to attract attention and get a message across. A good business letter, the argument goes, is more likely to interest someone than a good résumé.

Some of our clients have enjoyed high success rates with marketing letters, landing ten or more interviews by sending out one hundred letters. Others have found that the tactic didn't work well at all, even lagging behind the typical 1 to 2 percent response rate of standard résumé and cover letter mailings.

We believe that two factors probably account for such disparate return rates: first, the qualifications of the individual, and, second, the effectiveness with which these abilities are communicated in the marketing letter. If you have a great story to tell, and if you can tell it well, then a campaign of marketing letters may be a very effective search tool.

If you choose to write one, you'll need to create a vigorous and energetic business letter that sells your qualifications unequivocally. You should base the letter on solid accomplishments: "I've been cutting costs for more than fifteen years, and I've saved more than $30 million in the process." There is no room for modesty or reticence in a good marketing letter.

The first paragraph of such a personal sales document should tell what you've done and how well you've done it. Include numbers and percentages wherever possible. Then, in the body of your letter, expand and embellish this introduction, continuing to be as specific as you can about your achievements.

Close the letter with a quick sales pitch that indicates the action you would like a reader to take—an invitation to discuss personally how your experience might benefit his organization. Think of your letter as a direct-mail marketing brochure. You are the product, and you want your audience to act by contacting you for an interview. Use the sample letters that follow as guides for creating one of your own.

Marketing Letter

2841 Narrow Street
San Francisco, CA 94333
March 23, 1991

Ms. Nancy C. Slater
President
Food Service Incorporated
Commerce Center
Albuquerque, NM 87199

Dear Ms. Slater:

As the Regional Vice President for Westco Services, I directed the development of Northern California and the Southwest. Working from a 10-year plan, the company anticipated developing 30 units and $65 million in new revenues. We achieved the plan in five years, developing 33 dinner houses and specialty theme restaurants, and $68 million in revenues.

In Southern California we concentrated on developing three areas, Newport Beach, San Diego, and Riverside. These areas are directed and controlled from San Diego, utilizing the commissary cluster unit approach. Three major facets of this concept are: control over the quantity and quality of the food; storage and warehousing of inventories to reduce costs to individual units, and the reduction of suppliers to a manageable number with an increase in items supplied by them. This reduction has saved the firm $600,000 annually.

The enormous success of this approach encouraged us to utilize the same concept in Phoenix and Albuquerque. These units have also prospered. Along with our new commissary in Phoenix, we have established three dinner houses and one theme restaurant. In the Albuquerque area, we established a commissary, three coffee shops, and two dinner houses.

As a result of my role in successfully developing the Southwest, I was promoted to Vice President of Operations. I currently have responsibility for 90 restaurants located nationwide with $140 million in revenues.

My varied and proven experience in the food service industry is only briefly touched on in this letter. I would appreciate the opportunity to personally explore with you in greater detail how my experience might benefit your company.

Please write me at my home address shown above or telephone either my home or office.

Sincerely,

Marvin S. LeBrun

Office: (415) 555-1000
Home: (415) 555-2468

Marketing Letter

Harold Stormer
676 Archer Avenue
Miami, Florida 33100
(305) 800-1616

<u>PERSONAL AND CONFIDENTIAL</u>

Mr. Vance Mitchell
Chairman
The Reflex Group
1400 Pilgrim Street
Lowell, MA 01899

Dear Mr. Mitchell:

As President of Telnet, Inc., a subsidiary of Anso Incorporated, a $1.4 billion diversified world leader in the manufacture and distribution of electronic components, I was responsible for a $30 million operation producing stereo components for consumer markets. In this capacity, I turned the operation from a loss position into the black after being on the job only three months. Specifically, I increased gross profits by more than 50% (over $400,000 in profit contribution). I also reduced inventories by more than half in less than one year, a reduction of over $2 million.

My record demonstrates an ability to cut through difficult problems and reduce them to simple common denominators. My contemporaries consider me to have a strong numbers sense, providing direction in moving my company to become profitable and well controlled.

Telnet is being moved to South Korea due to high local labor costs and stiff competition from foreign markets. I have decided to seek another position to challenge my skills and abilities.

Some of my other achievements include:

Developed a long-range business plan at Telnet mapping future business efforts on short- and long-term marketing strategies to meet corporate goals and objectives.

Instituted cost-reduction programs which resulted in savings of more than $500,000 in each of the past three years. Among these were increased machine shop capability and increased computerization for automatic testing procedures.

Established an offshore manufacturing facility that resulted in over $100,000 in tax savings in one year. Savings over the next nine years are estimated to be $1.2 million.

As Director of Finance, along with the Division President, completed an acquisition that has increased the division's sales and earnings by more than 25% per year.

Prior to my current position, I worked 11 years at a medium-sized electronics subsidiary of Stiller, Gruhewald, Inc., a $1 billion multinational. I began as Controller, progressed in five years to Director of Finance, and was again promoted after two years to Director of Operations/General Manager of the division.

I graduated from college with a major in Business and was the Top Honor Graduate (GPA 4.0) in my MBA class at Pepperdine University. I am married and will relocate in the United States for a suitable position.

I would like to explore with you the contributions I can provide for your organization. Please contact me in confidence at my home.

Sincerely,

Harold Stormer

It is probably easier to write an excellent résumé and cover letter than it is to create a first-rate marketing letter. One way to determine which option you should choose, as a result, is to consider your own writing skills. If you're a good writer—and particularly if you are looking for work that demands excellent writing skills—then the marketing letter is an opportune way to demonstrate your abilities. Remember, however, that a badly written marketing letter may do you more harm than good.

You can't expect much success from either a marketing letter or a cover letter and résumé if your mailing doesn't get into the right person's hands. The second marketing letter sample, for example, is identified as "Personal and Confidential." Its writer hopes that this nomenclature will keep a secretary from arbitrarily consigning it to the personnel files.

The "Personal/Confidential" tag certainly won't help if it is followed by the salutation, "Dear Executive." Do your best to determine the identity of the individual who should receive your mailing at each company. This will usually be the head of your discipline at the firm.

Don't address your mailing to the director of personnel unless, of course, you are looking for a job in the personnel field. If you desire a position as a marketing manager, mail to the vice president of marketing at each company. That person may send your material straight on to the personnel director, but he or she might also attach a note saying, "This one looks interesting. I think we should take a look." Or the person could contact you directly.

If you want a job as vice president of operations, don't send a mailing to the company's vice president of operations. He or she is more likely to feel threatened than interested. Send your materials to the appropriate senior vice president or group head. If you're approaching a smaller company, go directly to the president or chairman.

There are several ways to find the names that go with these titles. Look at Appendix E, "Job Research Resources," at the back of this book. It lists business directories found in most good libraries. These books can help you determine the companies you should contact, and in many cases they will identify by name the people you should write to. You'll also find telephone numbers for the companies you've targeted. A call to each firm on your target list will get you current names and addresses for your primary contacts.

If you take the time to create a mailing, make every effort to do it properly. It won't hurt to assume that if you give a reader the slightest reason to disregard your mailing, he or she will do just that. Every letter, whether it's a cover letter or a full-blown marketing letter, should be carefully typed and proofread. Use quality stationery. If you don't use a personal computer yourself, you might call in a word processing service to create top-quality letters for you.

Executive Search Firms

Some people call them "executive search consultants," others refer to them as "body snatchers," and everyone knows them as "head-hunters." Whatever name they go by, executive search firms, along with the employment agencies that are generally considered to occupy a somewhat lower position in the placement business hierarchy, locate about 15 percent of the new jobs taken by our clients. While everyone has heard about these firms, many people really don't understand how they operate or how they can be worked into a job-search strategy.

Many people believe, for example, that search firms work for the individuals who approach them seeking jobs. The business actually works the opposite way. Search firms work for companies, not individuals. When a client has a position to fill, it contacts a search firm, pays the recruiter a healthy fee (often a flat 30 or 33 1/3 percent of the job's yearly starting compensation), and the search firm locates top candidates whose qualifications meet the specifications of the job.

Most openings are only listed with one search company. Search firms, no matter how reputable or well respected they may be, usually have no involvement with a search being conducted by some other recruiter. This means that individuals should contact as many search firms as they can to stand the best chance of turning up available positions.

Which search organizations should you contact? We advise our clients to get in touch with one hundred to one hundred fifty search firms. Targets can range from large, international search firms to small, one-person operations. The largest search firms have traditionally concentrated their energies on the highest paying jobs, focusing on positions with salaries of six figures and up. Smaller firms typically work below this level. Even at firms where accepting lower level assignments goes against official policy, however, there can be exceptions. If, for instance, a good client who has given the search firm a number of high-fee searches asks for help on a somewhat lower paying position, the request will probably be accommodated. Since the majority of your search firm contacts are likely to be made via a résumé mailing, don't spend too much time agonizing over which firms to target. Choose more rather than fewer.

How do you identify and contact these firms? If you've dealt with a search firm previously—either by having been contacted by one as a potential candidate for a search, or by retaining a firm to locate an executive for you—you should get in touch with the consultants you've worked with in the past. If you're a member of a professional organization, its staff may have search firm contacts. Call and ask. As you build a personal contact network, which we'll discuss shortly, you can ask the people you meet to recommend search consultants. You might ask the human resources manager at your former company for a contact at a search firm. (Don't be too proud to ask. The search firm might work a little harder for you if you are referred to them by a company they're trying to impress.)

Although it works to your benefit to have someone introduce you to a search firm, you can even walk into a firm's office and tell the receptionist you wish to register. You might be ushered into an immediate interview.

But to alert the greatest number of search organizations, you'll have to mail out résumés and cover letters. Don't waste any time anguishing over the style or content of your letter. Search firms work with résumés; cover letters are often discarded immediately. Mention a few key points about yourself and the kind of position you're seeking. Tell how you can be reached. Ask the firm to contact you if they are handling any relevant searches, and to keep your résumé on file should any pertinent assignments surface in the future.

What you don't say is probably more important than what you do mention in this type of cover letter. Don't prescreen yourself. You may decide to state a salary level, for example, but not if you think it might hurt your chances with the firm. In the sample letters that follow, the salary figures seem unlikely to raise eyebrows. In fact, in the second letter, mentioning a salary level is probably a very good idea. Depending on the company he or she works for, a marketing director might make from $50,000 to $450,000 a year, so a salary figure can give a search firm a good idea of the level at which an individual is equipped to work. But if you have concerns about any information in your cover letter, follow an old rule of thumb: When in doubt, leave it out.

The letter doesn't require a personal salutation and can be offset or photocopied. Of course, if you have someone's name at a particular firm, it makes sense to send a personalized letter.

Search Firm Cover Letter

2 Barnacle Way
Jones Bay, NC 28999
May 15, 1991

Search Consultant:

Enclosed is a résumé of my background and experience in general management.

In ten years as CEO of the Connerfield Corporation, whose net sales were $350 million, my achievements have been significant.

I am now seeking new and challenging responsibilities in an organization with similar needs. My income level is in the six-figure range.

Should you have a client assignment matching my background or like to set up an appointment, please contact me at the above address.

Sincerely,

Richard L. Jones
(919) 555-4514

RJ/bc
enc.

Search Firm Cover Letter

Anne C. Whitby
23-38 Sixth Avenue
Minneapolis, MN 55499
(612) 724-4321

Mr. Walter Mays
Execusearch, Inc.
32 South La Salle Street
Chicago, IL 60699

Dear Mr. Mays:

Enclosed is a copy of my résumé for review against your client assignments.

As the document shows, I have an excellent track record as Marketing Director in businesses with sales volumes of up to $100 million, and in industries ranging from electronics to optical products distribution. About half of my last 12 years has been spent as an effective line and staff manager in international businesses. My current compensation is $110,000.

During the business day, I can be reached at (800) 888-1707.

Sincerely,

Anne C. Whitby

AW/cd
enc.

Most search firms assign a given search to a single consultant. At the larger companies, unsolicited résumés are screened by researchers who know enough about their firm's current business to give whoever is handling a particular search assignment the résumés of people who seem to meet its requirements. The consultant looks through these résumés and decides whether to contact the individuals. At smaller firms, the consultant may be his or her own researcher.

Unsolicited résumés have become an increasingly important resource in the executive search business. If a résumé comes in that doesn't match a current search but looks as if it might meet future needs, the firm may keep it on file for about six months. After that period, it is considered out of date and is normally discarded. When a firm accepts a new assignment, the consultant's first move will be to check the files for appropriate résumés. A next step will be to contact people who have been reliable sources for good prospects in the past.

In a normal search, a consultant will turn up about fifty people who meet the job requirements to one degree or another. As résumés are compared, the field may be narrowed to half that number. The individuals who remain are called for a telephone interview screening.

If you receive such a call, you'll be asked specific questions about your résumé, track record, skills, and goals. If you didn't offer salary information when you contacted the search firm, you may be asked for it at this time. You may also be asked to give a more detailed description of your work experience than your résumé provides.

If you survive the telephone screening (in a normal search, eight to ten people probably will), you'll be asked to come to the search firm for an interview. Once again, the search executive will try to determine how well your abilities fit the requirements of the job he or she has been assigned to fill. The consultant will also want to learn whether you're articulate and will want to be reassured that you look presentable and act appropriately in interview situations.

Personal chemistry begins to enter the selection process at this point. The consultant probably isn't enough of a specialist to know all the specific requirements of the job in question, so he won't make his decision solely on the basis of skills and experience. Nor will he be able to determine just how the decision makers at the client company will react to you personally, so he can't reach a decision based on chemistry alone. It's likely that he'll draw a general conclusion about you and that it will color his recommendation. If you don't impress him, he won't send you on to see his client.

After this round of interviews, the search executive will narrow his list of candidates to three or four choices and inform his client of his selections. He may rank the finalists and pass along this information as well.

If you reach this stage of the process, you'll probably be invited to the company for an interview. If you are asked to return for a second interview, you're likely to be either the first or second choice for the job.

As you can see, the search process proceeds along specific lines. It uses a rifle-shot approach to match people to jobs. Search consultants have well-defined slots to fill, and they rarely deviate from these strict job specifications. In addition, the process is as much an art as it is a science. You can be removed from the search at a number of points along the way for a variety of subjective as well as objective reasons.

As a result, when you deal with search firms, you have to anticipate a high rejection rate, which you shouldn't take personally. Expect to receive form letters that begin, "We have nothing at this time . . ." or, in many instances, expect to hear nothing at all. Search firms receive stacks of unsolicited résumés each week, and many cut their paperwork substantially by contacting only those people whose résumés match the requirements of a current search.

If you land an interview with a search firm, exploit it. Don't think only in terms of a single job opportunity. Sell yourself to the search firm. If you don't get past a telephone screening, write a note thanking the search consultant for his or her interest and saying you hope you'll be able to work together in the future. Consultants do retain an interest in candidates who impress them, and they do like to increase their business. The combination sometimes prompts search executives to call one or more of their corporate clients to say, "I realize that you don't have any searches on right now, but I've just talked with someone I think may interest you."

Employment Agencies

Some companies choose not to pay the hefty fees that search firms command, sending their business to employment agencies instead. These agencies, which have traditionally handled lower level positions than search firms, earn their fees only when an individual they recommend is actually hired by a company. The client pays nothing up front and, as a result, can list an opening with multiple agencies. The fees charged by employment agencies are usually substantially less than those charged by search firms.

These agencies must, as a result, operate quite differently from search firms. They receive smaller percentages of lower starting salaries. They aren't paid until someone is hired. And they often compete with other agencies to fill the same jobs. For these reasons, they typically have to hustle to be successful.

If you visit an employment agency, don't expect much in the way of kid-gloves treatment. You'll probably be given a quick interview, where you'll discuss your résumé and career objectives with an agency representative. Don't expect anyone at an agency to be able to devote too much time to your cause. And certainly don't put up with anyone who tries to fast-talk you into an unsuitable job.

Be selective as you choose employment agencies. Make sure you have a clear understanding with a firm that it won't arbitrarily send your résumé to companies. If you list yourself with ten agencies and each shotguns your résumé indiscriminately, a single employer could conceivably receive your résumé ten times. This doesn't make you appear to be particularly exclusive, although it may show that you're serious about finding a job. More importantly, it may raise a real problem for a would-be employer. If he decides to hire you, which of the ten agencies gets the fee? Will all ten argue that they saw you first? An employer might resolve the issue by not hiring you, or not even interviewing you.

Be selective if you decide to contact employment agencies. Tell those you work with that you want to be considered only for appropriate openings.

Personal Contact Networks: The 70 Percent Solution

One job-search strategy, networking, accounts for 70 percent of all the jobs our career continuation clients accept. The job seeker constructs a search network by talking to friends and business associates who introduce him or her to a continually expanding circle of personal contacts. We've watched thousands of individuals find good new jobs by building networks that expand through the business universe until they find the jobs they have been seeking. It sounds mysterious, but it isn't.

You begin the process by making a list of thirty or fifty or even one hundred people with whom you are acquainted. Your first thought is likely to be, I can't possibly come up with that many names. You probably can. They don't have to come from the field or fields you've targeted for your search. You will simply want to explore whether they know anyone in or near those areas. If you're looking for a job in data processing, for example, your lawyer and your accountant would be excellent people to list, since they may have friends, clients, or advisers who work in the field.

Your list can include doctors, ministers, rabbis, next-door neighbors, old friends, girlfriends, boyfriends, casual acquaintances, former classmates, former teachers, former clients, placement officers, bankers, stockbrokers, people who work at professional organizations, consultants you've met at search firms, fellow club members, even your dentist. (Imagine the captive audiences he commands in a day.) Don't be restrictive. If a name comes into your head, write it down. You can always remove it later in the game if you want.

When you've exhausted your address file and your memory, divide the names into primary and secondary categories. If you decide there is a better than average chance that an individual will know someone in the field you've targeted, put that name in the primary file. If a person seems less likely to be able to assist you, the name goes on the secondary list. Don't get carried away or slowed down by this process. It's only a loose way to set priorities and organize the first level of your network.

Starting with your list of primary names, you'll contact each person you've identified and try to set up a short personal meeting. If the individual is a close friend or business acquaintance, you can pick up the phone and call for an appointment. As you expand your network to include the names of people you've never met, you may want to initiate contacts by sending out short letters and following up with phone calls to arrange meetings.

This is the point at which some of our clients balk. "Oh no," they say, "I couldn't ask any of these people for a job." They couldn't, and they shouldn't.

In fact, before they make their first calls or send out their first letters, we have them memorize the first two rules of networking: Never ask for a job; always ask for suggestions. Don't ask for favors; ask for advice.

Call and say, "I'm making a career change, and I'd like fifteen minutes to ask your opinions and get some advice." This approach removes the risk from the situation, because the person now knows that all you want is advice. *Everyone* loves to offer advice. People write books just to be able to give advice.

As you call people, don't let them even imagine that you might be about to ask them for a job. Say, "I want to reassure you that I'm not going to ask you to find me a job. I'd like information from you, and I'd like to learn whether you can recommend other people I should talk with."

That is the key to networking. Each time you meet a new contact, your hope is that he or she will be able to recommend you to someone else. This keeps your network growing. At some point in the process, it will cause a job opportunity to surface.

Try for face-to-face meetings. Ask to meet the person in his or her office. Avoid lunch meetings or getting together for a drink after work. In an office, you can take notes. Your contact can make notes, and will have at hand the tools you hope will be used—an address book and a telephone.

Keep the meeting brief and to the point. Try to take up no more than fifteen minutes of a contact's time. Spend that period concentrating on the subject at hand—your career.

Be prepared to deliver a two- or three-minute summary of what you've done and what you intend to do next in your career.

As you discuss your experience, mention a few of your major strengths and accomplishments. As you talk about the future, be as clear as you can about the direction you want to take.

If the contact works in your target industry, find out as much as you can about what is happening in the business. Is it expanding or shrinking? What companies are doing well? What might someone with your qualifications and objectives expect to receive in salary?

If the individual is not employed in the field you've targeted, ask whether he or she knows people who are. If not, be persistent. Ask for names of people he or she has dealt with who could introduce you to others who do work in your target industry. If you prepare a series of polite, open-ended questions of this type, your contact will probably find that he or she does, in fact, know one or two people who can help you move closer to your target.

What you want to hear is, "Yes, I can think of three people you might talk to." What you want your contact to do is to give these individuals a call on your behalf. If that happens, you've started to expand your network. If the person doesn't pick up the phone, ask whether you can use his or her name to call them on your own. This requires a bit of courage for many people, but remember that many people really do like to help others and are flattered when others seek their counsel.

Your goal is to come away from these appointments with two things. First, you want your contacts to remember you and your skills so that, if they hear about something in the future, or if they discover a need for someone with your abilities in their own organization, they'll think of you. Second, you hope that they will pass you along to two or three other people so you can continue the process.

Suppose you contact twenty-five people to start, and each introduces you to two more contacts. All of a sudden, your network has seventy-five members and is expanding geometrically. Your skills, interests, and availability become known to a larger and larger group of people. And since you're not passed along to just anyone, but to individuals who work in or near your targeted field, your network actually becomes more precisely defined as it grows. Both the quality and quantity of your contacts improve.

You have to be a good bookkeeper to keep the process functioning properly. If you let your network get away from you, it will self-destruct. Follow-up is all-important. You need to know which individuals to contact next and which are owed thank-you notes for having taken the time to help you. Keep a series of file cards or use a data base program in your personal computer to keep a tight rein on your network. Keeping track of the following information will help you stay on top of things.

NAME:

PHONE:

TITLE/COMPANY:

INTRODUCED BY:

INITIAL CONTACT (DATE AND HOW FOLLOWED UP):

ADDITIONAL CONTACTS (DATES AND NATURE OF CONTACTS):

It's also important to prepare yourself in advance for every stage in the networking process. Suppose you're ready to telephone someone at the suggestion of one of your primary contacts. Plan the conversation by anticipating the direction it might take and preparing questions and answers to keep it on track.

You might begin by saying, "I'm calling at the suggestion of John Jones, an associate of mine who speaks very highly of your expertise in data processing."

Your contact might reply, "It's nice of John to say that. Why did he refer you to me?"

This is the time to ask for advice: "I'm looking for an objective viewpoint from someone with your background about the future of several segments of the data processing industry. I'd also like advice about opportunities you think are out there, since I'm in the process of making a career change. Let me make it clear that I'm not calling to ask for a job, just for information."

Your new contact is likely to say, "I'd be happy to talk with you." In that case, you've gained your first objective—his or her involvement.

You might respond, "Before I start my job search in earnest, I'd appreciate some thoughts and comments about my résumé. I want to make sure my objectives come across clearly, and I'd like to be certain the personal accomplishments I mention are in line with the needs of the industry. Can we schedule a fifteen-minute meeting to talk in your office?"

If the person agrees to the meeting, you've added another layer to your network. Or he or she may ask instead, "Do you have any questions I can answer over the phone?" Be ready with several, and give some thought to the order in which you ask them, regardless of whether you raise them in person or on the phone.

Start with *yes* questions or inquiries your contact should be able to answer with ease. You might ask, "What's the direction of data processing in the '90s?" Or, "What companies are having trouble keeping up with the industry?" Or, "Do you know of any companies that are growing rapidly and may be expanding their operations?" You can expect that the individual will be able to come up with answers to all these questions.

Then you can move along to "possibly no" questions, queries that the contact may not be able to answer. You might say, "In the course of my research, I've selected five companies that appear to have excellent data processing operations. I don't know a great deal about them, however, and I wonder if you can tell me anything about their operations and style of management."

The sequence of your questions is important. If you begin by asking a string of questions your contact can't answer, you run two risks. He may wonder, Why am I being asked questions I know nothing about? Is this person dumb? Or you might put him on the defensive: Why don't I know the answers to these questions? Am I dumb? Either way, you're likely to lose.

If the contact doesn't raise the issue, your final question should be "Will you help me with introductions to some of the people we've discussed?" If no names have come up, ask whether your contact can supply any. You are trying, of course, to continue the expansion of your network.

If, on the telephone, you have trouble getting past a protective secretary, try calling very early in the morning or very late at the end of the day. The secretary may come to work at 9:00 and go home at 5:00. The individual you want to contact may arrive earlier and stay in the office much later, answering his or her own calls at those times.

If you choose to introduce yourself to a new contact by writing a letter, make it specific. First, tell how you got to this individual by naming the person who brought up his or her name. Then get straight to the point. Describe your background in a short paragraph. Define your career goals in another. Say that you would appreciate getting some information about companies and individuals in the field you have targeted. Ask if the person will take fifteen minutes to talk with you. Say that you'll call for an appointment.

As you move from contact to contact, be sure you don't embarrass anyone. Get clearance before you use someone's name to get in touch with someone else. If someone isn't willing to help, don't say, "Well, Harry said you'd be happy to see me." Be sensitive to the fact that you are now representing other people.

The Evolution of a Job

As you consider the idea of personal contact networks, you may wonder, Why am I spreading myself out among all these people? I need a job, not an extended family.

To understand how and why the process works, it will help to look at how jobs evolve. Imagine that you are at the other end of the process: you have an opening to fill.

That's a problem. You or someone else in your organization must cover that slot and perform those duties until the position is filled. You probably have more than enough to occupy your days as it is. At the same time, filling that position entails a certain amount of risk, because you'll have to live with the consequences.

You're contending with conflicting forces. First, with time: the longer it takes to hire someone, the more additional work you and your staff must do. So you want to fill the position quickly. But you also need to reach a knowledge and comfort level with anyone you might consider for the spot. You're looking for skills, you need to assess motivation, and you have to make decisions about chemistry and how well the person will fit into your organization.

The first thing most people do in this situation is call their friends and business associates. They announce how desperate they are to find someone, and they ask whether their friends know anyone who might fit the bill. If someone they respect says, "I know *just* the person . . ." they've cut their risk and lessened their anxiety considerably, and in a very short time. They have an expert, trusted opinion about a candidate.

Consider their alternatives. Their firm's human resources department may hand them a stack of résumés. If they publish a Want Ad, they're likely to be swamped with applicants who may or may not meet their needs. There's no real way to find out without conducting endless interviews. Going to a search firm will improve their odds to a certain degree, but that is an expensive proposition. And how can they be sure a search consultant will really understand their needs?

Their best option seems to be to get in touch with everyone they know.

The Advantage of Networking

Now return to your own situation and consider your position as a job seeker. The more contacts you've made as you've built your network, the more likely it is that your name will come up in such an "I know just the person" conversation. And as you're introduced to more and more people in your target industry, the chances improve that you'll walk into the office of someone who already needs your services.

The value of the networking process is that you are constantly advertising yourself. It's comparable to putting up point-of-purchase displays at the end of the aisle in a supermarket. You're not just sitting on the third shelf from the left waiting to be recognized. You're creating your own recognition points.

You talk to John, and he sends you off to see Mary. When John and Mary meet for lunch two weeks later, John may ask Mary whether she saw you. Mary may say, "Yes, but you know,

now that I think of it, I should have put him in touch with Joe." So Mary calls you back, your network continues to grow, and, all of a sudden, someone you've contacted hears about a job and thinks about you. You land an interview—and that is the goal of your marketing strategy.

The Hidden Job Market

Another benefit of networking is that it admits you to that almost mythical region, the hidden job market. The term refers to a substantial part of the employment universe in which changing organizational needs have not yet crystallized into official job openings.

Such opportunities are likely to surface in:

- Organizations that are performing poorly and could stand new leadership.
- Departments that have fallen behind in their assigned responsibilities because of a lack of adequate staff or a shortage of competent leaders.
- Companies where growth, expansion, new products, or new services have created a need for new positions.
- Organizations confronted by competitive change which demands in response new skills and new people.

Until needs are defined and become openings in the visible job market, such opportunities obviously can't be advertised in newspapers or listed with search firms. A company mailing might trigger someone's thought processes, but it's much more likely that, as an individual expands his or her network, the spreading knowledge of the person's skills and availability will reach someone who wonders, Could that person help us out?

Many people are misled by discussions about this "hidden" job market. It does not refer to hundreds or thousands of existing job openings that, for some dark reason, have been kept secret. It doesn't represent empty chairs or vacant offices waiting for bodies to fill them.

But it does exist, occurring when organizations face new needs that haven't been planned for. You can capitalize on this phenomenon because, as you meet more and more people through the networking process, you give them the opportunity to match your skills to their needs. You're not trying to fit yourself into someone else's predetermined slot. You're describing what it is that you're looking for. This gives you flexibility that other job-search techniques simply don't offer.

CHAPTER 16

The Interview

The selection interview is certainly the most important event in the job search and, for many people, the most intimidating step in the entire career continuation process. Once the decision has been made to seek employment working for others, the activities that lead to this result—from creating a résumé to building contact networks—aim for one common goal: landing interviews with targeted companies or organizations. At this point the focus shifts and a new objective emerges: using the interview to get the job itself.

The position is won or lost in the interview. No matter how well you plan your search or prepare yourself during the weeks leading up to the interview phase, all that time and energy really pay off only when you get the job you've been aiming for. This is accomplished in the job interview, which is why the event can be such an unnerving, "do-or-die" experience.

It doesn't have to be, though. In fact, by following the systematic process we've been describing throughout this book, you not only work toward arranging interviews, but you also prepare yourself to turn these meetings to your advantage. If you think of an interview as an isolated incident in the campaign to find a new job, it certainly can inspire terror. But if you realize that everything you've done during the career decision-making process, and everything you've done to land the interview, have also prepared you to conduct it effectively, then it becomes merely the logical next step in a well-managed campaign.

Take, for instance, a common interview request that can turn aggressive business people into stutterers. "Tell me about yourself!" an interviewer demands with a menacing grin. If you haven't thought about the question, it may stump you. What is the interviewer really looking for? What should you say about yourself? How long should you talk? How on earth can you distill your life into a single coherent answer?

But even if you haven't anticipated the question, you really have given it a substantial amount of thought. As you've completed the lengthy process of introspection set forth in this book, you may have come to know yourself—and your values, skills, and needs—better now than at any time in years. If you've recently lost a job, you've dealt with difficult emotions and weathered a real psychological storm. You've investigated your past as you've listed career accomplishments and prepared your résumé. You've anticipated your future by considering your personal and professional needs. You've identified the principal sources of satisfaction and dissatisfaction in your life.

You may even have practiced your answer. As you've built your personal contact network, you've undoubtedly been describing yourself to the people you've met. You probably refined your comments in each subsequent meeting, distilling your responses as you learned what was most persuasive and what seemed to miss the point. As you discovered what worked and what didn't, you became more confident with your answers and more comfortable in your discussions.

Now, as you prepare for formal selection interviews, you can adapt several activities from this comprehensive process to improve your performance during job interviews. Specifically, you can:

- anticipate questions,
- prepare answers, and
- practice, practice, practice.

A job interview is typically a planned event in which the interviewer seeks to obtain various kinds of information about the candidate. This data doesn't change a great deal from one interview to another. As a result, the questions are fairly predictable, and preparing in advance can remove much of the uncertainty from the actual interview situation. If you have a good idea beforehand of the questions that are likely to be asked, you needn't be caught flat-footed, without any response or rambling on incoherently as you search for an acceptable answer.

Having prepared your answers, you can practice them so that you will respond confidently and concisely in a real interview. This practice can include not only what you say but also the manner in which you present yourself and the way you deliver your answers.

Anticipation

Think back to your school days. Didn't you imagine how nice life would be if only you knew the questions on the next day's test? Here's your chance.

A good interview is not a haphazard event. A competent interviewer will have planned the occasion carefully, dividing the interview into sections, preparing questions to be asked in each segment and, in general, orchestrating the affair so that a variety of predetermined subjects and lines of inquiry will be covered in detail.

A Model Interview

To discuss this topic, we'll draw from an interview model created for Drake Beam Morin by Henry Morgan and John Cogger.[1] Not all interviewers show such professional preparation, but almost any hiring discussion will touch on many of the subjects described

1. Morgan and Cogger's *The Interviewer's Manual,* published by Drake Beam Morin, investigates the ways professional interviewers plan and conduct interviews in greater detail than we mention here. For information on how to obtain a copy, contact Drake Beam Morin, Inc., 100 Park Avenue, New York, NY 10017.

below. In general, the better trained the interviewer, the more closely the interview will approximate this format.

Morgan and Cogger divide their model interview into six general sections: an introduction, a section on work experience, questions about education, a discussion of present activities and interests, a summary of strengths and shortcomings, and a brief period of closing remarks.

The Introduction. The introductory section of the interview begins, understandably enough, with a greeting. A good interviewer acts like a gracious host, introducing himself and offering a cordial greeting and firm handshake. This begins to establish the warm relationship that marks superior interviews, as the interviewer attempts to reduce anxiety and characterize the session as a friendly, rather than an adversarial, event. The effective interviewer's greeting is genuine, not contrived. He knows that an insincere atmosphere can cripple the confident exchange of information that is the basis of a productive interview.

Next the interviewer devotes a few moments to small talk. If he notices on your résumé that you're interested in sports, he might discuss a recent event. If he's acquainted with people at one of the companies you've worked for in the past, he may try to discover whether you have friends in common. This part of the interview is also designed to reduce the tensions that are natural to the situation. During the warm-up period, the interviewer phrases his questions so that you do most of the talking. He realizes that the simple act of hearing your own voice can relax you and make you feel less self-conscious.

Once the conversation appears to be flowing smoothly, the interviewer moves on to the next section of the interview with one or two opening questions. These initial queries may explore your expectations about the job, or they may deal with events that led to the interview. The questions can range from the ubiquitous "Tell me about yourself" to one or more of the following possibilities:

- What's been your contact with our organization?
- What do you know about this job and this company?
- How did you become interested in this job?

- What's your understanding of the purpose of this interview?
- Tell me, what led up to your coming to see me today?

The interviewer uses your answers to determine whether you and he are operating from the same set of assumptions about the purpose of the interview. He either confirms or attempts to alter your expectations so that you and he establish a joint goal for the meeting.

While this part of the interview seeks to relax you and set the stage for questions to come, it also addresses several important priorities. In the opening moments, the interviewer is likely to watch you and interpret your initial responses in an attempt to draw conclusions about your appearance and general manner, your skills for self-expression, and your responsiveness to the situation. Right from the start, he begins to form an impression.

In fact, many people argue that the most critical portion of an interview is the first five minutes. The interviewer has already seen your résumé. He may have talked to a search firm representative about you. If this isn't your initial interview with the organization, he may have discussed you with other people in the firm. So he knows a substantial amount about you before you've even walked into his office. Now, beginning with the first handshake, he's looking carefully to see how you handle yourself.

As the interviewer begins the body of the interview, he may say something like:

> Let's talk about your background and experience. If I get to know you well—both what you've done and what you hope to do— we can judge whether there are opportunities in our organization suited to your talents and interests. I'd like to hear about your jobs and schooling, your hobbies and interests, and anything else you'd like to tell or ask me. Perhaps the best place to start is with your work experience.

This opening recognizes the fact that a good interview is a shared discussion. The interviewer expects to find out certain things about you, and he understands that you expect to find out certain things about the organization.

Work Experience. Next, the interviewer begins his questions about your work experience. In this section of the interview—as in each subsequent area of inquiry—he is likely to begin with a prepared "lead" question. These questions announce clearly and briefly what he expects to discuss in the particular interview segment. The lead question in the section about work experience might be:

> Tell me about the jobs you've held, what your duties and responsibilities were, and what you liked or didn't like about them. I'm also interested in your level of earnings, any special achievements you may have had, and what you think you gained from these jobs.
>
> Let's begin with your earliest jobs—those you may have had after school or during summer vacations. What do you remember about your very first job?

From these early jobs, the interviewer will proceed to details about your military service (if applicable), to the full-time positions you have held, and to volunteer work you have done. As he probes your career, he'll draw from an arsenal of specific questions:

- What things did you do best in that job?
- What things did you do less well?
- What things did you like best there?
- What did you dislike?
- What were your major achievements in that position?
- How did you achieve them?
- What were the most difficult problems you faced?
- How did you deal with them?
- In what ways do you think you were most effective with people there?
- Were there ways in which you were less effective?
- What was your level of earnings?
- What did you learn from that work experience?
- What were you looking for in that job?
- What are you looking for in your career?
- What are your short- and long-term goals?

The interviewer is unlikely to ask all these questions about each job you've held. Some may not be raised at all. But if he is a good interviewer, he'll ask questions like these to determine how your work history can be related to the job being discussed. Is what you've done in the past relevant to this job? Has your work experience given you sufficient expertise for it? Do you seem to possess the skills and competence called for by this position?

He'll also be evaluating your adaptability, productivity, and apparent motivation. He'll consider your leadership qualities, and he may try to assess the degree of growth and development that has characterized your career.

Education. The next topic in the model interview is education. Here, the lead question might be:

> You've given me a good picture of your work experience. Now let's discuss your education. I'd like to know a little about your early schooling and then, of course, more about your more recent education, including any specialized training you've had. I'm interested in such things as the subjects you preferred, those you didn't like, as well as your grades, the extracurricular activities you were involved in, and any special recognition you received. Let's begin with your earliest schooling. What was it like?

In this section, the interviewer might refer all the way back to your elementary schooling, then spend somewhat more time talking about your high school and college years, and conclude the section by investigating specialized training you may have received or recent courses you have taken. He may ask such questions as:

- What were your best subjects?
- In which subjects did you do less well?
- What subjects did you like most?
- Which did you like least?
- How did you feel about your teachers?
- What kinds of grades did you receive?
- How much effort did you put into getting them?
- What were some of the reasons for choosing that school?
- What was your major field there?
- What special accomplishments did you record?

- What were the toughest problems you faced?
- What extracurricular activities did you engage in?
- How did you finance your education?
- How do you think your education relates to your career?
- How do you feel about further schooling or specialized training?

As he asks these questions and considers your answers, the interviewer thinks in terms of the relevance of your education to the job. He considers the sufficiency of your schooling and tries to take some measure of your intellectual abilities. He looks at the breadth and depth of your knowledge and the level of accomplishment you achieved during your school years. He considers versatility, motivation, and specific interests. He may try to determine how your education might affect the way you react to authority, and he may also think about leadership qualities and teamwork abilities.

Activities and Interests. The next part of the model interview is devoted to present activities and interests. This is often considered an optional topic, as many organizations are not too interested in hobbies or leisure pursuits. In any event, this sort of personal information is only relevant if it can be related to the job under discussion. The lead question might be:

> We've talked about your work and schooling. Now let's talk about your leisure activities—your interests and hobbies. What do you do for fun and recreation, either on your own or with others?

Here the interviewer covers special interests and hobbies, as well as civic and community affairs that might be relevant to the job. He may discuss issues related to your health and energy, and he could use this section to ask about your geographical preferences. His questions may include:

- What kinds of things do you like to do in your spare time?
- To what extent are you involved in your community?
- Do you have any health problems that might affect your job performance?
- What would be your reaction to relocating?

- How do you feel about business travel?
- Can you think of any circumstances that might influence your job performance?

As he asks these questions, the interviewer looks for such things as vitality, maturity, and good judgment. He is interested in determining how well you manage your time, your energy, and even your money. He is concerned about intellectual growth, cultural breadth, and the diversity of your interests. He thinks in terms of the social effectiveness of how you act and what you do outside your job. He may use the questions to assess interpersonal skills and interests, your sense of leadership, even your basic values and goals as they are reflected in your leisure activities.

Strengths and Shortcomings. Next the interviewer moves to one of the most important parts of the interview, a summary of strengths and shortcomings. He may divide this discussion into two parts, and he will probably begin each with a lead question. He starts with your strengths:

> Now let's try to summarize our discussion. As you think about what we've covered, what would you say are some of your chief strengths? What are some of the assets that would make you a good prospect for any employer?

Specific questions could include:

- What do you bring to a job?
- What are your main assets?
- What do you think your major talents are?
- What outstanding qualities do you see in yourself or do others see in you?
- What makes you a good investment for an employer?

Then the interviewer moves to the other side of the subject, perhaps with the aid of this lead question:

> You've shown me some real strengths. Now, what about some of your qualities that aren't so strong? All of us have a few areas we'd like to improve in. In the past you may have had constructive criti-

cism from friends, supervisors, or other people who've come to know you well. Thinking of the future, what areas or what personal qualities need improvement for you to be fully effective in your job or career?

The specific questions here might include:

- What are some of your shortcomings or limitations?
- What areas do you think you should improve?
- What qualities would you like to develop further?
- What kinds of constructive criticism have you received from others?
- How might you be a risk to an employer?
- What kind of further training or experience do you think you might need?

As he asks you both sets of questions, the interviewer weighs apparent strengths against apparent weaknesses and asks himself three additional questions. First, *can* this person do the job? (Do you have the talents, skills, knowledge, and energy for the position?) Second, *will* this person do the job? (Do your interests and motivation mesh with the requirements of the position?) Third, how will this person fit in? (Will your personal qualities, character, and apparent effectiveness in social settings fit the organization's style?)

Closing Remarks. The final section of the interview is devoted to closing remarks. Here a likely lead question might be:

> You've given me a good review of your background and experience. I've enjoyed talking with you, and I appreciate your sharing this information with me. It will be of considerable value as we make our decision. Before we close, is there anything else you would like to cover? What questions would you like to ask about the job, our organization, or anything else?

The interviewer invites a dialogue in this last part of the interview, answering your questions, reviewing the job and the opportunities it offers, perhaps even trying to sell you on the organization. He also identifies further contacts you should make with the

286   *Parting Company*

organization and outlines the next steps to be taken. Finally, he offers a cordial parting, and the interview is over.

This model presents a particularly thorough selection interview. Most are not likely to be so comprehensive or intense. No one can promise that you'll run into skilled interviewers everywhere you go. A trained personnel manager or human resources management executive may be expected to go into this sort of detail, taking you all the way back to your early days in school, for example, but it is less likely that a potential boss or immediate superior will take the time, or possess the interviewing expertise, to conduct this complete an interview. But if you prepare for this in-depth interview experience, you'll probably succeed at any interview.

Types of Interviews

There are four general types of interviews you can expect to encounter as you move closer to a particular job: screening, in-depth, multiple (or "beauty parade"), and final. Each seeks to develop a somewhat different set of information, and each is likely to be conducted somewhat differently than the others.

The Screening Interview. Typically, the screening interview, the first in the series, is conducted by a member of the organization's human resources management or personnel department. This individual cannot possibly know enough of the details about every specific position in the organization to be able to match an individual's precise qualifications to the exact demands of each job. But he or she can and will reach conclusions about the candidate's general experience. The interviewer will attempt to decide whether the person has the right personality for the job and the organization. He or she will identify strong and weak points and, assessing them, compare and perhaps rank the individual with others being considered for the position.

Don't underestimate the importance of the screening interview. It's particularly unwise to assume that you can breeze through it and begin to take things seriously when you get to the "real" boss. If you approach a screening interview in anything but a serious and well-prepared frame of mind, the chances are that you'll never get to see that "real" boss.

The In-Depth Interview. If you perform well in the screening interview, you will be invited back for an in-depth interview, which is normally conducted by the functional head or line manager in your discipline. This interview is overwhelmingly task-oriented. The manager is likely to get right down to business. He needs to satisfy himself that you know what you're talking about. The interview concentrates on the specific dimensions of the job, and the interviewer tries to find out how well you fit them. Because you and this interviewer are likely to share a great deal of job-related knowledge, this interview normally moves quickly. The interviewer grasps the points you make as readily as you understand the questions that are asked. The discussion focuses both on your technical expertise (specific job-oriented skills and experience) and on interpersonal skills.

In some situations, the order of the screening and in-depth interviews may be reversed. If you are being considered for a high-level position, for instance, you may speak first with the functional superior and later, if all goes well, be asked to meet with a representative of the personnel or human resources staff.

The Multiple Interview. Since many organizations look for consensus before hiring people, successful completion of the first two rounds in the interview process is likely to result in a series of multiple interviews which are often collectively referred to as a "beauty parade." In these interviews, you meet a number of people from the department or area in which you would work, individuals from higher levels, perhaps, as well as some of those who would be your peers and subordinates within the organization. In small companies, these interviews might be scheduled with people throughout the firm.

You may be asked to take part in a series of short private interviews with each individual, or you might find yourself sharing lunch with a small group of people. Because they are often relaxed and unstructured affairs, these interviews can be deadly. Capable individuals have talked themselves out of good jobs by making unguarded or inappropriate comments. Anything you say in an interview is likely to be scrutinized. Welcome an interview conducted in a relaxed atmosphere, but don't be lulled into making ill-considered remarks.

The Final Interview. If you pass this round of interviews, you're probably very close to landing the job and will be asked back for a final interview. Loose ends may be wrapped up at this time, and an offer may be made to you.

In addition to these four general types of interviews, you may encounter other formats. You could be asked to a psychological interview, for instance, and spend some time talking with a psychologist from the organization. You may be able to gain an interesting perspective about the job by asking this professional for his or her observations about the organization.

In general, of course, the more interviews you take, the better your chances of landing the job. Not only does being asked back indicate that the company continues to be interested in you, but, as you talk to more people there, you improve your ability to make a good decision about whether the job suits your skills and needs.

The Stress Interview. There is one kind of interview that you certainly don't want to be asked to complete: the stress interview. Once quite fashionable, the stress interview has gone out of fashion more recently. But there are undoubtedly some people who continue to believe that, because anxiety and stress are part of any demanding job, it may be a good idea to create stress in interviews to test the reactions of candidates. If a job involves selling a product to difficult customers, for instance, why not see how well the candidate can sell himself to a hostile interviewer?

There are several problems with this approach. First, creating stress in an interview is usually counterproductive. The candidate becomes defensive and resistant. The information that is elicited is limited and less candid than it would be in a more congenial atmosphere. A principle of the model interview presented earlier is that it seeks to reduce anxiety between the interviewer and the candidate, as that tends to be the most effective way to produce the greatest amount of useful information.

Stress interviews may provoke complaints of unfair selection procedures. And since the selection interview often sets a precedent for the future relationship between employer and employee, a stress interview has the potential to create the undesirable situation in which a new employee starts a job full of hostile feelings for the company.

Finally, since stress encountered on the job is usually different from that which can be created in an interview, a stress interview may not even be effective in determining a candidate's ability to deal with difficult work situations. It is much more productive to review the person's past behavior and attitudes about working under stress to discover this information.

How do you know if you've landed in a stress interview? The interviewer might not look at you but instead stare out the window throughout the discussion. You might give a careful answer to a straightforward question, only to have the interviewer respond, "No, no, you missed the point entirely." An interviewer might ask embarrassing personal questions.

In a discussion of strengths and weaknesses, it is perfectly proper for an interviewer to ask about shortcomings. But if the interview begins with the question, "What gives you the idea that you're good enough for this job?" then you're most likely in for a difficult session.

To deal with a stress interview, meet the situation head-on. Let the interviewer know that you know what is taking place. Do not, under any circumstances, sit and try to answer demeaning questions. Don't put up with impolite behavior. If the interviewer is obviously trying to goad you by contesting your answers or actively trying to make you uncomfortable, consider leaving the interview. You might say, "Look, there's a lot I'd like to find out about this company, and I'm sure there's a lot you'd like to learn about me. If you can't cooperate with me on that, I think we should end this interview. If you're trying to determine whether I can deal with aggressive situations, the answer is yes, but if you think such an aggressive approach will produce an effective interview, I can't agree with you."

The interviewer will most likely drop the pose and continue the interview on more considerate terms. You'll have shown that you can deal with aggression, and will have passed the test.

But even if you do pass, remember that an organization using stress interview techniques is likely to have an extremely aggressive management style. Ask yourself whether you really want to get involved with such a company. If you're an aggressive person yourself, a stress interview might not bother you at all, and the organization's style might be well suited to your own. You may even feel challenged by the situation. But be honest with yourself.

We recall one instance in which a job candidate created his own stress situation. He was being interviewed for a job as a corporate labor negotiator. The interviewer, a member of the company's personnel department, was probing into his shortcomings and weaknesses. The man answered, "I'm a labor relations expert, I have a great deal of experience, I get the job done, and I won't answer that question."

When the interviewer reported back to the vice president of labor relations the next day, he gave the man a negative appraisal. But when the vice president learned the details of the encounter, he contacted the candidate for another interview and ultimately offered him the job. That kind of behavior was exactly what he was looking for. He needed someone who wasn't afraid to say no and who wouldn't avoid taking an unpopular stand in a difficult negotiation.

There is obviously a substantial amount of risk involved in this approach, however. Unless you really crave stress situations (and some people honestly do), you would be well-advised to avoid creating them and to refuse to put up with them in interviews.

Preparing Answers

As we've indicated, most interviews are conducted along more positive and supportive lines. You don't have to worry too greatly about being bushwhacked. But, at the same time, you must realize that it is the interviewer's job to discover just how effective you might be in a specific position. To be objective and impartial, he or she will give you every opportunity to prove yourself or to hang yourself. While a relaxed atmosphere promotes open communication, it can also lull you into lowering your guard and saying something you hadn't intended to say. Always think before you speak.

You can start this thought process by taking the questions that are likely to be asked and preparing solid answers for them. You'll need to be able to answer what are often intricate questions articulately and convincingly. You need to appear knowledgeable and enthusiastic about the organization and, of course, about yourself as well.

In this section, we'll present a number of questions that are often asked in interviews. Many of them give you a chance to plant a foot firmly in your mouth. By preparing answers before you get into an interview, you can substantially reduce the likelihood of making this sort of misstep. As we pose each question, we'll offer suggestions that may help you prepare answers.

When you've worked your way through these questions, go back to the model interview and try to prepare answers for those questions as well. The more subjects you can discuss intelligently in an interview, the less likely you are to be unpleasantly surprised.

Before you begin, consider a few general guidelines. First, make your answers as brief and concise as you can. Don't ramble. Don't over-elaborate. When you've answered the question, stop talking.

Most people worry that they won't find enough to say during an interview. Often, the exact opposite occurs: people continue to talk long after they have answered the question. This is often caused by simple nervousness. Someone feeling tense may speak quickly and race through a number of topics, hoping sooner or later to touch on something the interviewer will appreciate. Sometimes candidates simply assume that their role in an interview is to talk, and if they aren't speaking constantly, they aren't doing their job. It's astonishing to learn how often interviewers sum up unfortunate sessions with the lament, "If he'd only shut up sooner."

Second, as you prepare your answers, use positive terms whenever you can. Don't talk about a "problem." Call it a challenge or an opportunity instead.

Third, do your homework on the company. Tailor your answers to the apparent needs of the organization. Use specific details to show how you can help the potential employer. Whenever they are available, get annual reports and 10-K statements for the companies you interview. Talk to people who work for, sell to, or are in any way involved with the organization. If you've worked through a search firm to land the interview, ask the search executive for information about and impressions of the company.

Not only will this investigating help you prepare specific responses, but it will also help you answer an important question of your own: is this the right job with the right organization? You'll want to impress the interviewer, but you deserve to be impressed as well.

Finally, as you consider these questions, you may wish to make notes or jot down phrases to remind you of important points you wish to cover. Avoid writing out complete answers, however. It's important to appear spontaneous and enthusiastic in an interview, qualities that are difficult to achieve when you repeat memorized answers. If you're comfortable with main points and key phrases, you can tailor your exact responses to the specific conditions of the interview and to the personality of the interviewer.

HOW WILL I ANSWER THE DIFFICULT QUESTIONS?

Think about an appropriate response for each of the following questions. Make notes of the main points to remember or key phrases you will use if you're asked the question during an interview.

1. Tell me a little about yourself.

Because this is often the opening question in an interview, be very careful that you don't run off at the mouth. Keep your answer to a minute or two at most. Cover four topics: early years, education, work history, and recent career experience. Emphasize this last subject. Remember that this is just a warm-up question. Don't waste your best points on it.

_____

_____

2. What do you know about our organization?

You should be able to discuss products or services, revenues, reputation, image, goals, problems, management style, people, history, and philosophy. But don't act as if you know *everything* about the place. Let your answer show that you have taken the time to do some research, but don't try to overwhelm the interviewer, and make it clear that you wish to learn more.

Give your answer a positive tone. Don't say, "Well, everyone tells me that the company's in heaps of trouble, and that's why I'm here"—even if that *is* why you're there.

---

3. Why do you want to work for us?

The deadliest answer you can give is "Because I like people." What else would you like—animals?

Here, and throughout the interview, a good answer comes from having done your homework so you can speak in terms of the company's needs. You might say your research has shown that the company is doing things you would like to be involved with, and that it's doing them in ways that interest you. For example, if the organization is known for strong management, your answer should mention that fact and show that you would like to be a part of that team. If the company places a great deal of emphasis on research and development, emphasize the fact that you want to create new things and that you know this to be a place in which inventiveness is encouraged. If the organization stresses financial controls, your answer should mention a reverence for numbers.

If you feel that you have to concoct an answer to this question, then you probably shouldn't be taking the interview, because you probably shouldn't be considering a job with that organization. Your homework should include learning enough about the company to avoid approaching places where you wouldn't be able or wouldn't want to function.

4. What can you do for us that someone else can't?

Here you have every right, and perhaps obligation, to toot your own horn and be a bit egotistical. Talk about your record of getting things done, and mention specifics from your résumé or inventory of career accomplishments. Say that your skills and interests, combined with this history of getting results, make you valuable. Mention your ability to set priorities, identify problems, and use your experience and energy to solve them.

_____

_____

5. What do you find most attractive about this position? What seems least attractive about it?

List three or four attractive features of the job, and mention a single, minor, unattractive item.

_____

_____

6. Why should we hire you?

Create your answer by thinking in terms of your ability, your experience, and your energy. (See Question 4.)

_____

_____

7. What do you look for in a job?

Keep your answer oriented to opportunities at the organization. Talk about your desire to perform and be recognized for your contributions. Orient your answer toward opportunities rather than personal security.

_____

_____

8. Please give me your definition of (the position for which you are being interviewed).

Keep your answer brief and task-oriented. Think in terms of responsibilities and accountability. Make sure that you really do understand what the position involves before you attempt an answer. If you aren't certain, ask the interviewer; he or she may answer the question for you.

---

9. How long would it take you to make a meaningful contribution to our firm?

Be realistic. Say that, while you would expect to meet pressing demands and pull your own weight from the first day, it might take six months to a year before you could expect to know the organization and its needs well enough to make a major contribution.

---

10. How long would you stay with us?

Say that you are interested in a career with the organization, but admit that you would have to continue to feel challenged to remain with any organization. Think in terms of "As long as we both feel achievement-oriented."

---

11. Your résumé suggests that you may be overqualified or too experienced for this position. What do you think?

Emphasize your interest in establishing a long-term association with the organization, and say that you assume that if you perform well in this job, new opportunities will open up for you.

Mention that a strong company needs a strong staff. Observe that experienced individuals are always at a premium. Suggest that because you are so well qualified, the company will get a fast return on its investment. Say that a growing, energetic company can never have too much talent.

---

12. What is your management style?

You should know enough about the company's style to know that your management style will complement it. Possible styles include: task-oriented ("I enjoy problem solving, identifying what's wrong, choosing a solution, and implementing it"); or results-oriented ("Every decision I make is determined by how it will affect the bottom line"). The participative style is also popular: an open-door method of managing in which you get things done by motivating people and delegating responsibility.

As you consider this question, think about whether your style will let you work happily and effectively within the organization.

---

13. Are you a good manager? Can you give me some examples? Do you feel that you have top-management potential?

Keep your answer achievement- and task-oriented. Rely on examples from your career to support your statements. Stress your experience and your energy.

---

14. What do you look for when you hire people?

Think in terms of skills, initiative, and the adaptability to be able to work comfortably and productively with others. Mention that you like to hire people who appear capable of moving up in an organization.

---

15. Have you ever had to fire people? What were the reasons, and how did you handle the situation?

Admit that the situation wasn't easy, but say that it worked out well, both for the company and, you think, for the individual or individuals involved. Show that, like anyone else, you don't enjoy unpleasant tasks but that you can resolve them efficiently and, in the case of firing someone, humanely.

---

16. What do you think is the most difficult thing about being a manager or executive?

Mention planning, execution, and cost control. The most difficult task may be to motivate and manage employees to get tasks routinely planned and completed on time and within budget.

---

17. What important trends do you see in our industry?

Be prepared with two or three trends that illustrate how well you understand your industry. You might consider technological challenges or opportunities, economic conditions, the current competitive situation, or even regulatory demands related to the direction in which your business is heading.

---

18. What are the frontier or cutting-edge issues in our industry?

Be prepared with two or three key issues.

_____

_____

19. Why are you leaving (did you leave) your present (last) position?

Be brief, to the point, and as honest as you can without hurting yourself. Refer back to the planning phase of your job search, where you considered this topic as you thought about reference statements. If you were laid off in a staff reduction, say so; otherwise, indicate that the move was your decision, the result of your desire to advance in your career. Don't mention personality conflicts.

The interviewer may spend some time probing you on this issue, particularly if it's clear that you were terminated. Be as positive and honest as you can. The "We agreed to disagree" approach suggested earlier may be useful. Don't fabricate a story for an interview: even in today's reference-shy climate, your story might be checked.

_____

_____

20. In your current (last) position, what features do (did) you like the most? The least?

Be careful and be positive. Describe more features that you liked than disliked. Don't cite personality problems. If you make your last job sound terrible, an interviewer may wonder why you've remained there until now, or whether you have an attitude problem that would be likely to show up in a new job, too.

_____

_____

21. In your current (last) position, what have been (were) your five most significant accomplishments?

Have specific examples ready. If you're asked for five examples, don't cite ten. If you want to show that you were responsible for more than five major achievements, you can say, "I've given you the five that seem most important to me. There are others, if you'd like to hear about some other area of my work." Then, if the interviewer asks for additional accomplishments, you can give them without appearing to boast.

22. Why haven't you found a new job before now?

Say that finding a job isn't difficult, but that finding the *right* job deserves time and demands careful planning.

23. Did you think of leaving your present position before? If so, what do you think held you there?

You might say that the challenge of the job held you in the past but, as that seemed to diminish, you reached the decision to investigate new opportunities.

24. What do you think of your (former) boss?

Be as positive as you can. A potential boss will anticipate that you might talk about him or her in similar terms at some point in the future.

25. Would you describe a few situations in which your work was criticized?

Be specific. Don't be emotional. Think in terms of constructive criticism. Show that you responded positively and benefited from the criticism.

_____

_____

26. If I spoke with your (former) boss, what would he or she say are your greatest strengths and weaknesses?

Name three or four strengths and only one weakness. Be honest but not negative.

_____

_____

27. Can you work under pressure and deal with deadlines?

Observe that both are facts of business life. Take examples from your list of accomplishments to show how you have dealt successfully with pressure and deadlines in the past.

_____

_____

28. Did you change the nature of your job?

Tell how you improved it.

_____

_____

29. Do you prefer staff or line work?

Say that it depends on the job and its challenges.

_____

_____

30. In your present (last) position, what problems did you identify that had previously been overlooked?

Be brief and don't brag. Indicate the positive changes your suggestions or leadership resulted in.

---

31. Don't you think you might be better suited to a different size company? To a different type of company?

Tailor your answer to the job being discussed. Say that your preferences for size or type of company generally depend on the job in question. Note that your research has shown you that this organization and this job meet your criteria.

---

32. If you could choose any job at any company, where would you go?

Talk about the job and company for which you are being interviewed.

---

33. Why aren't you earning more at your age?

Say that this is one reason why you're conducting this job search. Don't be defensive.

---

34. What do you feel this position should pay?

Salary is a delicate topic. We suggest that you defer tying yourself to a precise figure for as long as you can do so politely.

You might say, "I understand that the range for this job is between $X and $Y. That seems appropriate for the job as I understand it." You might answer the question with a question: "Perhaps you can help me on this one. Can you tell me if there is a range for similar jobs in the organization?"

If you're asked the question during an initial screening interview, you might say that you feel you need to know more about the responsibilities involved before giving a meaningful answer. Here too, either by asking the interviewer or doing research during your investigation of the company, you can try to find out whether there is a salary grade attached to the job. If there is, and if you can live with it, say that the range seems right to you.

If the interviewer continues to probe, you might say, "You know that I'm making $X now. Like everyone else, I'd like to improve on that figure, but my major interest is in the job itself." Remember that the act of taking a new job does not, in and of itself, make you worth more money.

If a search firm is involved, your contact there may be able to help with the salary question. A search firm representative may even be able to run interference for you. If, for instance, this person tells you what the position pays, and you respond that you are earning that amount now and would like to do a bit better, he or she might go back to the employer and propose that you be offered an additional ten percent.

If no price range is attached to the job, and the interviewer continues to press the subject, then you will have to respond with a number. You can't leave the impression that it doesn't really matter, that you'll accept whatever is offered. If you've been making $96,000 annually, you can't say that a $42,000 figure would be fine without sounding as if you've given up on yourself. (If you're making a radical career change, however, a substantial disparity may be more reasonable and understandable.)

Don't sell yourself short, but continue to stress the fact that the job itself is the most important thing in your mind. The interviewer may be trying to determine just how much you want the job. Don't leave the impression that money is the only thing that is important to you. Link questions of salary to the work itself.

But, whenever possible, say as little as you can about salary until you reach the final stage of the interviewing process. At that point, you know the company is genuinely interested in you and that it is more likely to be flexible in salary negotiations. For more information on this subject, refer to Chapter 18.

_____

_____

35. Do you have any objections to psychological tests?

Say you would feel comfortable taking them.

_____

_____

36. What other jobs or companies are you considering?

Restrict your answer to fields that are similar to the one in which this company operates.

_____

_____

37. Do you speak to people before they speak to you?

The interviewer is probably trying to determine your ability to deal with unstable or unanticipated situations. Say that your actions depend on specific circumstances. While you wouldn't normally start a conversation with a stranger in the street, for example, you feel comfortable initiating discussions with people you don't know in normal business or social settings.

_____

_____

38. What was the last book you read? Movie you saw? Sporting event you attended?

Try to show that you lead a balanced life when answering questions about outside activities.

_____

_____

39. Will you be out to take your boss's job?

Say that while you certainly hope to win additional responsibility in the organization, you've always focused on getting the current job done.

_____

_____

40. Are you creative?

Be prepared with work-related examples of creativity.

_____

_____

41. How would you describe your own personality?

It may be wise to say that you're the proud owner of a balanced personality.

_____

_____

42. Do you consider yourself a leader?

Take examples from your work experience.

_____

_____

43. What are your long-range goals?

Refer back to the self-assessment phase of your career continuation efforts. Don't answer, "I want the job you've advertised." Relate your goals to the company you're interviewing for: "In a firm like yours, I would like to . . ."

---

44. What are your strong points?

Present at least three. Use concrete, work-related examples to illustrate them. Try to relate your answer to the interviewing organization and the specific job opening.

---

45. What are your weak points?

Don't say that you have none. But try to make a negative sound like a strength carried just a bit too far: "I sometimes get impatient and become too deeply involved when a project is running late."

Don't offer a list of weaknesses. A good interviewer is likely to press you a bit by saying, "Is there anything else?" You might answer, "No, I don't think so on that topic." If the interviewer persists, come up with a second weakness, but only if you are asked for it. Don't offer negative information unnecessarily. If the interviewer continues on and asks for a third weakness, say politely that you really can't think of anything else.

Finally, show that you are working to correct your weaknesses.

---

46. If you could start your career again, what would you do differently?

The best answer is, "Not a thing." You should try to present yourself as an individual who is happy with his or her life. You've enjoyed its ups and learned from its downs. You would not, as a result, want to change the things that brought you to where you are today. Mention that it is your past, after all, that has prepared you for this position.

_____

_____

47. What career options do you have at this moment?

You should try to identify three areas of interest, one of which includes this company and job. The other two should be in related fields.

_____

_____

48. How would you define success?

Think in terms of a sense of well-being. Consider opportunity and responsibility as components of success.

_____

_____

49. How successful do you think you've been so far?

Say that, all in all, you're happy with the way your career has progressed. Given the normal ups and downs of life, you feel that you've done quite well and expect to continue to succeed in the future.

Present a positive and confident picture of yourself, but don't overstate your case. An answer like "Everything's wonderful; I'm overjoyed!" is likely to make an interviewer wonder whether you're trying to fool him or yourself. The most convincing confidence is usually quiet confidence.

"I Speak Your Language"

When we introduced this list of questions, we suggested that, although it's a good idea to jot down key words or phrases as you prepare answers, it's probably unwise to write out complete responses. Our point was that if you appear too well prepared, you may sound mechanical in an actual interview. There is another reason to avoid casting your answers in stone: the need to remain flexible and adaptable.

Since no two people are exactly alike, no two interviewers are the same. Each is likely to interpret your answers and assess your abilities in terms of his or her own experience and personality. In fact, trained interviewers learn that the only way to conduct objective and impartial interviews is to take into account their own subjectivity in the process.

So while you should give careful thought and preparation to the content of your answers, you should also try to remain flexible in responding to a specific interviewer's personal style.

Most of us react instinctively to obvious manifestations of personal style. If an interviewer fidgets, frowns, and looks away, we may equate her impatience with a need to get to the point, and be more direct in our answers. If she looks at her watch, we assume she has a limited amount of time to spend with us and react accordingly. If, on the other hand, she leans back in her chair, spends more than a few minutes engaging in small talk, and seems in no hurry at all, then we may guess that she wants to move slowly, methodically, and intensively through the interview. We adapt to her pace. (This should not, however, be considered an invitation to ramble.)

Our reactions to style go well beyond these responses to body language. From our earliest years when, for instance, we learned that what works with a father does not always work with a mother, we tailor our actions and reactions to specific situations and differing individual needs.

At Drake Beam Morin we've developed a communications system based on a study of personal styles. We call our system "I Speak Your Language," and we've found it to be an extremely useful tool, both in job interviews and in a variety of other work-related and personal situations. It helps people understand how others act and react, both in normal circumstances and under stress conditions.

Drawn from psychological theories developed by Carl Jung, "I Speak" is based on four major personality styles that individuals adopt in their characteristic approach to work and life. Each style is associated with a predominant behavioral function:

Style	Function
Senser	Relating to experience through sensory perceptions
Feeler	Relating to experience via emotional reactions
Thinker	Analyzing, ordering
Intuitor	Conceiving, projecting, inducing

Sensers are present-oriented. They respond to things they can feel and touch. They are the "doers" in our world.

Feelers rely on emotions, on gut feelings. They thrive on human contact and enjoy people.

Thinkers are logical, systematic, orderly, and structured. They are data-oriented.

Intuitors look to the future. They are concerned with planning and setting goals.

Most people blend all four of these styles together, with one or two styles being characteristically more prominent. These are called their *dominant* and *secondary* styles. No one uses a single style in a vacuum. To place too much emphasis on one style, therefore, is to deal in stereotypes. But understanding an individual's dominant style can supply fascinating clues and insights about his or her actions and reactions.

WHAT'S MY "I SPEAK YOUR LANGUAGE" STYLE?

Answering the following questions will provide a sketch of your "I Speak" style.

Instructions: For each self-descriptive statement, rank the four listed endings. 4 = most like you; 3 = a lot like you; 2 = somewhat like you; 1 = least like you.

1. I am likely to impress others as:
____a. practical and to the point
____b. emotional and stimulating
____c. astute and logical
____d. intellectually oriented and complex

2. When I work on a project, I
____a. want it to be stimulating and involve lively interaction with others
____b. concentrate to make sure it is systematically or logically developed
____c. want to be sure it has tangible "pay out" that will justify my time/ energy
____d. am most concerned about whether it breaks ground or advances knowledge

3. When I think about a job problem, I usually
____a. think about concepts and relationships between events
____b. analyze what preceded and what I plan next
____c. remain open and responsive to my feelings about the matter
____d. concentrate on reality, as things are right now

4. When confronted by others with a different point of view, I can usually make progress by
____a. getting at least 1 or 2 specific commitments on which we can later build
____b. trying to place myself in the other person's shoes
____c. keeping my composure and helping others to see things simply and logically
____d. relying on my basic ability to conceptualize and pull ideas together

---

1. "I Speak Your Language: A Survey of Personal Styles" © 1972 by Drake Beam Morin, Inc.

5. When communicating to others, I may
_____a. express unintended boredom with talk that is too impersonal
_____b. convey impatience with those who express ideas that they obviously have not thought through carefully
_____c. show little interest in thoughts and ideas that exhibit little or no originality
_____d. tend to ignore those who talk about long-range implications and instead direct my attention to what needs to be done now

ANALYSIS OF ANSWERS

To determine your dominant communication style, enter your rankings for each question.

	Intuitor	Thinker	Feeler	Senser
Question 1	_____	_____	_____	_____
	d	c	b	a
Question 2	_____	_____	_____	_____
	d	b	a	c
Question 3	_____	_____	_____	_____
	a	b	c	d
Question 4	_____	_____	_____	_____
	d	c	b	a
Question 5	_____	_____	_____	_____
	c	b	a	d
TOTALS	_____	_____	_____	_____

The column with the highest total indicates your favored communication style. The next highest column represents your secondary style. The column with the lowest total is your least used style.

In an interview, insights into communication styles can help an individual communicate more effectively with an interviewer and make the parties more comfortable with each other. The interviewer has a better chance of gaining the necessary information, and the candidate is able to present his or her case as effectively as possible.

As soon as you enter an interviewer's office, you can begin to look for clues to his or her communication style. First, look at the person's desk.

A *senser's* desk is likely to be cluttered and disorderly.

A *feeler's* desk may be covered with personal memorabilia: family photographs, vacation souvenirs, even a sports trophy.

A *thinker's* desk is likely to be neat and orderly. You'll probably find a calculator on it or a computer nearby.

An *intuitor* commonly has books and reports piled on his or her desk. These materials may be organized into two stacks for the purpose of comparison. Look for scholarly publications.

Next, you can scan the office itself.

The *senser's* office is likely to be a mess. The floor and bookcases may be cluttered with books and reports. If there is art on the wall, it's likely to be action-oriented—a sailing scene, perhaps.

The *feeler's* office is personalized. The walls may be adorned with family photos or community- and company-oriented mementos.

The *thinker's* surroundings are likely to be neat and simple, even sterile. Look for charts on the walls and stacks of computer printouts in the bookcase.

An *intuitor's* office may have abstract art on its walls. The books in the bookcase are likely to have theoretical titles.

Third, you can observe the interviewer's dress style.

Most *sensers* dress simply, but many are too busy to be very neat. Male sensers are likely to have their jackets off, ties loosened, and shirt sleeves rolled up. Female sensers are likely to dress casually.

Feelers tend to be extremely fashion-conscious. They favor colorful clothes. Look especially for interesting patterns in men's ties or striking women's styles.

Thinkers dress neatly and give careful consideration to color coordination. Men lean toward traditional dark business suits. Women may wear conservative suits.

Intuitors are not fashion-conscious. They may look suspiciously like an absentminded professor. They may wear remarkably unusual outfits.

Fourth, you can look for clues about communication style in the interviewer's opening questions.

The *senser* is likely to get right down to business and speak about problems and practical solutions.

The *feeler* may begin by focusing on your relationships with others or might ask whether you get personal satisfaction from your work. He or she may start the interview with a discussion of such diverse topics as family, hobbies, the weather, vacations, or new movies, and may digress at any point in the interview.

The *thinker* is interested in facts and figures. What was your college grade point average? How much did you save your last company?

The *intuitor* may try to tie your past to his or her future. Look for questions about your long-range goals and objectives.

Once you have a good idea of the interviewer's communication style, you can tailor your responses to meet his or her needs and expectations.

For example, since time is of the essence to the *senser,* don't ramble. You might ask how long the interviewer has to talk with you. Expect to be interrupted by telephone calls. Be concise, candid, and factual in your answers. Stress your problem-solving abilities. Talk about getting the job done.

The *feeler* is interested in interpersonal relationships, so stress your skills and interest in working with people. Take advantage of the digressions that are likely to occur during the interview. If you find that you share a common family or community interest with the interviewer, your position may be strengthened if you mention this common ground. Feelers often seem informal or even casual in interviews. Don't assume that this makes them pushovers. They are often the most exacting interviewers of all.

The *thinker* deals in well-ordered data, so stress facts and figures. You might lead the thinker step-by-step through your interview. He or she is likely to seem aloof, but don't take this to mean indifference. Be specific with your answers, and avoid digressions. Don't be emotional.

In an interview with an *intuitor,* stress the future. Ask questions about company goals. Try to link your job experience to the demands of the position you are discussing. Don't dwell on the past.

Suppose, for example, that you're in the middle of an interview and are asked the question, "Where do you see yourself going in the next two years?"

If you're talking to a *senser,* emphasize getting the current job done. "I want to grow with the company, but getting this job done would be my first priority."

Stress personal relationships with an interviewer who is a *feeler:* "My experiences with people have always been most fulfilling, and that makes me see myself doing . . ."

If a *thinker* asks the question, mention the past, present, and future: "Based on my experience, I'd want to take care of this assignment and then . . ."

With an *intuitor,* focus on the future: "As soon as I accomplish this task, I see myself moving forward to . . ."

The "I Speak" styles are useful guides.[1] But don't try to rely exclusively on them as judge and jury. Note also that any style can be used constructively or destructively. An intuitor may be original, or he may be unrealistic. A thinker can be prudent or gun-shy. Feelers can draw out the feelings of others, or they can stir up conflicts. Sensers may be pragmatic or shortsighted.

You must be the judge of the person beneath the style. If, for example, you are a senser and you run into an intuitor in an

1. Drake Beam Morin has developed a resource package of "I Speak Your Language" materials: a self-administered questionnaire that lets you investigate your own styles in greater detail than the short instrument reproduced in this chapter permits; a manual that explains the system and the four styles in detail; and a book of self-development exercises to sharpen your skills of identifying and dealing with the personal styles of others. For information on how to obtain this resource package, contact Drake Beam Morin, Inc., 100 Park Avenue, New York, NY 10017.

interview, he or she may seem entirely too impractical, out of
touch, or even devious for your practical, results-oriented style. If
this individual is an interviewer in the human resources department and you're a marketing manager, the differences in style
probably won't have long-range consequences for you, because
you wouldn't work together regularly. But if the person were to
become your immediate superior, you might have legitimate concerns about potential chemistry problems. Would you want to
work with this person day in and day out?

Don't settle on an answer too quickly. The two of you could
make an excellent team, as your practical focus and his or her
creativity might complement each other. Many successful managers reinforce their own strong suits by attracting others whose
strengths balance their shortcomings. A creative manager may
search out a detail-oriented second-in-command. An analytical
thinker might avoid being too cautious by working alongside a
more spontaneous feeler.

At the same time, if you're a deliberate, prudent, and rational
thinker, and you can see that your potential boss is an impulsive,
sentimental, and subjective feeler, you might be correct to assume
that taking the job would unleash a torrent of problems for you.
Refuse to consider a job that places you in a "no-win" situation.

Careful consideration of personal communication styles can
help you make these important choices. "I Speak" styles shouldn't
make decisions for you, but they can help show you what to
consider as you make these choices for yourself.

The Importance of Practice

Information on personal styles and lists of questions that are likely
to be asked remain theoretical tools until you're able to deal with
the material confidently in real-life interviews. You may know
more about a company than its founder, but if you aren't skilled
at sharing the information, you won't be able to capitalize on it.

Just as actors and dancers spend long hours in rehearsal stu-
dios and athletes spend their days on practice fields, you need to
prepare yourself for interviews by practicing in a realistic environment. Each time you review your preparations and presentation,

you will reinforce your strengths and learn from your mistakes.

At our company, we rely heavily on videotape training to prepare our clients for interviews. Our consultants take the interviewer's role, engaging the client in question and answer sessions modeled on real interviews, and then reviewing the results, pointing out weaknesses, suggesting changes, and reinforcing effective interview techniques. If you own or can borrow a video camera, it can be a great asset to your own interview training. If you can't obtain video equipment, you can certainly find an audio cassette recorder and use it to preserve your responses for review following practice interviews.

You'll need a partner to practice with, someone willing to play the interviewer's role. Ask your spouse or a friend for help.

If you approximate actual interview conditions as closely as you can in practice, you're likely to be much more relaxed and well prepared when you get into a real interview. When the first question is asked, rather than searching for words, you'll realize that you answered much the same question in a mock interview. That's an exceptionally reassuring discovery.

If you use audio equipment to record your practice interviews, ask your partner to be particularly observant of your physical appearance and reactions. Do you seem relaxed and in control of the situation, or do you appear apprehensive? Do your gestures and postures suggest that you're alert and confident, or are they disconcerting, making you seem wary or unsure of yourself? Do you gesture too frequently? Do you maintain good eye contact, or does your gaze dart nervously around the room? Do you stare woodenly at the interviewer?

As the practice interview unfolds, try to conduct yourself just as you would in a real interview. Listen carefully to each question. (Many people are so concerned about answers that they never listen to the questions.) Don't interrupt the interviewer. Let him or her run the interview: that's the interviewer's job. Don't blurt out your answers. Take a moment to marshal your thoughts, think of key points, and then respond as clearly and concisely as you can.

When you complete a trial interview, go back through the tape to review your performance. Are you satisfied with your voice (and, if you've used videotape, with your image as well), or do you seem nervous or hesitant? If you do, additional practice will provide increased self-assurance. Do your answers sound original, or do you seem to be spewing out memorized responses? Do you speak clearly and articulately, or do you rush through answers uncertainly?

Study the content of each response. If a question had two parts, did you remember to answer both? (Trained interviewers may ask multipart questions to test your ability to organize your responses.) Is each answer as concise and to the point as you can make it? Or do you stumble around for a few sentences before getting to the heart of the question? Additional practice will help you tighten your answers.

In your answers, do you refer to your skills, accomplishments, and goals consistently? Do you seize opportunities to make comments about your strengths and your experience without sounding like an egomaniac?

If you can, conduct test interviews with more than one partner. In this way, you can gain experience dealing with different communication styles. As you become more adept with your answers in successive interviews, try to polish them so that, on each occasion, you seem more alert, more original, better prepared, and more energetic than you were the previous time out.

Remember that the rest of your job search doesn't stop while you're getting ready for your first interview. As you continue to expand your personal contact network, you can ask the individuals you meet to help you with your interview skills. At the end of a discussion, ask for comments and suggestions about the way you handled yourself. Say that you've scheduled several important interviews for the near future and would appreciate honest feedback on your speaking style, mannerisms, and general interview habits.

Taking an Interview

Practice is invaluable, but it can never duplicate the real thing precisely. As you practice your interview methods, the suggestions that follow may help you improve your performance.

We've talked about the importance of doing your homework before showing up for an interview. It's even a good idea to visit the company before the day of the interview to look things over and check the tempo of the organization. You don't have to sneak around. Tell the receptionist that you're going to have an interview there in a few days, and ask for an annual report, recruiting brochures, or any other materials she can think of that might help you learn more about the organization. She might be flattered by your interest in her company. She'll also probably remember you on the day of the interview, when the words "Well, hello again!" can be especially comforting.

During this quick visit, look around you. How are people dressed? Are they scurrying from one place to another, or does their pace seem calm and measured? Is the reception area elaborately furnished, or is the atmosphere Spartan? Is the receptionist busy or idle? Digesting these bits and pieces of data will help you begin to form a picture of the organization's style.

Before you leave home on the day of an interview, look yourself over carefully. Remember that everyone you meet during an interview will look very closely at you. What may be a favorite pair of comfortable old shoes to you may impress someone else as an indication that you really don't care too much about your appearance. That interpretation may be entirely false, but it certainly won't help your cause. Wear conservative clothes unless a prior visit to the firm convinces you unequivocally that some other style is called for.

Arrive at least five minutes before the interview is scheduled to start. If you haven't had a chance to reconnoiter the company, ten or fifteen minutes spent sitting in the reception area can be useful. Talk to the receptionist, if only to hear yourself speak.

If a secretary appears to usher you into the interview, shake hands. Talk about the offices, the weather, or the view. Don't be a lump. It's entirely likely that, as soon as you leave the interview, the interviewer will ask the secretary, "Well, what was your impression?" Secretaries are often their bosses' confidants. They can help your cause or hurt it.

If someone offers you coffee, decline politely until you see a cup in the interviewer's hands. If the interviewer does have coffee, accept a cup if you think it will relax you. But avoid it if you feel particularly nervous. Your hands may shake, or you might worry about spilling it.

Remember that it's an interviewer's job to be particularly observant. Things that might normally be overlooked will be noticed. A limp handshake or appearing five minutes late probably has never gotten anyone fired, but they've probably never gotten anyone hired, either.

Don't smoke.

Body language has a great deal to do with the overall impression you make in an interview. How and where you sit can be important. Wait for the interviewer to ask you to sit, and if you're not sure which chair to take, ask whether the interviewer would like you to sit somewhere in particular. Don't just plop yourself down anywhere: Murphy's Law of Interviews dictates that you'll have chosen the interviewer's chair.

Sit so that you can focus easily on the interviewer. If additional people are present, sit so you can conveniently see everyone. Don't cut anybody out. Sit forward in your chair. That suggests eagerness and energy. Don't slouch into the folds of a comfortable couch.

Look around the office. If you see personal items, mention them. If there is a boat model on a table, for example, ask about it. If pictures of children adorn the walls, ask about them. Try to determine whether you and the interviewer share things in common that you might chat about for a minute or two. If, by contrast, the office is decorated with flowcharts and computer printouts, prepare yourself to get right down to business.

Be positive from the start. Don't begin by saying that the weather certainly is lousy or wondering aloud why traffic is so deadly. (We've seen people walk into someone's office for the first time and introduce themselves by saying, "What an ugly plant!") Remember that you're on stage during every minute of an interview.

Try to build a sense of rapport with the interviewer right from the beginning. Help set the positive tone that is characteristic of good interviews by being alert, energetic, and outgoing.

Finally, remember that no matter how well you've prepared yourself, you must let the interviewer lead the discussion. People who say, "I really took that interview over and turned it around," usually didn't. Don't wrestle for control.

If you run into a poorly trained interviewer—and sooner or later you will—you'll simply have to live with the situation and do whatever you can to make the interview work. He's the only interviewer you have at the moment, and however dismal a job he does, he can probably still see to it that you never get any further at that organization. Work with him, not against him. If, for example, your interviewer spends most of the time talking about the company, he hasn't prepared himself to conduct a proper interview. The best you can do is show that you're knowledgeable and enthusiastic about the organization. Ask questions about the firm. You want that person to leave the interview thinking good thoughts about you.

As the questions begin, remember to be a good listener. First, make sure that you've heard each question correctly. If a question isn't clear, ask for clarification. Don't simply jump in and embarrass yourself by answering a question that wasn't asked. If you can't answer a question, say so.

Respond directly to each question and only to that question. Don't volunteer information unless it is both positive and pertinent to the question that has just been asked.

Above all else, be brief. If you find that you're talking in five-minute stretches, stop. If the interviewer wants to know more about a subject than you've offered, he or she will ask for elaboration. Or, if you give a concise answer but wonder if you have in fact satisfied the interviewer's curiosity, ask if your answer covered the subject or if you should provide additional details. Make it clear that you want to answer each question fully but do not want to bore the interviewer.

Don't go to extremes, however. If your responses consist of single syllables, or if the interviewer asks you to elaborate on every question, spend more time on your initial answers.

Although it's the interviewer's responsibility to lead the discussion, it's your job to make certain you present yourself well.

Weave strengths and accomplishments into your answers. Be positive about everything you say. Show the interviewer that you've done your homework on the company.

There may be some subjects you'll have to raise yourself. If, for instance, you walk into an interview and the interviewer realizes for the first time that you're in your sixties, you'd better deal with the issue. Interviewers can't ask about your age without breaking laws. But don't imagine they won't be thinking about it. Meet the issue head-on by talking about your experience and track record.

Toward the end of the interview, you'll probably be asked if you have any questions about the job or the organization. If anything important has been left out of the discussion, here is where you can introduce the subject.

You should also be prepared with several questions for the interviewer. But give them some thought. If you're talking to a potential new boss, for instance, and have spent the past hour convincing this person of your interest in the job and the excitement and opportunity you think it offers, don't finish by asking about health benefits or pension plans. He or she may leave the interview wondering whether you're more interested in the job or your personal security. If you're speaking with a personnel manager, these can be valid questions. But identify them as details, not as burning central issues.

Here are some general questions that may help you prepare your own:

- What are some of the more important objectives that you'd like to see accomplished on this job?
- What's most pressing? What would you like to see done in the next two or three months?
- What freedom would I have to determine my own objectives, deadlines, and methods of performance measurement?
- What are some of the most difficult problems someone would face in this position? How do you think they could best be handled?

- What might some possible sources of satisfaction be in this job?
- How would you describe your (or "my future superior's") management style?
- How does that compare with your (or his/her) boss and those above, particularly the organization's chief executive officer?
- Where could a person who is successful in this position go in the organization? Within what time frame?

At the conclusion of the interview, make sure to find out what your next step should be. Will someone contact you? Should you make an appointment to talk with someone else in the organization? When might you expect to hear something? Should you provide any additional materials or information?

Be sure to thank the interviewer for his or her time and interest.

After the interview, you may be able to take some action to further your cause without appearing too anxious or seeming to meddle. You should certainly send the interviewer a short thank-you note. If an important point you think should have been mentioned comes to mind following the interview, you might raise it in this letter.

You should also critique your own performance while the details of the interview remain fresh in your mind. Were you relaxed but alert? Were you well enough prepared so that your answers were clear without seeming rehearsed? Were you surprised by any questions? Did you ramble, or were your answers concise and to the point? Overall, how did you feel about your performance? You'll undoubtedly find ways to improve your presentation for future interviews.

CHAPTER 17

Nothing's Working!

Finding a job and reading a book about finding a job are not the same thing at all. In books, topics can be arranged, manipulated, and introduced so that one subject follows another swiftly and logically. Things never seem to be quite so well ordered in real life.

Suppose you're two months into your job search. The first month wasn't bad. Perhaps because you couldn't have felt much worse immediately after you lost your job, your spirits generally improved in the first five or six weeks. You had straightforward, relatively mechanical things to do: putting a résumé together, producing a mailing, answering want ads. You began to feel hopeful as you started to receive encouraging comments about your campaign.

Then you suddenly realize that nine weeks have passed since you lost your job, and nothing meaningful seems to be happening. Your mailbox is empty of everything except bills. You haven't heard a word from 98 percent of the search firms you approached. A close friend hasn't returned your phone call. Yesterday, you met with an executive who spent forty-five minutes tearing apart your résumé. In the middle of an interview, an executive from one of the two search firms that did respond to your inquiry announces, "I'm not so sure you're in the right field, after all." Things seem shaky, and you may begin to doubt your plans and yourself.

Stick to Your Plan

Perhaps you should quit the rat race entirely and start a sailboat charter business in the Caribbean. You feel alone and forgotten. "I guess I really don't have any friends," you think. "The people I counted on certainly haven't come through."

You begin to doubt your résumé, so you rewrite it, hoping that a different document might work some new magic. You abandon your contact network and withdraw into yourself. You ask yourself a question you thought you'd answered affirmatively weeks ago: "Am I ever going to find another job?"

You will, if you stick to your plan. Almost any job search, like virtually anything else in life, is a series of peaks and valleys. It's perfectly normal to receive one or two leads for every one hundred letters you mail. That's the expected response rate, so you're not being realistic or fair with yourself if you consider it an unacceptable return. You ought to expect that 97 percent or even 100 percent of the search firms you contact won't have anything for you at any given time. Your personal contacts will dry up from time to time. It isn't that they don't like you or haven't thought of you. It's that they don't have anything for you. They look around and find that not only do they not have a job to offer you, but they also can't think of anyone else to send you to.

When you're worried that your severance is dwindling, the thing that will pull you through such hard times is your perseverance. If you just keep plugging away, something will surface, often when you least expect it. Two or three important doors open, and your whole campaign picks up. This cycle, incidentally, may be repeated two or three times during the course of your job search. When you find the right job, of course, you reach a new peak. But even that doesn't last forever. You soon jump to the new set of highs and lows that are a normal part of any occupation.

It's easy for us to deliver a "stick to it" sermon, and it may be very difficult for you to accept the message, particularly if it comes at a point in your job search when you feel worried or demoralized.

But giving in to the situation can be dangerous. If you decide that your search won't work, you'll never find a job, and you may as well give up, you could wind up digging a very deep hole for yourself. We suggest that the best way out of this dilemma is to stick with your plan and get back to the basics of your job search.

Give It Some More Gas

Go to the library and look up new companies to contact. Get back to work on your network of personal contacts. Check back with the people you've already talked with, not to cry on their shoulders, but to tell them how you're progressing and to let them know that you're still available. You might start these conversations by saying that you have a number of plans going, that your investigations have prompted you to alter your thinking somewhat, and that, as a result, you're now heading in a direction that is somewhat different from the one you last talked about.

Look through any rejection letters you received when you sent out a company mailing. Call the individuals who signed them and talk to them about their companies. The results may amaze you. Most people will admire your tenacity and appreciate the fact that you're sufficiently interested in their company to get in touch with them. You might even discover that the employment situation has changed at the organization.

If you sent a résumé and cover letter to fifteen or thirty search firms, mail materials to forty or sixty or a hundred more. If more than two months have passed since your first mailing, send another package to the search organizations you've already contacted. Many will have discarded your résumé as soon as they determined they had no current searches corresponding to your skills and experience. And even the largest firms with the most sophisticated filing systems often throw out résumés after a couple of months.

Don't assume that any organization is so efficient that it knows it isn't interested in you, or that it is sufficiently impressed by your credentials to keep your résumé on file. Your materials may have been lost, misrouted, or never returned to someone who passed them along to an associate. Don't suppose that you've been forgotten; but at the same time, don't imagine everyone remembers you, either. Jog memories. Realize that it's your responsibility to keep yourself visible.

We believe that for at least the first six months of your job search, it's much wiser to stay with your original plan than change your program dramatically. If things still don't seem to be working at the end of six months, then it's time to reassess and perhaps change your plan. But don't scrap it. Review your program by examining the way you've implemented it.

Are you maintaining regular monthly contact with fifty members of your network? Do you check in with an additional fifty people every two or three months? Are you answering an average of three newspaper or trade journal advertisements each week? Have you sent a direct mailing to one hundred companies? Have you contacted one hundred fifty search firms? If you haven't maintained this level of activity throughout the first six months of your search, it is highly likely that your *execution,* not your *planning,* needs to be improved!

Rethink Your Options and Keep Planning

If, after eight or nine months, your search seems seriously stalled, then you should go back and completely reassess your plan. Are you perhaps one job away from the job you really want? Should you accept free-lance or consulting work on a project basis to pull you through this difficult period without getting locked into an undesirable job? Have you unnecessarily limited your search by identifying your needs too narrowly? For example, is geographical location as important to you now as it was eight months ago? By doubling the size of the area in which you would be willing to work, you might markedly increase your chances of finding the job that's been eluding you.

We counseled one man who had been the president of a major consumer organization. For months he worked his plan diligently but continued to finish second in one search after another. Finally we encouraged him to accept a job that was obviously a bit below his needs and abilities but would help him survive emotionally and weather the doldrums he seemed unable to escape. Meanwhile, he continued his search by keeping his contact network open and, within a few months, he found another position that fit his skills and experience perfectly.

That was an extreme situation, however, and we would certainly counsel anyone to think long and hard before making such a decision. Don't settle for just any job if you've been out of work for three or four or even six months. If economic conditions make waiting for the right job an impossible luxury, then you'll obviously have to consider interim employment. But hold on to your plan for as long as you can. Give it time to work.

We know one man who lost his job with a large company, sat for three months without doing a thing, and then, with no thought or planning, took the first job that was offered to him. He lasted six months in a situation where even a cursory examination would have alerted him to the serious chemistry problems he would encounter as soon as he joined the company. When he was fired for the second time in less than a year, his spirits were understandably low. He became even more panicked than he had been the first time around, refused help, and landed in an inextricable trap of despair. It is impossible to overemphasize the importance of planning.

Outside support may help when things aren't going well. Many churches and community organizations run programs for people who are looking for jobs. These can help in two ways. First, sharing fears and experiences with others can be very reassuring. At our company, the informal support and friendship our clients give one another prove to be potent resources in their searches.

Second, these informal groups often serve as clearinghouses for specific details about the mechanical aspects of the job search. One member points another to a new contact or search firm.

We don't suggest that you look to these groups for real vocational counseling, however. Don't let a well-meaning acquaintance shape your future for you. If you're not comfortable with your own plans at this stage, contact a professional counselor for help.

We've watched thousands of people find new jobs. We've worked with people who are geniuses and many more who are not. We've counseled men and women with serious physical or psychological problems. We've discovered that the ease or difficulty with which virtually all of them found jobs was linked to their acceptance of the job search as a systematic process. The people who stick to the process find jobs most easily. No matter how intelligent or experienced or energetic they may be, those who don't make plans or won't stay with the plans they've made have the most trouble finding good jobs.

You can't absolutely control the process. Timing has too much to do with finding a job: a position must be available for you to take it, and you must be aware of it to find it. But by pursuing your plan relentlessly, by adding layer upon layer of contacts who know that you are skilled and available, you can expand your search universe and multiply your chances until you ultimately succeed in your search for an exciting, satisfying job.

CHAPTER 18

Negotiating an Offer

If the selection interview is the most important event in the job-search process, negotiating an offer can be the most delicate. You reach a critical stage in your search when you realize that a prospective employer is serious about wanting to hire you. Until this happens, you're most likely to present yourself in terms of what you can offer the employer. But when an employer indicates interest in hiring you, you should be ready to discuss the things you need in return. Many people find it far easier to say, "Here's what I can do for you" than to assert, "Here's what I'd like you to do for me."

You have every right to expect reasonable rewards for the work you'll do and the responsibilities you'll accept in a new job. Still, determining what these rewards should be and reaching agreement with an employer about them are not always easy.

The negotiating process can be simple and straightforward. You may receive an offer that exceeds your expectations for a job that more than meets your needs. Your response is likely to be, "When do I start?"

Incidentally, if that should occur, don't fall into a common trap: "That was too easy; why didn't I ask for more?" The point of negotiating an offer is not to break the bank but to strike a deal that satisfies you and the company. If you reach that point in the first round of negotiations, so much the better. You should feel secure knowing how well attuned you and your new associates are to each other.

But when you consider the number of variables involved, it seems likely that you and your prospective employer will have to discuss the terms of the deal in some detail, so that everyone will be comfortable with them.

Money is the most obvious consideration. On the subject of compensation, in addition to salary you may think about such items as bonuses, health and life insurance, a pension or annuity, a profit-sharing plan, an expense account, a club membership, a company car, a relocation allowance, a stock option plan, or some other incentive program.

Important negotiable areas may not be related to finances. You could find it necessary to settle questions about your title or job responsibilities. You may want to discuss the size and composition of your staff, or to inquire about an employment contract. You may wish to talk about where you'll fit into the company's organizational chart. You might want to discuss technical support: computers or other systems you'll need to succeed at the job.

You may even have to negotiate things *out* of the job, refusing to take on duties that don't fit your professional skills, for instance, or responsibilities that don't mesh with your personal needs.

The Basic Principle of Negotiating

The key to effective negotiating is to link each negotiable item to the job itself. How does what you want relate to the position and the company? How might it affect your ability to perform effectively? How will it affect your satisfaction with the job and your new employer?

Suppose that you're trying to determine the title you should hold. You want to join the company as a vice president. Ask yourself why.

If you want to be a vice president simply because you've always liked that title and think that now would be a good time to have it, you're on thin negotiating ice. But suppose you want to be a vice president because you realize that you'll spend most of your time dealing with other vice presidents and you'll be able to perform effectively only if you can approach them on an equal corporate footing. Now you have an acceptable, performance-related reason for raising the issue.

Suppose you decide that you want a certain salary because you believe that an individual with your background doing this job at this company in this industry deserves this level of compensation. You're thinking reasonably. That doesn't mean the company will necessarily agree with you, but you certainly have a legitimate negotiating concern. If you want a certain salary because you'd like to buy a bigger house or a fancier car, you're not on solid negotiating ground.

The Importance of Timing

As soon as you sense that you're getting warm with a company, you'll probably begin to think about these subjects. But don't raise them until an appropriate moment. Good timing is crucial to good negotiating.

Don't move too quickly. Making a demand or even airing a suggestion before an employer has decided that he or she really wants you to join the organization is dangerous. Suppose you say, "I'd really like to come in at $100,000 a year." On one day, a potential employer might think, What's wrong with this person? I haven't even decided to hire him, and he's asking for six figures. On the next day, his reaction might be, Well, I am leaning toward this person, but I haven't entirely ruled out my second choice, either. And we did set a $90,000 level for this job. Maybe I should think some more about the other candidate.

Had you waited one additional day, the employer might have decided, I've made up my mind. I want this person on board. I can go to $95,000 or even a little higher if I have to. I think we can work out the numbers.

If you wait until a clear interest to hire you surfaces, you've shifted the focus. The employer may now feel an increased willingness to bargain with you.

How do you tell when the time is ripe for negotiation? If you're asked to return to a company for successive rounds of interviews, you're getting warm. If you seem to be talking with decision makers on these occasions, you're drawing closer. When you hear a definite expression of interest from a company representative, you ought to be prepared to negotiate.

The tip-off might be a comment like "We're interested in you. What kinds of concerns do you have about us? We'd really like to see whether we can get closer to a final decision." Or the approach may be direct: "What's it going to take to get you to come with us?" Obviously it's your move. Don't wait too long to make it.

You can't make a final decision about whether a job is the right position for you until you understand the details and conditions surrounding it. So you need to deal with all negotiable items before accepting or rejecting an offer. If you accept a job and then turn around and say, "By the way, do you think you could throw in a country club membership?" your new company may think you're trying to renege on the deal. Had you asked the question earlier, the most negative reaction you'd have risked might have been, "No, we've just never offered that sort of fringe."

If trying to negotiate after you've accepted an offer is ill-advised, attempting to negotiate after you start work generally makes even less sense. Suppose that in your second week on the job, you decide you should have asked for an additional $5,000 in salary. You bring the issue to your boss's attention: "You know, the more I think about this job, the more I think I deserve another $5,000." You're no longer negotiating your salary; now you're asking for a raise.

Or suppose you say, after your first month at work, "At my last job I had a company car. What are the chances of getting a car here?"

The reply might be, "Sorry, but we have a firm policy: no company cars." Had you thought to raise the issue before accepting an offer from the company, you could have continued the discussion: "OK, if that's corporate policy, I understand. But I figure my company car represented another $5,000 annual income at my last job. Can you work with me on salary to adjust for that?" You might not have gotten your wish, but you would at least have raised the issue in an appropriate context.

The only topics that might still be worthy of negotiation at this point will probably be linked directly to the job at hand. "I know we agreed that I'd have a staff of six professionals, but the more I learn about what really needs to be done, the more I realize that we need to think about adding to that number."

Preparing to Negotiate

However important timing may be, knowing when to speak up is only the first step. You need to know what to say as well, and that calls for careful preparation.

What topics should you stress as you try to reach agreement on an offer? What subjects are less important to you? Should you be rigid or flexible in your demands? What is the cut-off between an agreement that satisfies you and one that does not?

To answer these questions, you need to review the target you created as you focused your job search, think about the specific details of the job you're now considering, and compare the two. By rating a specific offer in terms of the values you think are important, you can determine whether it hits or misses your target. If it hits, how close is it to the bull's-eye? If it misses, can you negotiate additional items into the offer to move it within your targeted range?

If you refer back to Chapter 13, you'll find the Career Targeting Grid on which you ranked the importance of a number of variables in terms of your needs. Now, by using the information you've gained through research and interviews, you can rate a specific job in terms of these variables. For each category, rate the company from 1 to 10, where a 10 indicates that you and the company see absolutely eye to eye on the subject, and a 1 signifies that you are in total disagreement on the issue.

Some of the values you assign for the company may be unsubstantiated just yet. You can certainly be precise in rating the organization's size, for instance, but as you consider an item like compensation base, you may have to rely on an educated guess unless a firm salary figure has already been established. As you move through the negotiating process, you can verify your estimates and, where necessary, alter your ratings accordingly.

For the sake of simplicity, consider this short version of the chart, which gives only three variables.

Criteria	My Needs	Job Option A	Job Option B	Job Option C
Decision-making authority	6	9		
Size of company	7	4		
Compensation base	8	9		

Start by looking at nonnegotiable items—company size, perhaps. You can't alter a nonnegotiable item, so if it makes a job unacceptable, you have no choice but to turn down the offer. You might as well find that out before negotiating anything.

The individual in our hypothetical example gave "Size of company" a personal value of 7, indicating that company size is important, but not absolutely critical to him. In giving Job Option A a rating of 4 in this category, he would conclude that there is a meaningful discrepancy between his needs in this area and the situation at the company. Perhaps he prefers the intimacy or flexibility of a very small company, and Company A is a medium-sized firm. His next move will be to decide whether the difference is great enough to make the job unacceptable, or whether other variables might tilt the scales back in favor of accepting the offer.

Suppose he had assigned a value of 10 to company size, and Company A earned a 1 in that category, a situation that might occur if an individual who is convinced that he needs a small organization to enjoy and succeed at his job is offered a job at IBM or Ford. No matter how greatly other considerations might sweeten the offer, it would probably be foolish for such an individual to accept a position at a place so at odds with his own needs.

People frequently consider these nonnegotiable topics in much less deliberate, but no less effective, fashion. If you walk out of an interview telling yourself, "No way on earth I'd work for someone like that," you've gone through exactly the same process, perhaps deciding that the organization's management style, which you couldn't change, is entirely at odds with your own needs.

It's absolutely critical to deal with these issues honestly and not let negotiable considerations blur their importance. Many people get themselves into real career trouble by accepting jobs that are basically wrong for them. Usually they decide that some negotiated item will compensate for the position's underlying unalterable shortcomings.

This occurs most frequently when substantial amounts of money prompt people to ignore their better judgment and accept positions for which they're ill-suited. Statements like "For that kind of money, I'll do whatever they want," or "At that salary, I'll learn how to do the job," are tip-offs to this perilous situation.

But, to return to our illustration, let's assume that the difference between the two numbers is not great enough to make this individual categorically reject an offer on the basis of company size alone.

He moves on to negotiable variables. Here, the first is decision-making authority. He has rated himself with a 6. The ability to make decisions is important to him, but certainly not an overriding employment factor. He ranks the position he is considering very highly in this area, giving it a 9. This indicates that, to the best of his knowledge, the decision-making requirements of the position would exceed his own needs somewhat. If he felt there would be absolutely no decision-making opportunities in the new job, or if he decided that there would be so many decisions required that he'd feel very uncomfortable in the new job, he might have given the company a 1 or 2 in this category.

The final variable in our example is base compensation, and things look fine here as well. If these were the only criteria involved in the situation, our individual might take the data and reason, "The size isn't perfect, but everything else is so close that, if I'm offered the base compensation I anticipate, I'll accept the job."

In an actual situation the decision would be much more complex, of course, given all the additional variables to consider. But the example does illustrate the value of understanding both your own needs and all the details of an offer in order to reach a good decision about accepting or refusing a job.

As you prepare your own negotiating position, then, your deliberations should include as many variables as you can develop. You might start with your last job. What were the conditions of employment there? Are you looking for different arrangements here? Do you deserve the same employment package? Should you receive more?

Are there any special considerations that should be included in the negotiations? If, given your age now and the age at which you anticipate retiring, you wouldn't build adequate retirement benefits in the company's normal program, should you try to negotiate a supplementary retirement plan? If you surrendered a substantial life insurance policy that was a fringe benefit of your last job, should you attempt to get this company to replace it?

When you've considered as many variables as you can think of, from job title to vacation policy, you should also think about how flexible you're willing to be as you negotiate. This varies from one job to another and is linked to your target. If the job is near or at the center of your target, you can afford to be extremely flexible; you're looking at an opportunity that is close to an "I'd give anything for that job" situation, and, while you won't give *anything,* you can afford to be generous. The job will still offer enough positives to fall well within the boundaries of your search plan.

As you consider jobs that are further removed from your bull's-eye, you have less room to bargain. When you reach the edge of your target, giving away anything might make the offer unacceptable. Finally, if you're trying to salvage a position that doesn't even land within your target, not only do you have nothing to barter away, but the company will have to make concessions to get you to accept an offer.

Since negotiating is a process of compromise, obviously the more flexible you can be, the more likely you are to reach agreement.

The Negotiating Process

You've done your homework and completed your preparations. You know what an ideal offer would involve, and you know what you can accept and still be satisfied. Your potential employer has given you a clear signal that it's time to negotiate. What do you do now?

First, relax a bit. For many of us, the word *negotiate* prompts visions of all-night sessions in which management and labor attack each other. In contrast, by this point you've probably located a job you want very much and an employer who wants you very much. The two of you still need to reach agreement about a number of things, but you'll begin the process from this very positive point of departure.

Reaching agreement may call for compromise. Still, if you have to give a little (a fringe benefit you were originally interested in, or even a certain amount of starting salary, perhaps) to gain a great deal (a job you'll find satisfying and rewarding), the net result will be a substantial gain. You'll have to set limits on your generosity to avoid landing yourself in an unacceptable job, but as long as you know and respect those limits, you can think of negotiating in terms of two parties aiming for the same goal.

Perhaps the employer will open the discussion by asking, "Well, just what would you need from us to join the company?" He or she is probably thinking about dollars, but you may wish to preface your remarks with a more general statement.

"Before we go into details," you might say, "it would make sense for me to review my understanding of the position. Several things seem clear: you're looking for a marketing vice president, who will report directly to you, who will manage a staff of about twenty-five people and a budget of $19 million, and who will be responsible for all the marketing-related activities of this division.

"Additional observations may be assumptions on my part, but I believe that you see two immediate priorities for this individual: getting two new products, both of which are now behind schedule, into and well known in the marketplace, and beginning to strengthen the marketing staff so that similar delays won't disrupt future plans. Those are exactly the challenges I'm looking for, so I hope that's a fair assessment of the situation."

You should get quick agreement from the employer. If you don't, you may have a problem. You can't negotiate if you're talking about one job, and he or she is discussing another. But at this stage in the selection process, that's unlikely.

You've done several things with your statement. First, you've opened the discussion with a subject that you're both almost certain to agree on. That's a good positive start. Second, you've tied the entire negotiating discussion to the job itself.

Now you can approach the thorny subject of compensation. You might begin by saying, "I'm as interested in money as anyone else, I suppose, but I'm more interested in the job. My primary concern is getting the opportunity to get in and prove myself. If I do, I'm sure the money will take care of itself." This statement links financial considerations to performance-related job issues.

You certainly don't want to give the impression that you care less about the job than about what it will pay you, and you don't want to make a prospective employer think that you're looking for financial ways to make the position attractive enough to accept. But it's just as risky to avoid the topic or to undersell yourself. You can't say, "I'm not sure what I'm worth. What do you think?"

Here is where the importance of good preparation becomes so evident. You should have both a salary goal and a lowest acceptable figure in mind, and you should be able to tie your goal to your own experience and to the demands of the job.

If your research has shown that there is a definite salary range for the job, you might say, "As I understand it, this job pays between $93,000 and $102,000 at your company. I would find the top figure in that range acceptable. It's about 7 percent more than I earned at my previous job, and I think that the added responsibility of this position more than accounts for the difference."

If there is no salary range, it's usually best to fall back on your past compensation history: "I was earning $95,000 when I left my previous position," you might say, "and like anyone else, I'd like a bump. More to the point, considering the additional demands of this job, I'd like a 10 percent increase over that figure."

If the company representative says, "No problem," you can move on to the next topic. (And don't kick yourself. You got what you asked for. Don't try to get more.)

But suppose he or she doesn't agree. The most important thing is not to get stuck this early in the negotiation. Let the employer's response dictate your reaction. If he or she says, "I'm not sure I can quite match that, but we shouldn't be too far away from each other," don't belabor the subject. Say something like, "Fine. Then let's move on to some other concerns, and perhaps they'll help us agree on an exact salary figure."

Suppose your would-be boss's reaction is, "I think we may have a real problem here. I don't think we can come anywhere near that figure."

Don't get rigid or defensive or give up on the job. Probe a bit: "Well, how far apart are we?" Say that he or she tells you that the position is budgeted at no more than $90,000. You might reply, "That certainly could be a problem, but this certainly is the job I want, too. Let's put salary aside for the moment and see if there are some other areas where we can make up the difference." There is probably no way you're going to get a $15,000 salary concession at this early stage of the game, so move to another topic for now.

You could, after all, be pleasantly surprised later in the discussion. You might say, "I'd like to know whether we could choose some way to measure my performance on the job and link an appropriate bonus system to it." The company representative might answer, "You mean no one told you about our bonus plan? Why, it has averaged 26 percent of base salary in each of the last four years."

Or you might be able to make up the difference in increments: mortgage assistance for the house you'll have to buy to relocate in the area, a term life insurance policy that would have cost you $1,500 annually, and immediate vesting in a pension plan in which 7.5 percent of your base salary is automatically deposited each year.

Suppose that, at the end of your talk, you feel you've found an additional $7,000 in annual benefits. That would leave you about $8,000 away from your original salary goal (or perhaps less if tax considerations were figured in). You could say, "The only problem I see remaining is that question of salary. Do you think we could split the difference? I could live with $97,500 to start. It's only marginally above my previous salary, but the benefits here are somewhat better than I anticipated, and I do want this job. I think I'll be able to make up the difference pretty rapidly once I get to work here."

The employer might answer, "That would still create problems in terms of internal salary parity. I think the best I could do would be $96,000."

Added to your $7,000 of found benefits, you would only be about $1,500 away from your original goal. That's a small price to pay for a satisfying job. In addition, you would have shown your new boss that you're exceptionally reasonable and determined to have that job.

Starting salary is important, particularly since many raises are based on percentages. If you join a company at a high level, you get large dollar-amount raises. It's more difficult to make this sort of headway after you come on board, because your percentage increase is likely to be tied to those of the people around you.

You could try to build an earlier than normal review into your agreement if you can't get together on salary: "Could we move the first review date up to three months from now?"

"That's too short a time," the employer might say. "What about six months?"

"Fine," you answer.

You could even encounter a situation in which the problem is too much salary, not too little. We counseled a man in his thirties who had been earning about $75,000 a year in his previous job and was being considered for a position paying nearly twice that salary. The employer had narrowed his search to two candidates: our client and another individual in his forties whose most recent salary was much closer to the new pay level.

The company was close to making a decision, and the momentum appeared to be shifting in favor of the other candidate. The reasoning was apparently that the man's last salary, and perhaps his age, made him seem the "safer" candidate. The company had developed an informal ability quotient, linking the man's age and income to the new job. They began to wonder how our client could be ready to step up to this new job, even though he had already impressed them enough with his experience and maturity to reach the final round of the search.

Our client dealt with the problem by tailoring his negotiating strategy to the situation. He said, "Obviously you're evaluating this by looking at a number of issues. My experience in judging people has been to consider their job-related skills, their experience, their motivation, and personality factors to determine how well they would fit into the organization.

"With respect to those factors, I think I fit your needs. I have all the job-related skills you're seeking. I have the energy level to bring a lot of innovations to the job. I'm well enough motivated to have reached a pretty decent salary level at a pretty early age—and, even then, I don't think my last job paid me as much as I'm worth. In terms of personality, I feel very comfortable with the organization, and I sense that you feel comfortable with me, too. Finally, I know that I can do the job you want done."

By helping to move the decision along, he got the job. His argument was "If you agree that I'm qualified, then I'm worth the money you anticipate paying."

The Value of Outside Counsel

If negotiating an offer involves discussing many separate and complex topics, you might be well-advised to seek the counsel of a compensation specialist or an attorney who is familiar with compensation issues and negotiating strategy. Consider the subject of employment contracts, for example, which guarantee employment at certain compensation levels for a certain length of time. They have become increasingly popular, particularly at and above the upper-middle-manager level. More and more people ask for them, both to document the agreed-upon results of negotiation and because, in theory at least, they add security to a job.

They can be two-edged swords. They frequently contain "noncompete clauses," which may limit the individual's future employment flexibility in return for making his or her current position more secure and financially rewarding. Depending on how they're drafted, these contracts may not be much better than a more traditional handshake. On the one hand, overly broad noncompete clauses have been overturned in court cases. On the other, since most contracts allow the employer to disregard their terms if the employee is fired "for cause" (illegal or unethical behavior), a company might try to turn a slight technical irregularity into grounds for dismissal if it is particularly unhappy with a covered employee.

Kenneth Asher is a New York attorney with special expertise in financial planning, compensation issues, and other employment-related topics, who counsels some of Drake Beam Morin's senior-level clients as they approach new jobs. He offers an interesting perspective on this issue. Suppose you leave a company and start to look for another job in your industry. Your lawyer tells you that the noncompete clause you signed will never hold up in court. But a potential employer asks, "Is there anything you know of that might affect your ability to work for us?"

You reply, "Well, there's this noncompete clause I agreed to, but my lawyer assures me it could never be invoked."

The employer might think (though perhaps not say), "But if the other company does sue this person, valuable time will be spent taking care of that, not doing the job for me. And the other company might even sue me, too. Maybe I should look for someone else."

If you neglect to inform this potential new employer of the situation, accept a job, and get sued by your former company, your new employer could conceivably turn around and sue you, too.

Employment contracts are often complex, intricate legal documents. If you're considering or confronted by one, enlist a lawyer's help before signing it.

If you don't see an employment contract on your horizon, you may wish to add another negotiating item to your list. Can you expect any compensation or assistance if, six months after you accept the job, you and your employer agree that it wasn't a good decision? This can be tricky. An employer might wonder why you're worried about losing a job before you've even accepted it.

But if you can demonstrate a legitimate reason for raising the issue, it's a valid bargaining point. If accepting the job means that you and your family will have to move across the country, for example, you probably have reason to ask for some form of commitment from the company.

Be Flexible

However important a single item on the negotiations agenda may be, the ability to remain flexible will probably determine the overall acceptability of the agreement you reach. Suppose that you will have to relocate to start the new job. You ask for details of the company's relocation assistance package and learn, to your surprise, that no such thing exists. You've determined that moving your family will cost about $20,000, and you know that you simply can't absorb that amount no matter how much you want the job.

You might say, "I can understand that you may feel unable to set a precedent about relocation allowances, but I don't see how I can handle it on my own. Could you consider giving me a one-time, up-front bonus to cover the move? You won't have to set a precedent, as it wouldn't be a recurring expense like a salary increase. And it would let my family and me make the move without bankrupting ourselves."

Flexibility also involves knowing when to get off a subject. When you sense that you're approaching the brink on some topic, move to another. If you see hostility in someone's face, or if the company representative changes the subject abruptly, that may be a signal that there is nothing more to be said on that subject at that time. If it's a critical negotiating point, come back to it later in the meeting, perhaps acknowledging the fact that you're dealing with a delicate, but important, issue.

People lose job offers by over-elaborating minor points. Office space and vacation time may be important to you, but if you talk about them too much, a potential employer may conclude, "This person is worrying about paper clips when I need someone to make some major changes around here."

At the end of the negotiating session, it's likely that the company representative will need to refer some of your requests to his or her superiors. If you've brought a list of concerns into the meeting with you, you might leave a copy so that nothing is missed. In a subsequent meeting you can reach final agreement on outstanding items. Then you'll be able to make a decision about accepting or rejecting the offer that results.

Even if all your concerns are settled immediately, however, and you are asked whether you'll accept the offer on the spot, it may be wise to wait a day or two. You could say, "I think you know how much I want this job, and I think that we've settled all the details. But I'd feel more comfortable if I took a day or two to go back over everything, just so I know we haven't neglected anything. This is a great opportunity and a very important decision for me, so I think it deserves that little extra thought."

No one should have a problem with that request. You can't ask for too much time, however. If, after weeks or months of convincing the company you want very much to work for them, you turn around and react to a firm offer with "I'll let you know in two weeks," you might be considered indecisive at best and, at the worst, a little crazy.

Reaching a Decision

During that one- or two-day period between receiving an offer and announcing your decision, you need to have a conversation with yourself. If you're out of work, you'll naturally want a new job. That pushes you toward accepting an offer. But how can you be sure you've reached a good, not just an easy, decision?

Play the devil's advocate for a moment. Picture yourself losing this new job because it was a poor decision to accept it. Imagine yourself spending the next couple of years in an unpleasant, stressful situation because you made the wrong choice. Slow down and make sure this offer really is a good one for you.

Good decisions end up feeling right. You won't have nagging doubts about your choice. You'll feel a sense of excitement, not just about being back at work, but about the opportunities the new job offers you.

344

Parting Company

Taking One Job to Get Another

But suppose you've been out of work for ten months, you received your last severance payment seven weeks ago, you see nothing else on the horizon, and you're offered a job that seems all right but doesn't really excite you. What should you do?

After assuring yourself there really is nothing else on the horizon, you can consider taking this job to get another job. Therapeutically, it may be an excellent idea to get back to work, as long as you don't convince yourself to stick with this position permanently.

Keep your search going. And don't confuse this kind of tactical move with the "brass ring" syndrome: jumping from one job to another in the blind hope that eventually you'll land someplace interesting. By this time, you should have a pretty good idea of what "the right job" means for you. Don't settle for anything less, even if you decide to accept an interim position for personal or economic reasons.

Give the interim job all the effort and energy you can muster. By accepting the position, you make a serious commitment to your new employer, who deserves your best efforts for as long as you remain with the organization.

Multiple Offers

What happens if, after you've been figuratively starving for eight months, you suddenly receive two offers and have to choose between them? As job-search campaigns gather momentum, this situation occurs much more frequently than most people imagine, and it gives some individuals a false sense of euphoria: "I can get two jobs now. Imagine what will happen if I wait another couple of months!"

If you receive two offers, refer back to your original target once again, and determine how each job matches with your needs. At the outset, put questions of salary, perks, benefits, and titles out of your mind. Think about fundamental, nonnegotiable items: the people you'd be working with at each place, the location, and the projects you'd be working on. How do the two positions measure up against each other in these respects?

Then turn back to the Career Targeting Grid in Chapter 13, and rate each job in terms of applicable criteria. This time, multiply each job option value by the corresponding personal value you assigned the item. If you total the columns that result for each job option, the option with the highest sum—in theory, at least—is the one that best meets the needs that are important to you.

The chart can serve as a helpful guide or starting point, but you probably won't—and shouldn't—base a major career decision on it alone. You're ultimately much more likely to sit back, take a deep breath, and go with your gut feelings. That is often the best solution: consciously or not, you've probably been weighing the two organizations against each other all along. Still, being as analytical as possible as you near that decision can be helpful.

As you think about each job, ask yourself whether you'll be able to handle its responsibilities, whether you think you'll be successful at it, and whether you assume that you'll get along well with your new associates. How well do you think you'll interact with your new boss in each situation? Where might each job take you in your career?

If, after all this thought, both offers still interest you about equally, consider going back to both companies and saying as much. If you do, be sure to announce at the start that you're not trying to set off a bidding war. Give that impression, and both offers might be withdrawn. No one likes to be held up. But you can try to get each company to help you decide to work for it.

One of our clients with two offers to pick from was inclined to accept the second choice position because he wasn't sure how well he'd get along with his new boss—the company president—at the other organization. We advised him to schedule a meeting with the president.

The two discussed the fact that they had very different personalities, and our client came away with a clear understanding that the president considered this a strength rather than a drawback. He wanted our client's personality to counterbalance his own, and he had concluded that the two would be able to work exceptionally well together.

Up to that point, our client had worried that perhaps the boss wouldn't back him in a fight. Reassured, he accepted the job.

If you think you're about to get a second, more interesting offer, you have fewer options. You can try to delay your response to the first company, but you have to be careful. If you ask for a couple of weeks to deliberate, the offer could be withdrawn. Even if you ask for a week, you might leave the impression that you have trouble making decisions. Then, if you finally do accept, you might start the job with a question mark over your name.

You might say you need a week or two to discuss the decision with your family, particularly if the new job necessitates a move. Or you could say that you've owed your family a vacation for several years, you intend to take it now, and you'll be back in town, with an answer, in two weeks.

But be alert to the employer's reaction. If you sense a chill, realize that you might jeopardize the offer by trying to delay your decision too long.

If you can gain some time from the first company, let the company you actually prefer know that you're genuinely close to making a decision about another job. You must be honest and straightforward about this. If the second company thinks you're playing with them, they probably won't join in the game.

It might be wise to say, "I feel uncomfortable bringing this up, but I've received a firm offer from another company, they need my answer within a week, and I'd honestly like to hear from you in the meantime." Be very sensitive to what you say and how you say it in this situation.

Turning Down an Offer

When you make your decision between two offers, or if you decide that a single offer misses your target, you need to say something more than "No, thanks" to the company you're rejecting. You've gone far enough along in the search process, shown enough interest in the company, and taken enough of its time, to owe the employer a simple explanation. Remember that the business world can be a very small place.

Make a final, clean statement. Don't leave any impression that you might be bought off. Make a phone call and follow it with a letter. Say how difficult it was for you to reach your decision. Don't discuss specifics unless you're asked for them. Even then, try to limit your remarks to statements like "I felt I could bring a bit more to Company B." "I really appreciate the way you handled the entire selection process." "Your company looked awfully good to me, and it was a tough choice."

Near Misses

Suppose the tables are turned and, thinking you're close to being offered a job, you find instead that you're out of the running. What happened?

It may have had nothing to do with you, so don't take it too personally. Another attractive candidate may have surfaced at the last minute. Top management could have failed to approve the position or the salary. The company might have instituted a sudden freeze on all hiring. A merger or takeover threat could have paralyzed management. Perhaps the individual you dealt with wasn't the actual decision maker. Maybe someone decided an internal promotion would be a more suitable way to fill the position.

Even if you're convinced you blew your chance at the last moment, don't be too hard on yourself. You were probably the company's number one or number two choice by that late date, and someone may have decided that your competitor had a bit more experience or a slight edge in skills. None of that makes you any less worthy or valuable. But focusing on it can be destructive.

Handle the situation with dignity. Leave the company's representative thinking that he or she just might have made a mistake. If you get a phone call telling you that you missed out, for instance, you might ask for feedback: "I'm just as interested as ever in working for a company like yours, so anything you can tell me about the way I handled myself might help me in the future."

Don't press the issue. If you're told, "It was a tight race and, in the end, we just leaned the other way," accept the explanation. Say, "Thanks for giving me the opportunity to come so close, anyway. By the way, I hope I can count on you for some ideas about other people in the industry I might talk to." What's a person going to say when he or she has just shot you down?

Accepting an Offer

You should have no difficulty deciding what to say when you accept an offer. But you may want to consider a detail or two. You might ask to have the conditions of your agreement put in writing, so that you and your new employer are 100 percent certain you're talking about the same responsibilities and the same rewards. Include everything from title and salary to responsibilities, reporting procedures, company car, and relocation allowances in this document. It will clarify what's going to be expected of you, as well as what you can expect in return. Many things have been said during the selection process. Now is the time to see them in writing so that you and your new associates will have no lingering misunderstandings.

Having such a memo may seem even more important to you if you've turned down another offer to accept your new job. You certainly don't want any surprises before you start work or during your first months on the job.

When the deal is signed and sealed, you obviously have cause for celebration. You've weathered a major storm in your life and turned it to your advantage.

CHAPTER 19

Starting a New Job

Beginning a new job is always exciting and sometimes intimidating. There is the invigorating feeling of a fresh start and a clean slate: you face new challenges and draw on a renewed sense of energy as you approach them. But you may also feel apprehensive about this new adventure. Will it actually turn out as well as you hope? You're entering a strange environment, and you'll have to learn to work with new associates. If you were fired from your last job, you may feel particularly sensitive. Could that happen again?

Making a Smooth Transition

Here are ten simple suggestions that may help you make the transition to a new job more enjoyable and less stressful.

1. Know Yourself. During the career continuation process you've recently completed, you spent a great deal of time and energy getting to know and understand yourself. You investigated the things you do best, the things you enjoy most, and the things you would like to accomplish in the future. You also thought about what happened at your last job.

Now that you're back at work, don't abandon that useful perspective of self-interest and self-examination. Remain alert to yourself and your needs.

Many of the insights you gained during your job search are

directly transferable to your new job. Don't forget them by going off to the first day of work thinking, Whew, that's over.

2. Set Priorities. As soon as you start work, sit down with your immediate supervisor to discuss priorities. As you interviewed with him, her, or other individuals during the selection process, you undoubtedly talked about a number of things that need to be done. But if you did talk to several people, they may not all have had similar thoughts on the subject, so you could have come away with an imprecise picture of what you should be doing at the outset.

When one of our clients starts a new job, we suggest that he or she try to get the boss to join in a simple exercise. The two sit down and independently make a list of the five most important priorities they think the employee should attend to immediately. Typically, when they compare notes, they discover that they have agreed on two or three items.

A new employee who starts work without going through such an exercise could spend 40 to 60 percent of his or her time and energy attending to duties that the superior either doesn't know about or doesn't think are particularly important.

You could learn that your boss wants several small things done immediately, things that were never mentioned as the two of you discussed long-term objectives during your interviews. A major project might have been completely overlooked in the abnormal atmosphere of the selection process. Your boss may want you to generate revenue; you may have thought he or she was worried about controlling costs. You pinch pennies while your boss hopes you're selling things.

For example, more than once in the past when our company has opened a new office, we've felt that our people spent entirely too much time organizing things—looking at various brands of copying machines, or getting the office in shape. We wanted them to be out knocking on doors, getting to know the companies in their area, and making people aware of the services we provide. We got upset; they got upset; and the insidious thing about the situation is that we wondered why things weren't getting done, while they thought things were moving along perfectly splendidly.

Having a priority-setting discussion will also give you an idea of the pace your boss would like you to set at the start. You may want to jump in and show everyone how well you can do the job. He or she may want you to hang back at first, study the overall picture, and become familiar with the organization before making any major moves. If you don't understand each other, your boss may wonder what on earth you're up to.

After you compare lists, set priorities for the items on which you've both agreed. Then decide what your remaining objectives should be.

3. Study the Organization's Style. If the "I Speak Your Language" personality styles proved useful in the interview phase of your search, you may find them equally helpful as you start your new job.

Consider your boss, his or her superiors, your peers, your subordinates, and even the organization as a whole. What do these people emphasize? Are they numbers-oriented? Sales-oriented? People-oriented? Are they thinkers, feelers, sensers, or intuitors? Does the organization have an overall style of its own?

Don't start a job thinking that everyone is going to match or bend to your personality. You're the new kid on the block. That doesn't mean you should try to change your personality. But you may have to adapt your behavior to the company's style. Don't think of giving up any of the things that make you unique, but be sensitive to the style of the people you're working with now. They'll be watching closely as you begin this new stage of your career.

They'll probably reach a preliminary decision about you within a month, but you'll be on parade for six months or so. Heighten your sensitivity to the *people* side of your new job during this period.

4. Listen. Don't think you have to jump into a new job and prove yourself in the first week. Watch what is going on around you. Listen carefully. Don't make sudden moves until you understand how your new company really works.

Even if you're convinced you know exactly what needs to be done, be careful how you act. Unless your boss has specifically told you, "Go in there and clean up that mess by Tuesday," move cautiously. You won't cement a good working relationship with superiors or peers, not to mention subordinates, by being labeled a know-it-all.

Don't make statements like "Well, at [your former company], we did it this way." Don't suggest to people at your new company that things are done better somewhere else. Even if that's true, it's undiplomatic to point it out. Make the suggestion your own idea: "I wonder if this might work?"

5. Do Small Things Well. Although it may be unwise to initiate major projects when you first join a company, you don't have to sit idly by and drink in the atmosphere of the place for your first six months on the job. You can show how responsive you can be, how well you attend to details, how disciplined you are, and how willing you are to accept unglamorous but necessary projects if you start your new career by doing small things quickly and well.

We know one man who may have assured himself a successful career with a major food corporation simply by being willing to tag meat. It wasn't in his job description, and he had no experience organizing food lockers, but soon after he joined the company his new boss asked him to make some sense out of a freezer room full of meat.

Our friend said, "Fine," put on a heavy coat, went into the storage room, and devised a system of color-coded, dated tags that showed which meat had arrived at the facility on which date.

When he returned to his office and told his new boss what he'd done, his superior was overjoyed. Our friend didn't understand the jubilation, but he didn't mind it, either. The freezer room had obviously been a thorn in his boss's side for some time. The boss concluded on the spot that his new hire was the brightest person to come along in years.

You don't have to save humanity in your first month on the job to earn yourself a solid reputation.

6. Don't Knock Your Former Employer. You refrained from attacking your former employer throughout your job search. Don't give in to the impulse now. First, no one at your new company is likely to be interested. Second, those who are may wonder whether you might describe them in similar terms in the future. Others may ask if you ever got over leaving your last job. They may worry that a preoccupation with the past could cut into your current effectiveness.

7. Learn What Happened to Your Predecessor. During the interview process, you should have determined how your new position became available. If you didn't, look for that information now. What happened to your predecessor? If he was promoted or moved elsewhere in the organization, he may be able to provide valuable information about the job. If he was fired, what went wrong? What should you do differently?

Even if you did cover this ground during an interview, it won't hurt to ask again. You're an insider now, and you may get an insider's answer that is markedly different from a response offered for public consumption. Or, you may get the same answer, but be able to interpret it differently from your new insider's perspective.

Don't approach this information thinking that if the person who last held the job got fired, the odds are greater than normal that you will too. Use what you've learned to determine what it will take to be a success in the job.

8. Transform Warning Signals into Guidelines. Refer back to the danger signs that show that a job isn't secure. Each can be turned around and made into a positive guideline for successful employment. Remain aware of them in this optimistic context from your first day on the job.

You may recall that the first and most important warning sign is the feeling that you hate your job. As you start your new job, refuse to abdicate responsibility for yourself. Instead of avoiding the subject, make it a continuing personal concern to monitor your satisfaction with your job. If you begin to sense displeasure, you'll be able to do something about it. At the very least, you'll be in a position to act and not be acted upon. Rather than discover at some future time that you have lost your voice at the company, dedicate yourself to creating effective communications and good visibility in your new job.

Don't hide from feedback or wait passively for reports from peers or superiors. Actively seek out comments from the people around you. By doing so, you'll not only show how seriously you take your job, but you'll also be able to correct minor issues so that major problems don't develop.

Look at all seven warning signs and figure out how to turn them to your advantage so that you're never surprised by their outcome. Use all available feedback to remain on top of the situation.

9. Respect Your Peers and Subordinates. When you start a new job, deal as conscientiously with your peers and subordinates as you do with your superiors. The people who work for and with you, after all, are the individuals who can make you great. Deal with the people side of your business before immersing yourself in business decisions.

10. Enjoy Yourself. This sounds obvious, but for many people, doubling sales or introducing a new product is child's play compared to accepting the right to enjoy their work. All jobs involve bad days and unpleasant duties. But, beginning with day one, if you can't sit back at any time and honestly reflect that, all in all, you're happy with what you've done and are doing, you may not really be able to consider this new job—or yourself—a success.

A Parting Word

This book isn't about leaving one job and finding another, about starting a business of your own, or about planning and enjoying a rewarding retirement. Its subject is much broader: understanding and securing a sense of personal satisfaction in a world where success is often measured by professional accomplishments.

You deserve to enjoy whatever new course you carve out for yourself. And if you are guided by personal satisfaction and strengthened by professional competence, the choice you make is almost certain to bring you a great reward: the comfortable knowledge that you're doing exactly what you want to do. To this end, let your real job be a relentless determination to learn about and listen to yourself so that, in this new stage of your life, and in all that follow it, you direct your career and your future. Refuse to settle for anything less.

Entrepreneurial Readiness
Self-Assessment

Starting a business of your own demands expertise across a range of diverse business areas. On the pages that follow, you will find a series of self-assessment instruments that will help you determine:

- Your knowledge of important aspects of new business development; and
- The potential importance of this knowledge to the success of your venture.

You can use the information you develop in these exercises to identify areas in which you should seek expert assistance or improve your skills.

MARKET ANALYSIS: Rate yourself in knowledge of these marketing factors.

	Knowledge Level					Importance to Success of Enterprise				
	Low			High		Low			High	
1. Size of market now	1	2	3	4	5	1	2	3	4	5
2. Size of future market	1	2	3	4	5	1	2	3	4	5
3. Potential market share	1	2	3	4	5	1	2	3	4	5
4. Physical factors influencing market (location, weather)	1	2	3	4	5	1	2	3	4	5
5. Economic and social factors influencing market	1	2	3	4	5	1	2	3	4	5
6. Market trends	1	2	3	4	5	1	2	3	4	5
7. Your competition	1	2	3	4	5	1	2	3	4	5
8. Methods for calculating sales volume	1	2	3	4	5	1	2	3	4	5
9. Methods for calculating profit margin	1	2	3	4	5	1	2	3	4	5
10. Financial practices, guidelines for your industry	1	2	3	4	5	1	2	3	4	5

MARKETING PLAN: Rate yourself in knowledge of these marketing factors.

	Knowledge Level					Importance to Success of Enterprise				
	Low			High		Low			High	
1. Sales forecasting	1	2	3	4	5	1	2	3	4	5
2. Product mix	1	2	3	4	5	1	2	3	4	5
3. Pricing	1	2	3	4	5	1	2	3	4	5
4. Distribution	1	2	3	4	5	1	2	3	4	5
5. Sales methods and techniques	1	2	3	4	5	1	2	3	4	5
6. Advertising	1	2	3	4	5	1	2	3	4	5

	Knowledge Level					Importance to Success of Enterprise				
	Low			High		Low			High	
7. Customer relations	1	2	3	4	5	1	2	3	4	5
8. Product/service warranty	1	2	3	4	5	1	2	3	4	5
9. New product development	1	2	3	4	5	1	2	3	4	5
10. Market planning	1	2	3	4	5	1	2	3	4	5

OPERATING FUNCTIONS: Rate yourself for how much you know and what abilities you possess in basic operating functions of the business you are planning to start or buy.

	Knowledge Level					Importance to Success of Enterprise				
	Low			High		Low			High	
General										
1. Supplier relations	1	2	3	4	5	1	2	3	4	5
2. Industry contacts	1	2	3	4	5	1	2	3	4	5
3. Purchasing	1	2	3	4	5	1	2	3	4	5
4. Inventory control	1	2	3	4	5	1	2	3	4	5
5. Site selection	1	2	3	4	5	1	2	3	4	5
6. Layout of premises	1	2	3	4	5	1	2	3	4	5
7. Security of building	1	2	3	4	5	1	2	3	4	5
8. Production technology	1	2	3	4	5	1	2	3	4	5
Retailing										
1. Merchandising	1	2	3	4	5	1	2	3	4	5
2. Customer services (refunds, repairs)	1	2	3	4	5	1	2	3	4	5
3. Displays (fixtures, lighting, signs)	1	2	3	4	5	1	2	3	4	5

THE ORGANIZATION PLAN: Rate your knowledge of the following organizational factors.

	Knowledge Level					Importance to Success of Enterprise				
	Low			High		Low			High	
1. Types of legal entity	1	2	3	4	5	1	2	3	4	5
2. Business formation requirements	1	2	3	4	5	1	2	3	4	5
3. Liability exposure	1	2	3	4	5	1	2	3	4	5
4. Contracts and leases	1	2	3	4	5	1	2	3	4	5
5. Tax laws for corporation, partnership, or sole owner	1	2	3	4	5	1	2	3	4	5
6. Licenses	1	2	3	4	5	1	2	3	4	5
7. Local, state, and federal laws governing business practices	1	2	3	4	5	1	2	3	4	5

INSURANCE AND STAFFING: Rate your knowledge in these areas.

	Knowledge Level					Importance to Success of Enterprise				
	Low			High		Low			High	
Insurance										
1. Risk management	1	2	3	4	5	1	2	3	4	5
2. Fire	1	2	3	4	5	1	2	3	4	5
3. Auto	1	2	3	4	5	1	2	3	4	5
4. Crime	1	2	3	4	5	1	2	3	4	5
5. Fidelity bonds	1	2	3	4	5	1	2	3	4	5
6. Liability	1	2	3	4	5	1	2	3	4	5
7. Product liability	1	2	3	4	5	1	2	3	4	5
8. Health and disability	1	2	3	4	5	1	2	3	4	5
9. Life insurance	1	2	3	4	5	1	2	3	4	5
10. Workers' compensation	1	2	3	4	5	1	2	3	4	5

	Knowledge Level					Importance to Success of Enterprise				
	Low				High	Low				High
Staffing										
1. Job descriptions	1	2	3	4	5	1	2	3	4	5
2. Recruiting	1	2	3	4	5	1	2	3	4	5
3. Hiring (selection, interviewing, evaluation)	1	2	3	4	5	1	2	3	4	5
4. Personnel policies (vacations, sick leave, performance evaluation, promotions)	1	2	3	4	5	1	2	3	4	5
5. Wage/salary policies	1	2	3	4	5	1	2	3	4	5
6. Employee benefits	1	2	3	4	5	1	2	3	4	5
7. Training	1	2	3	4	5	1	2	3	4	5

FINANCIAL PLAN: Listed here are factors related to financial stability and planning. How much do you know about the need, availability, and administration of these factors?

	Knowledge Level					Importance to Success of Enterprise				
	Low				High	Low				High
1. Total start-up capital needs	1	2	3	4	5	1	2	3	4	5
2. Long-term capital needs	1	2	3	4	5	1	2	3	4	5
3. Personal sources of capital	1	2	3	4	5	1	2	3	4	5
4. Outside sources of cash; bank loans	1	2	3	4	5	1	2	3	4	5
5. Local private investors	1	2	3	4	5	1	2	3	4	5
6. Leasing	1	2	3	4	5	1	2	3	4	5
7. Cash flow requirements	1	2	3	4	5	1	2	3	4	5
8. Profit/loss projections	1	2	3	4	5	1	2	3	4	5
9. Balance sheet	1	2	3	4	5	1	2	3	4	5
10. Analysis of financial statements and projections	1	2	3	4	5	1	2	3	4	5

APPENDIX B

Resources for Careers in Consulting

Bermont, Hubert Ingram. *How to Become a Successful Consultant in Your Own Field.* Rocklin, CA: Prima Publishing and Communications, 1989.

Block, Peter. *Flawless Consulting: A Guide to Getting Your Expertise Used.* Austin, TX: Learning Concepts, 1981.

Bolles, Richard. *The Three Boxes of Your Life.* Berkeley, CA: Ten Speed Press, 1978.

Fuchs, Jerome H. *Management Consultants in Action.* New York, NY: Hawthorn Books, 1975.

Hollander, Stanley C., and Stephen R. Flaster. *Management Consultants and Clients.* East Lansing, MI: Michigan State University Press, 1972.

Kelley, Robert E. *Consulting: The Complete Guide to a Profitable Career.* New York, NY: Charles Scribner's Sons, 1981.

Klein, Howard J. *Other People's Business: A Primer on Management Consultants.* New York, NY: Mason/Charter, 1977.

Kotler, Philip. *Marketing Professional Services.* Englewood Cliffs, NJ: Prentice-Hall, 1984.

Krannich, Ronald. *Re-Careering in Turbulent Times.* Manassas, VA: Impact Publications, 1983.

Kubr, Milan, ed. *Management Consulting: A Guide to the Profession.* Geneva: International Labour Office, 1986.

Lant, Jeffrey L. *The Consultant's Kit: Establishing and Operating Your Successful Consulting Business.* Cambridge, MA: JLA Publications, 1986.

Lippitt, Gordon L., and Ronald Lippitt. *The Consulting Process in Action.* San Diego, CA: University Associates, 1986.

Shenson, Howard L. *Complete Guide to Consulting Success.* Wilmington, DE: Enterprise Publishing, Inc., 1987.

———. *The Consulting Handbook: An Encyclopedia of Consulting.* Woodland Hills, CA: H. L. Shenson, Inc., 1982.

Steele, Fritz. *Consulting for Organizational Change.* Amherst, MA: University of Massachusetts Press, 1975.

Wilson, Aubrey. *The Marketing of Professional Services.* London, New York, NY: McGraw-Hill, 1972.

Wolf, William B. *Management and Consulting: An Introduction to James O. McKinsey.* Ithaca, NY: New York State School of Industrial and Labor Relations, Cornell University, 1978.

APPENDIX C

Retirement Information

General Retirement

American Association of Retired Persons. *Planning Your Retirement.*

> For copies of this pamphlet contact: AARP Fulfillment, P.O. Box 2400, Long Beach, CA 90801. Specify stock number PW 3729(987).

Chapman, Elwood. *Comfort Zones: A Practical Guide for Retirement Planning.* Los Altos, CA: Crisp Publications, 1987.

Comfort, Alex. *A Good Age.* New York: Simon & Schuster, 1976.

> A well-written analysis of the myths and stereotypes of aging.

Fromme, Alan. *Life after Work: Planning It, Living It, Loving It.* Glenview, IL: Scott, Foresman AARP Books, 1984.

> Author's point of view is that a happy life after fifty is more a product of attitude than opportunity or luck.

Kaufman, Sharon. *The Ageless Self: Sources of Meaning in Late Life.* New York: New American Library, 1986.

Shank, Howard. *Managing Retirement.* Chicago: Contemporary Books, 1985.

A thoughtful and provocative book for those planning, entering, or already in retirement.

Willing, Jules. *The Reality of Retirement: The Inner Experience of Becoming a Retired Person.* New York: Morrow Quill Paperbacks, 1981.

Personal account and down-to-earth approach to planning for the emotional and psychological realities of retirement. Emphasizes changes in personal values and relationships.

Organizations for Retirees

American Association of Retired Persons (AARP), 1909 K Street, N.W., Washington, DC 20049.

Mature Outlook, P.O. Box 1208, Glenview, IL 60025.

Adult Development/Transitions

Bridges, William. *Transitions.* New York: Addison-Wesley, 1980.

Carnegie, Dale. *How to Stop Worrying and Start Living.* New York: Simon & Schuster, 1984.

Carter, Jimmy & Rosalynn. *Everything to Gain.* New York: Ballantine Books, 1987.

Erikson, Erik. *The Life Cycle Completed.* New York: W.W. Norton, 1985.

LeShan, Eda. *Oh to Be 50 Again.* New York: Pocket Books, 1986.

Levinson, Daniel L. *The Seasons of a Man's Life.* New York: Ballantine Books, 1976.

Sheehy, Gail. *Passages.* New York: Bantam Books, 1976.

Vaillant, George. *Adaptation to Life.* New York: Little, Brown and Co., 1978.

Other Vocational Interest Inventories

The Lottery Exercise is only one approach to this important and complex topic. It emphasizes the importance of interests uncovered by your imagination when you have the time, money, and energy to accomplish whatever you wish. However, there are other approaches to help you generate this information. We recommend that you consider supplementing the Lottery Exercise with one of the excellent career interest inventories described here. Your local library may also be a good source of information.

Self-Directed Search

This is a widely used interest inventory developed by John Holland. It helps you discover your interests and the occupations that are most compatible with those interests. You answer a series of questions and are scored on six dimensions: Realistic, Investigative, Artistic, Social, Enterprising, and Conventional. These scores are, in turn, related to various occupations in the *Occupations Finder.*

This instrument can be obtained at most college career development and placement centers, and is most effective when a counselor assists in the interpretation. It is also available for a nominal fee from Psychological Assessment Resources, Inc., P.O. Box 98, Odessa, FL 33556. (813) 968-3003.

Strong Interest Inventory

The Strong Interest Inventory is a 325-item questionnaire that inquires about your interest in a range of occupations, hobbies, leisure activities, types of people, and school subject preferences. The answers are analyzed by computer and presented in a report profile. While the profile is self explanatory, it is helpful to discuss the results with a counselor who can provide greater understanding of the scores.

The profile results give five types of information:

- scores on six occupational themes
- scores on 23 Basic Interest Scales
- scores on 207 Occupational Scales, relative to your interests
- scores on Introversion/Extroversion and comfort with academic environments
- administrative indexes to identify unusual or invalid profiles

The interest inventory is available at most college career development and placement centers and is most often used in concert with career counseling specialists. Distributed by Consulting Psychologists Press, 577 College Avenue, Palo Alto, CA 94306.

Job Research Sources

To make the information-gathering process more manageable, we have grouped the many sources of information into the following categories:

- Business References and Directories
- Bureau of Labor Statistics Publications
- Specific Company Publications
- Additional Publications and Periodicals

Business References and Directories

Business references and directories will be useful to you in planning your job-search strategy. Those listed below can be found at your local business, public, college, and university libraries. In addition, local directories published by the chamber of commerce and government agencies are available in many urban areas. Start with the preface and table of contents of any reference book you use; it's the most efficient way to locate the information you are seeking.

These reference materials have been grouped in reverse order of specialization, from listings that contain general directory information all the way down to a listing of sources containing specific positions at a certain level. Knowing this, you can start at whatever level is most appropriate for finding the information you need.

Guides to Directories, Associations, and Publications

Guide to American Directories. B. Klein Publications, P.O. Box 8503, Coral Springs, FL 33065. 567 pp.

A listing and description of 6,000 directories with over 300 major industrial, professional, and mercantile classifications. Useful in locating membership names and titles. Calling the publisher or library and asking for specific information from the directory will expedite your research.

The Directory of Directories. Gale Research Co., Book Tower, Detroit, MI 48226. 2 volumes.

10,400 listings in three sections: directory, title and keyword index, and subject index.

Encyclopedia of Associations—National Organizations of the U.S. Gale Research Co., Book Tower, Detroit, MI 48226. 3,600 pp. in 2 volumes.

A guide to 22,000 national nonprofit organizations of all types, purposes, and interests, including commodity exchanges, public administration, military, cultural, patriotic, and scientific organizations, fraternities, sororities, and fan clubs. Gives contact names, headquarter addresses, telephone numbers, chief officials, number of members and chapters, descriptions of membership, aims, and activities. Includes lists of special committees and departments, publications, and a four-year convention schedule. Arranged by subject and cross-referenced by name of chief executive, geographic location, and organization name. Useful in locating placement committees, which can help you learn of specific job openings in your field of interest; getting membership lists of individuals in order to develop personal contacts; learning where and when conferences are being held so you can attend them.

Business Organizations, Agencies & Publications Directory. Gale Research Co., Book Tower, Detroit, MI 48226. Approx. 2,030 pp. in 2 volumes. Biannual.

Lists business names, addresses, and contact persons of approximately 24,000 organizations as well as publications that are important and varied sources of data and information on all areas of business, including trade, commercial and labor organizations, government agencies, stock exchange, diplomatic offices and banks, tourism, and publishing and computer information services.

Moody's Industry Review. Moody's Investors Service, Inc., Dun and Bradstreet Co., 99 Church Street, New York, NY 10007. Annual with weekly updates of 11 industries per issue.

Ranks 4,000 leading companies in 145 industry categories according to standard financial criteria: revenues, price-earning ratio, net income, profit margin, return on capital. Classified by industry. Arranged by company name.

U.S. Industrial Directory. A Reed International Publication. 8 Stamford Forum, P.O. Box 100277, Stamford, CT 06904. 3,500 pp. Annual.

Four volumes provide over 50,000 company names, addresses, trade names, phone numbers of industrial entries, as well as addresses and phone numbers of local sales offices and distributors.

Directory of Industry Data Sources. Ballinger Publishing Co., Harper & Row, Publishers, 54 S. Church Street, Cambridge, MA 02138.

Lists 3,000 publishers of industry data sources and includes bibliographic and source data bases, indexing and abstracting services, and market research firms. Describes monographs, surveys, periodical special issues, market studies, covering 65 industries. Lists company name, address, and phone. Arranged alphabetically and by type of publication service. Three volumes cover the U.S. and Canada. Two volumes cover western Europe.

National Trade and Professional Associations of the U.S. Columbia
Books, 1350 New York Avenue, N.W., Suite 207, Washington, DC 20005. 430 pp. Annual in January.

Lists 6,250 entries including name, address, year established,
name of chief executive, phone numbers of staff members,
budget, size of membership; date, location, and expected at-
tendance of annual meeting; publications; historical and de-
scriptive data. Arranged alphabetically and by geographic location, subject, budget, and acronym.

Directory of U.S. Labor Organizations. BNA Books, Bureau of
National Affairs, 1231 25th Street, N.W., Washington, DC
20037. 90 pp. Biennial, fall of even years.

Lists over 200 national unions and professional and state employee associations engaged in labor representation. Includes
name, address, names of elected officials and department
heads, publications, conventions, membership figures, number
of locals. Separate sections for AFL-CIO, railroad unions,
other federations, and for individual national unions.

Consultants and Consulting Organizations Directory. Gale Research Co., Book Tower, Detroit, MI 48226. 2 volumes.

Lists more than 14,000 consulting organizations and consultants. Includes name, address, telephone, principal executives,
staff size, purpose, and activity. Arranged by industry, by
consulting functional category, by geographic location, by personal name, and by consulting firm.

Directory of Consultants. National Association of Regulatory Utility Commissioners, Box 684, Washington, DC 20044. 230 pp.
Annual in December.

Lists 190 consultants and consulting firms active in utility and
transportation industries. Includes firm or individual's name,
address, and phone; names of regulatory agencies which engaged them in the past; purpose and dates of past engagements; areas of specialization; qualifications and experience.
Arranged alphabetically.

The Career Guide: Dun's Employment Opportunities Directory. Dun's Marketing Services, Dun and Bradstreet Corp., 49 Old Bloomfield Road, Mountain Lakes, NJ 07046. 4,000 pp. Annual in November.

Lists more than 5,000 companies that have 1,000 or more employees and that may provide career opportunities in sales, marketing, management, engineering, life and physical sciences, computer science, mathematics, statistics planning, accounting and finance, liberal arts fields, and other technical and professional areas. Also covers personnel consultants throughout the country. Includes some public sector employers (e.g., governments, schools) not found in similar lists. Based on data supplied by questionnaire and personal interview. Entries include company name, location of headquarters, other offices and plants (may also include name, title, address, and phone number of employment contact); disciplines or occupational groups hired; brief overview of company; types of positions that may be available; training and career development programs; benefits offered. Companies are arranged alphabetically; consultants geographically.

Directory of Jobs and Careers Abroad. Vacation-Work, 9 Park End Street, Oxford OX1 1HJ, England. Triennial, last edition January 1989.

Lists 500 agencies, consultants, associations, government agencies, overseas branches, affiliates, and subsidiaries of British companies and other organizations which offer or assist in locating permanent jobs abroad. Coverage is worldwide. Entries include organization name, address, phone, name of contact, geographic location, and career areas covered. Arranged by type of career, then geographically.

Dun's Directory of Service Companies. Dun's Marketing Services, Three Sylvan Way, Parsippany, NJ 07054.

Lists 50,000 of the largest service enterprises nationwide, including both public and private companies.

The Directory of Executive Recruiters. Kennedy & Kennedy, Templeton Road, Fitzwilliam, NH 03447. Annual, 616 pp.

Lists over 2,000 executive recruiter firms. Includes firm name, address, principals of firm, key contact, and salary level. Arranged by retainer and contingency categories of search, as well as by function, by industry, and by geographic location.

Corporate Ownership Ties

Directory of Corporate Affiliations. National Register Publishing Co., Macmillan, 3004 Glenview Road, Wilmette, IL 60091. 1,800 pp. Annual.

Provides detailed information on "who owns whom" as a result of mergers and acquisitions. Listings include companies on the New York Stock Exchange, the American Stock Exchange, the Fortune 500, and others. Total listing of 4,000 parent companies and 40,000 U.S. affiliates and divisions. Useful for learning the detailed corporate structure of a parent company, or for finding a company not listed in other directories because it is a subsidiary, division, or affiliate.

America's Corporate Families: Billion Dollar Directory. Dun's Marketing Services, Three Sylvan Way, Parsippany, NJ 07054. 10,000 pp. in 2 volumes. Annual.

Identifies over 8,000 major U.S. parent companies and their subsidiaries and divisions (over 44,000). Gives Dun number and state of incorporation for parent companies, as well as directory information for all companies; also lists Standard Industrial Classification (SIC) codes and stock exchange symbols; principal bank, accounting, and legal firms. To be listed, companies must conduct business in at least two locations with controlling interest in at least one subsidiary, and have a net worth of at least $500,000.

Standard and Poor's Register of Corporations, Directors, and Executives. 25 Broadway, New York, NY 10004. 5,200 pp. in 3 volumes. Annual.

A guide to the business community providing information on public companies of the U.S.

Volume I. Corporate Listings.
Alphabetical directory listing by business name over 45,000 corporations, including names and titles of officers and directors, Standard Industrial Classification (SIC) codes, and annual sales.

Volume II. Directors and Executives.
Biographies of 70,000 individual officers, directors, trustees, and executives; their principal business affiliations; fraternal memberships, if available; residential addresses; and year and place of birth.

Volume III. Indexes.
Listings are indexed by SIC codes and geographic location. An obituary section records recent deaths of executive personnel. New executives appearing for the first time are included with brief business biographies, as are companies appearing for the first time in Volume I.

Standard and Poor's Stock Reports. 800 pp. Revised weekly.

The stock reports of 800 companies traded on the American Stock Exchange.

Dun and Bradstreet Million Dollar Directory. Dun's Marketing Services, Three Sylvan Way, Parsippany, NJ 07054. 13,600 pp. in 5 volumes. Annual.

A guide to 160,000 public companies in the U.S. with net worth of $500,000 or more; includes industrial corporations, bank and trust companies, wholesalers, retailers, and domestic subsidiaries of foreign corporations. Alphabetical listings by business name include address, phone number, names and titles of officers and directors, SIC code, annual sales, number of employees, some division names of principal and secondary businesses, as well as principal bank, legal, and accounting firms. 5th volume lists the top 50,000 money-making companies.

Polk's Bank Directory—North American Edition. R. L. Polk Co.,
2001 Elm Hill Pike, Nashville, TN 37210. 3,500 pp. Semiannual.

A major detailed directory listing banks, other financial institutions, and government agencies by address; also includes
geographic indexing, names and titles of officers, financial information, names of discontinued banks, and maps. Useful for
corporations and government agencies.

Who Owns Whom. Dun and Bradstreet Ltd., Holmers Farm Way,
High Wicombe, Bricks HP12 44L, England.

Indicates ownership of subsidiary and associate companies
and how they fit into the corporate structure of their parent
companies.

Best's Insurance Reports, Property and Casualty. A. M. Best Co.,
Ambest Road, Oldwick, NJ 08858. 2,200 pp. Annual.

Gives in-depth analyses, operating statistics, financial data
and ratings, names of officers, and addresses for over 1,300
major stock and mutual property-casualty insurance companies. Provides summary data on over 2,000 smaller mutual
companies and on 300 casualty companies operating in Canada.

Best's Insurance Reports, Life and Health. 2,100 pp.

Supplies 1,800 individual company reports in addition to summaries of property and casualty reports for 600 smaller companies.

Standard and Poor's Securities Dealers of North America.
25 Broadway, New York, NY 10004. 1,700 pp. Semiannual,
with supplements published every 6 weeks.

Lists over 15,000 security dealers alphabetically and by geographic region. Gives names, titles, and addresses of company
officers; employer's I.D. number, and clearing facilities.

Thomas Register of American Manufacturers. Thomas Publishing Co., One Penn Plaza, New York, NY 10001. 33,000 pp. in 21 volumes. Annual.

Lists more than 140,000 specific product manufacturers, both large and small. Includes names of officers, capital assets, and parent or subsidiary company.

Volumes 1–11. List firms under their product headings (approximately 48,000 products).

Volume 12. Index to products and services.

Volume 13. Company profiles.

Volume 14. Index to manufacturers by their trade brand names.

Volumes 15–21. Bound catalogs of more than 1,400 manufacturing firms.

Organizations by Specific Category

Corporate Technology Directory. Corporate Technology Information Services, 1 Market Street, Wellesley Hills, MA 02181. 4,000 pp. in 4 volumes. Annual.

Contains more than 25,000 corporate profiles indexed by name, product, geographic location, and parent company. All companies listed manufacture/develop high tech products. Gives general listing data including names of key personnel, sales, and average revenues.

Directory of American Firms Operating in Foreign Countries. World Trade Academy Press, 50 E. 42nd Street, New York, NY 10017. 2,000 pp. in 3 volumes. Updated irregularly.

Lists 3,000 American corporations with factories and branch offices in 36 countries; names of key contact personnel are given.

Dun and Bradstreet's Principal International Businesses. 4,388 pp. in 1 volume.

Lists 50,000 prominent companies in 133 countries. Grouped by geographic location, product, and alphabetical order. Text appears simultaneously in English, French, Spanish, and German.

Standard Directory of Advertisers. National Register Publishing Co., Macmillan, 3004 Glenview Road, Wilmette, IL 60091. 1,800 pp. Annual, with supplements published 5 times yearly.

Lists 24,000 companies that place national and regional advertising. Includes company names, phone numbers, and products advertised, with brand/trade names; names of 80,000 executives and their titles, as well as the advertising agency handling the account, account executives, media used, and distribution. Published in 2 editions; in one volume, companies are listed by product classification or service; in the second volume, companies are grouped according to geographic location. Useful tool in locating marketing officers, names of parent companies, subsidiaries, and affiliates.

Standard Directory of Advertising Agencies. National Register Publishing Co., Macmillan, 3004 Glenview Road, Wilmette, IL 60091. 1,200 pp. Published 3 times yearly, plus monthly supplements.

Lists a total of 4,400 U.S. and foreign agency establishments. Various sections include:

Special Market Index. Summaries of agencies specializing in the fields of finance, medicine, resort and travel, black and Spanish markets, media service organizations, and sales promotion agencies.

Media Services. Lists sales promotion agencies, media services, and time-buying organizations. Includes alphabetical listing of advertising agencies, with branches, personnel, and accounts, and ranking of largest agencies by annual billings. Index also lists advertising agencies by geographic location.

The Rand McNally Bankers' Directory. Rand McNally Corporation, Financial Publishing Division, P.O. Box 7600, Chicago, IL 60608. 3 volumes. Updated every six months.

Two volumes devoted to U.S. banks include individual listings for head offices, branches, agencies, and representative offices. The third volume lists offices of international banks considered in foreign exchange or trade. Each listing contains key marketing, administrative, and operational information.

Pratt's Guide to Venture Capital Sources. Venture Economics, 16 Laurel Avenue, Wellesley Hills, MA 02181. 600 pp. Annual.

Lists over 700 venture capital firms, corporate venture groups, and small investment corporations mainly in the U.S. Includes the investment and industry preferences of each firm. Articles on investment and other related topics are also included.

O'Dwyer's Directory of Public Relations Firms. J. R. O'Dwyer Co., 271 Madison Ave., New York, NY 10016. 400 pp.

More than 1,900 U.S. and Canadian public relations firms are listed alphabetically. Overseas offices, clients, and billings are included, as is a list of the top 50 public relations firms. Indexed by firm specialty, client, and geographic location.

Management and Officers' Profiles

Dun and Bradstreet Reference Book of Corporate Managements. 3,500 pp. in 4 volumes. Annual.

Contains data on nearly 200,000 presidents, officers, and managers of 12,000 credit, personnel, and data processing companies. Includes date of birth, education, and business positions presently and previously held; for directors who are not officers, their present principal business connections are supplied. Gives an idea of the personality of a corporation by providing information not found in other directories on the technical background of its officers.

Middle Management Positions

Middle Management Report. E. C. S. Wyatt Data Services. 2 volumes. Annual.

Contains information on middle management positions contributed by over 1,800 businesses within 17 industries. Information includes ECS industrial classification guide; budget, merit, and general increase tables; salary structures; position descriptions; and a table of general wage information grouped by job title.

Bureau of Labor Statistics Publications

The Bureau of Labor Statistics (BLS) publishes a comprehensive line of bulletins and periodicals devoted to analyzing statistical information related to major occupational fields. Past employment figures and projections by major sector, selected industry, and broad occupational groups are available, as are other published data covering a broad spectrum of economic topics. Salary surveys are also available by industry, by level within an industry, and by geographic location. The Bureau's publications include a number of comprehensive guides to job titles/descriptions within specific areas (e.g., health services and environmental protection), as well as more general references (i.e., the *Dictionary of Occupational Titles*). These volumes are updated as necessary, as are all the materials containing dated information. Many BLS publications are carried by public and college libraries.

The *BLS Update,* a quarterly newsletter, is available by subscription. It may be the most valuable publication for job-search research, as it lists availability dates of updated and new publications that can be mail-ordered, as well as brief content summaries. Many of the publications are free; others sell for a nominal price. The *Update* also contains brief articles and current statistical information on all areas of the economic scene.

The BLS also offers summaries of statistical data over telephone hotlines across the country. A Bureau economist is available for questions at one of the hotline numbers, which you can obtain by calling your nearest Bureau/Library of Labor Statistics. These numbers are also published in the *BLS Update.*

Some of the data series are available on BLS Data Diskettes. These contain the specified data series, as well as the customary uses, if any, for the statistics. You will need an IBM compatible personal computer and Lotus 1-2-3, Version 1A or Version 2, to use the diskettes.

These sources will be valuable to you whether you are considering a career in a new and expanding industry, are looking within a stable, established field, or have yet to decide on the direction of your new career. A complete catalog and information on ordering BLS publications is available from:

> Bureau of Labor Statistics
> Inquiries & Correspondence
> 441 G Street, N.W.
> Washington, DC 20212

Some of the following BLS publications may be particularly helpful:

> *Dictionary of Occupational Titles*
> *Guide for Occupational Exploration*
> *Exploring Careers*
> *Occupational Outlook Handbook*
> *Geographic Profiles of Employment & Unemployment*
> *U. S. Dept. of Labor Statistics Employment & Earnings*
> *Projections 2000*
> *Monthly Labor Review*

Specific Company Publications

The Annual Report. In investigating any company, one line of research will be into statistics and information the company publishes about itself. In addition to the balance sheet and the auditor's report, a company's annual report contains a letter from the chairman which can reflect the personality, well-being, and direction of the company.

Additional Publications and Periodicals

In addition to the preceding, there are numerous industry, chamber of commerce, and Fortune 500 directories, trade journals, annual reports, and papers that may be found at your local business, college, or university libraries.

Business Periodical Index
Directory of Directors
Readers' Guide to Periodical Literature
Directories in Print
The College Placement Annual
Encyclopedia of Careers and Vocational Guidance
Congressional Directory
Congressional Yellow Book
Federal Directory
Federal Yellow Book
Taylor's Encyclopedia of Government Officials

Periodicals that may be useful include:

Barron's
Business Week
Business World
Buyouts and Acquisitions
Forbes
Fortune
Money
Nation's Business

Finding Answers to Commonly Asked Questions

In this section we have listed the types of questions job seekers usually ask, followed by a list of sources where answers can be found. The questions fall into the following general categories:

- Location
- Industries
- Companies
- Employment Organizations

	Questions	Source of Answers
Location	What companies are located in my area?	State Industrial Directories
		Dun and Bradstreet Reference Book of Corporate Managements
		Regional Development Agencies
		Chambers of commerce, state and local

Questions	Source of Answers
In what states does a company have facilities?	*Moody's Manuals* *Directory of Corporate Affiliations* Company annual reports and 10-Ks Other sources of company information may be used depending on the types of facilities sought (e.g., headquarters vs. manufacturing location).
Industries — What are the high-growth industries?	*Value Line Investment Surveys* *Predicasts* forecast manuals Refer to the *Directory of Industry Data Sources* for other sources
What are salary levels in specific industries?	American Compensation Association publications *The American Almanac of Jobs and Salaries* American Management Association surveys (Libraries may not have the American Compensation Association or American Management Association surveys.)
What companies are competitors in my field?	*Dun and Bradstreet Million Dollar Directory* notes other companies making the same product. *Standard and Poor's Industry Survey* *Business Periodicals Index* Other sources include industry *Buyers' Guides* and industry directories. Check the special issues index of each.

	Questions	*Source of Answers*
	What industries use specific types of professionals?	*Encyclopedia of Associations*
		National Trade and Professional Associations of the United States (Identify appropriate organizations, obtain membership lists, note companies and/or industries.)
		Directory of U.S. Labor Organizations (Identify associations, obtain names of elected officials and department heads.)
		The Career Guide: Dun's Employment Opportunities Directory Encyclopedia of Career and Vocational Guidance Occupational Outlook Handbook
Companies	How can a company's products be identified?	Company annual reports
		Moody's Manuals
		Thomas Register, company catalog volumes
		U.S. Industrial Directory
	What companies make certain products?	*Thomas Register,* product volumes
		Dun and Bradstreet's Million Dollar Directory
		Standard and Poor's Register of Corporations, Directors, and Executives
		Standard Directory of Advertisers

Questions	Source of Answers
How can consulting organizations be identified by field?	*Consultants and Consulting Organizations Directory* and companion directories
	There are also many industry-specific directories of consultants; see the *Directory of Directories*
What are sources of company reports and company stock analyses?	*Standard and Poor's Stock Report*
	Moody's Investors' Fact Sheets
	Value Line Investment Surveys *Wall Street Transcript*
	Some libraries may subscribe to other stock analysis services.
What are management's practices with regard to training?	Company annual reports, employee relations section
	Membership directories for training organizations (e.g., *American Society for Training and Development Directory*)
	The Career Guide: Dun's Employment Opportunities Directory
	Peterson's Guides
Who are key people in a company and what are their backgrounds?	*Dun and Bradstreet Reference Book of Corporate Managements*
	Standard and Poor's Register of Corporations, Directors, and Executives
	Who's Who directories
	Corporate proxy statements

	Questions	Source of Answers
	Who are the people in my line of business?	*Dun and Bradstreet's America's Corporate Families*
		State Industrial Directories
		Company annual reports
		Other directories (refer to the *Directory of Directories* and *Directory of Industry Data Sources*)
Employment Organizations	Which employment agencies and/or executive recruiters specialize in my field?	*The Directory of Executive Recruiters*
		There are other directories produced by state or local associations.
	What governmental employment opportunities exist?	State: *The State Administrative Officials Classified by Functions* has a section listing state employment offices and their phone numbers.
		Federal: The U.S. Office of Personnel Management (1900 E Street, N.W., Washington, D.C. 20006) is responsible for nationwide recruiting for Civil Service positions at GS levels 1–15. It maintains a network of federal job information centers in major metropolitan areas. Phone numbers are listed in the white pages under U.S. Government, Office of Personnel Management.

Resume/Job Listing

The following Internet Search Engines offer a wealth of information and assistance to the job hunter. The Internet is the world's largest network available for your use 24 hours a day all at your fingertips *so use it!* You can get assistance writing your resume and then post it to employers at no cost in most cases. You have access to the most current information available both locally as well as across the state, country or even the world.

YAHOO	**ALTAVISTA**
http://www.yahoo.com/	http://altavista.digital.com/
Yahoo finds all keywords matches, then sorts the results according to relevancy within each specific area. Results are ranked in the following manner.	AltaVista claims to access the largest Web index: 31 million pages on 476,000 servers, and four million articles from 14,000 Usenet news groups. AltaVista supports Simple or Advanced searching. Simple Search uses machine intelligence to force some of the features of Advanced Search. Advanced gives the searcher more specific control.
• documents matching more of the keywords will have a higher rank	
• documents matching words found in the title are ranked higher than those found in the body or URL	
• categories matching high in the Yahoo tree hierarchy (general categories) are ranked higher than those lower in the hierarchy	
EXCITE	**WEBCRAWLER**
http://www.excite.com/	http://www.webcrawler.com/
Excite claims to be the most comprehensive search tool on the Internet, indexing over 50 million Web pages, 60,000 categorized Website reviews, and recent Usenet postings. Its search engine uses ICE (intelligent concept extraction) to learn about word relationships. This enables a king of cross-referencing.	Webcrawler is an outstanding search engine that includes a catalog of pre-classified subjects (directory services). It implements a feature of further searching based on pre-set search terms from the subject catalog, very much like Excite.
	Webcrawler touts "natural language searching," so you can enter a search like "highest mountain in the world."